The Simple
Air Fryer Cookbook for Beginners

....

365 Healthy, Affordable, and Fast
Air Fryer Recipes for Everyday Homemade Meals.

Ralph James

Table of Contents

Chapter 5: Vegetarians Recipes 33

Chapter 6: Beef, pork & Lamb Recipes 40

Chapter 7: Fish And Seafood Recipes 55

Chapter 8: Poultry Recipes 69

Chapter 9: Vegetable Side Dishes Recipes 83

Chapter 10: Desserts And Sweets Recipes 96

Recipes Index 104

Chapter 1: Introduction

In the realm of culinary innovation, the air fryer has emerged as a transformative appliance that has redefined the way we cook, making it possible to enjoy our favorite fried foods with significantly less guilt. This revolutionary kitchen gadget has taken the world by storm, offering a healthier alternative to traditional deep frying while still delivering the crispy, golden perfection we all crave. In this comprehensive guide, we will delve into the world of air frying, exploring its benefits, functions, usage tips, and maintenance to help you harness the full potential of this versatile kitchen companion.

The Air Fryer: A Brief Overview

What is an Air Fryer?
An air fryer is a compact, countertop kitchen appliance designed to simulate the cooking process of deep frying using hot air circulation and a minimal amount of oil. It employs rapid convection cooking technology to cook food evenly and create that coveted crispy texture, making it a versatile tool for preparing a wide range of dishes, from classic fried favorites like french fries and chicken wings to healthier options such as roasted vegetables and seafood.

Air Frying vs. Deep Frying: A Healthy Alternative
One of the key distinctions between air frying and deep frying lies in the cooking method and the impact on your health.

Deep Frying
Deep frying typically involves submerging food in a large quantity of hot oil, resulting in a crispy exterior but also a significant absorption of oil by the food. This method can lead to high calorie, fat, and cholesterol content in the finished dish, which is why deep-fried foods are often considered indulgent treats best enjoyed in moderation.

Air Frying
Air frying, on the other hand, accomplishes a similar crispy texture using a fraction of the oil required in deep frying or, in some cases, no oil at all. Instead, it relies on the circulation of superheated air to cook food quickly and evenly, producing a crispy exterior while retaining moisture within. This reduction in oil consumption translates to lower calorie and fat intake, making air frying a healthier alternative without compromising on taste and texture.

The Benefits of Air Frying

1. Healthier Eating
One of the most significant advantages of using an air fryer is its ability to promote healthier eating habits. By using little to no oil, air frying significantly reduces the calorie and fat content of your favorite fried dishes, making them more suitable for those looking to manage their weight or make healthier food choices.

2. Reduced Risk of Health Issues
Lowering your intake of fried foods cooked in excessive oil can contribute to a decreased risk of health issues such as heart disease, high blood pressure, and obesity. Air frying allows you to enjoy the flavors and textures of your favorite fried treats while minimizing the negative health impacts associated with deep frying.

3. Versatility in Cooking
Air fryers are incredibly versatile appliances that can handle a wide variety of foods. From frozen appetizers to

fresh vegetables, proteins, and even desserts, you can use an air fryer to cook an array of dishes with ease. This versatility makes it an essential tool in any kitchen.

4. Time Efficiency
Air fryers are designed to cook food quickly and efficiently. The rapid hot air circulation means shorter cooking times compared to conventional ovens, saving you valuable time in the kitchen. Whether you're whipping up a weeknight dinner or preparing snacks for a gathering, an air fryer can help you get the job done swiftly.

5. Energy Efficiency
Compared to traditional ovens, air fryers are more energy-efficient. They require less preheating time and consume less electricity, making them an eco-friendly choice for cooking. Additionally, their compact size allows for efficient use of space in your kitchen.

Functions of an Air Fryer
Air fryers come equipped with a range of functions and settings to cater to various cooking needs. Understanding these functions will enable you to make the most of your air fryer's capabilities.

1. Air Frying
The primary function of an air fryer is, of course, air frying. This mode circulates hot air at high speeds to cook food quickly and evenly. It is ideal for achieving a crispy exterior and tender interior in dishes like fries, chicken tenders, and even homemade doughnuts.

2. Roasting
Many air fryers offer a roasting function that allows you to cook larger cuts of meat, whole poultry, or vegetables with a roast-like texture. Roasting in an air fryer is efficient and can produce succulent, evenly cooked results.

3. Baking
Air fryers can also function as miniature convection ovens. You can use them to bake a wide range of goods, including cookies, muffins, and even cakes. The precise temperature control ensures consistent baking results.

4. Grilling

Some air fryer models come with a grill function that mimics the effects of grilling. This is perfect for achieving grill marks and that smoky flavor on items like burgers, steaks, and kebabs.

5. Dehydrating
For health-conscious individuals and those who enjoy making their own dried fruits or beef jerky, certain air fryers feature a dehydrating function. This mode uses low heat and airflow to remove moisture from foods, preserving their flavors and nutrients.

6. Reheating
Air fryers excel at reheating leftovers. They can revive cold pizza, french fries, and other dishes, restoring their crispiness and flavor. Say goodbye to soggy microwave reheats!

Tips for Using an Air Fryer
To achieve the best results with your air fryer, consider these helpful tips:

1. Preheat When Necessary
While some recipes may not require preheating, it can be beneficial for achieving consistent results. Preheat your air fryer for a few minutes before adding your food, especially for items that require a crispy texture.

2. Use the Right Amount of Oil
While air frying is known for using less oil, some recipes benefit from a light coating of oil to enhance flavor and texture. Invest in a quality oil sprayer to evenly distribute oil over your ingredients.

3. Avoid Overcrowding
To ensure even cooking, avoid overcrowding the air fryer basket. Overlapping or stacking food can hinder the circulation of hot air, resulting in unevenly cooked dishes.

4. Shake or Flip
For foods like french fries or chicken wings, shake the basket or flip the items halfway through the cooking time. This helps ensure that all sides of the food achieve that desirable crispiness.

5. Monitor Cooking Progress
Keep an eye on your food as it cooks. Adjust the temperature or cooking time as needed to prevent

overcooking or undercooking. Many air fryers come with transparent doors or baskets, allowing you to monitor your food's progress easily.

6. Experiment and Explore
Don't hesitate to experiment with recipes and flavors. Air fryers offer a versatile cooking platform that encourages creativity. Try different seasonings, marinades, and ingredients to discover new favorite dishes.

Cleaning and Maintenance of Your Air Fryer
Proper care and maintenance are essential to keep your air fryer functioning optimally and prolong its lifespan. Follow these cleaning and maintenance tips:

1. Unplug and Cool Down
Before cleaning your air fryer, ensure it is unplugged and has cooled down completely to avoid burns or electrical accidents.

2. Remove and Clean the Parts
Most air fryers have removable components like the cooking basket, tray, and pan. Remove these parts and wash them with warm, soapy water. Some parts may be dishwasher-safe, making cleanup even more convenient.

3. Wipe the Exterior
Use a damp cloth or sponge to wipe the exterior of the air fryer. Avoid using abrasive cleaners or scouring pads, as they can damage the appliance's finish.

4. Clean the Heating Element
Check your air fryer's manual for instructions on cleaning the heating element. Some models have accessible heating elements that can be cleaned with a brush or cloth.

5. Address Tough Stains
For stubborn stains or residue, create a paste using baking soda and water. Apply this paste to the affected area and gently scrub with a soft brush or cloth.

6. Regular Maintenance
Perform regular maintenance by inspecting your air fryer for signs of wear and tear. Replace any damaged or worn-out parts to ensure safe and efficient operation.

7. Store Properly
When not in use, store your air fryer in a cool, dry place to prevent dust accumulation and damage. Ensure that the appliance is stored safely to avoid any accidental damage.

Conclusion
The air fryer has revolutionized the way we approach cooking, offering a healthier alternative to deep frying without sacrificing flavor or texture. Its versatility, speed, and efficiency make it a must-have appliance in any kitchen. By following the tips for usage, cleaning, and maintenance outlined in this guide, you can fully harness the potential of your air fryer and enjoy delicious, crispy dishes with ease, all while promoting a healthier lifestyle. Embrace this culinary innovation, and let the air fryer elevate your cooking experience to new heights.s.

Chapter 2: Measurement Conversions

BASIC KITCHEN CONVERSIONS & EQUIVALENTS

DRY MEASUREMENTS CONVERSION CHART
3 TEASPOONS = 1 TABLESPOON = 1/16 CUP
6 TEASPOONS = 2 TABLESPOONS = 1/8 CUP
12 TEASPOONS = 4 TABLESPOONS = 1/4 CUP
24 TEASPOONS = 8 TABLESPOONS = 1/2 CUP
36 TEASPOONS = 12 TABLESPOONS = 3/4 CUP
48 TEASPOONS = 16 TABLESPOONS = 1 CUP

METRIC TO US COOKING CONVER SIONS
OVEN TEMPERATURES
120 °C = 250 °F
160 °C = 320 °F
180° C = 360 °F
205 °C = 400 °F
220 °C = 425 °F

LIQUID MEASUREMENTS CONVERSION CHART
8 FLUID OUNCES = 1 CUP = 1/2 PINT = 1/4 QUART
16 FLUID OUNCES = 2 CUPS = 1 PINT = 1/2 QUART
32 FLUID OUNCES = 4 CUPS = 2 PINTS = 1 QUART = 1/4 GALLON
128 FLUID OUNCES = 16 CUPS = 8 PINTS = 4 QUARTS = 1 GALLON

BAKING IN GRAMS
1 CUP FLOUR = 140 GRAMS
1 CUP SUGAR = 150 GRAMS
1 CUP POWDERED SUGAR = 160 GRAMS
1 CUP HEAVY CREAM = 235 GRAMS

VOLUME
1 MILLILITER = 1/5 TEASPOON
5 ML = 1 TEASPOON
15 ML = 1 TABLESPOON
240 ML = 1 CUP OR 8 FLUID OUNCES
1 LITER = 34 FL. OUNCES

WEIGHT
1 GRAM = .035 OUNCES
100 GRAMS = 3.5 OUNCES
500 GRAMS = 1.1 POUNDS
1 KILOGRAM = 35 OUNCES

US TO METRIC COOKING CONVERSIONS
1/5 TSP = 1 ML
1 TSP = 5 ML
1 TBSP = 15 ML
1 FL OUNCE = 30 ML
1 CUP = 237 ML
1 PINT (2 CUPS) = 473 ML
1 QUART (4 CUPS) = .95 LITER
1 GALLON (16 CUPS) = 3.8 LITERS
1 OZ = 28 GRAMS
1 POUND = 454 GRAMS

BUTTER
1 CUP BUTTER = 2 STICKS = 8 OUNCES = 230 GRAMS = 8 TABLESPOONS

WHAT DOES 1 CUP EQUAL
1 CUP = 8 FLUID OUNCES
1 CUP = 16 TABLESPOONS
1 CUP = 48 TEASPOONS
1 CUP = 1/2 PINT
1 CUP = 1/4 QUART
1 CUP = 1/16 GALLON
1 CUP = 240 ML

BAKING PAN CONVERSIONS
1 CUP ALL-PURPOSE FLOUR = 4.5 OZ
1 CUP ROLLED OATS = 3 OZ 1 LARGE EGG = 1.7 OZ
1 CUP BUTTER = 8 OZ 1 CUP MILK = 8 OZ
1 CUP HEAVY CREAM = 8.4 OZ
1 CUP GRANULATED SUGAR = 7.1 OZ
1 CUP PACKED BROWN SUGAR = 7.75 OZ
1 CUP VEGETABLE OIL = 7.7 OZ
1 CUP UNSIFTED POWDERED SUGAR = 4.4 OZ

BAKING PAN CONVERSIONS
9-INCH ROUND CAKE PAN = 12 CUPS
10-INCH TUBE PAN =16 CUPS
11-INCH BUNDT PAN = 12 CUPS
9-INCH SPRINGFORM PAN = 10 CUPS
9 X 5 INCH LOAF PAN = 8 CUPS
9-INCH SQUARE PAN = 8 CUPS

Chapter 3: Appetizers And Snacks Recipes

Fried Kale Chips

Servings: 2
Cooking Time: 10 Minutes
Ingredients:
- 1 head kale, torn into 1 ½-inch pieces
- 1 tbsp. olive oil
- 1 tsp. soy sauce

Directions:
1. Wash and dry the kale pieces.
2. Transfer the kale to a bowl and coat with the soy sauce and oil.
3. Place it in the Air Fryer and cook at 400°F for 3 minutes, tossing it halfway through the cooking process.

Stuffed Prunes In Bacon

Servings: 6
Cooking Time: 20 Minutes
Ingredients:
- 12 bacon slices, halved
- 24 pitted prunes
- 3 tbsp crumbled blue cheese
- 1 tbsp cream cheese

Directions:
1. Cut prunes in half lengthwise, but do not cut all the way through. Add ½ tsp of blue cheese and cream cheese to the center of each prune. Wrap each prune with a slice of bacon and seal with a toothpick.
2. Preheat air fryer to 400°F. Place the prunes on the bottom of the greased frying basket in a single layer. Bake for 6-8 minutes, flipping the prunes once until the bacon is cooked and crispy. Allow to cool and serve warm.

Savory Ranch Chicken Bites

Servings:6
Cooking Time: 15 Minutes
Ingredients:
- 2 boneless, skinless chicken breasts, cut into 1" cubes
- 1 tablespoon coconut oil
- ½ teaspoon salt
- ¼ teaspoon ground black pepper
- ⅓ cup ranch dressing
- ½ cup shredded Colby cheese
- 4 slices cooked sugar-free bacon, crumbled

Directions:
1. Drizzle chicken with coconut oil. Sprinkle with salt and pepper, and place into an ungreased 6" round nonstick baking dish.
2. Place dish into air fryer basket. Adjust the temperature to 370°F and set the timer for 10 minutes, stirring chicken halfway through cooking.
3. When timer beeps, drizzle ranch dressing over chicken and top with Colby and bacon. Adjust the temperature to 400°F and set the timer for 5 minutes. When done, chicken will be browned and have an internal temperature of at least 165°F. Serve warm.

Cheesy Stuffed Mushrooms

Servings:4
Cooking Time: 8 To 12 Minutes
Ingredients:
- 16 medium button mushrooms, rinsed and patted dry
- ⅓ cup low-sodium salsa
- 3 garlic cloves, minced
- 1 medium onion, finely chopped
- 1 jalapeño pepper, minced
- ⅛ teaspoon cayenne pepper
- 3 tablespoons shredded Pepper Jack cheese
- 2 teaspoons olive oil

Directions:
1. Preheat the air fryer to 350°F (177°C).
2. Remove the stems from the mushrooms and finely chop them, reserving the whole caps.
3. In a medium bowl, mix the salsa, garlic, onion, jalapeño, cayenne, and Pepper Jack cheese. Stir in the chopped mushroom stems.
4. Stuff this mixture into the mushroom caps, mounding the filling. Drizzle the olive oil on the mushrooms. Air fry the mushrooms in the air fryer basket for 8 to 12 minutes, or until the filling is hot and the mushrooms are tender.
5. Serve immediately.

Roasted Jalapeño Salsa Verde

Servings:4
Cooking Time: 20 Minutes
Ingredients:
- ¾ lb fresh tomatillos, husked
- 1 jalapeño, stem removed
- 4 green onions, sliced
- 3 garlic cloves, peeled
- ½ tsp salt
- 1 tsp lime juice
- ¼ tsp apple cider vinegar
- ¼ cup cilantro leaves

Directions:
1. Preheat air fryer to 400°F. Add tomatillos and jalapeño to the frying basket and Bake for 5 minutes. Put in green onions and garlic and Bake for 5 more minutes. Transfer it into a food processor along with salt, lime juice, vinegar and cilantro and blend until the sauce is finely chopped. Pour it into a small sealable container and refrigerate it until ready to use up to five days.

Fried Mozzarella Sticks

Servings: 7
Cooking Time: 5 Minutes
Ingredients:
- 7 1-ounce string cheese sticks, unwrapped
- ½ cup All-purpose flour or tapioca flour
- 2 Large egg(s), well beaten
- 2¼ cups Seasoned Italian-style dried bread crumbs (gluten-free, if a concern)
- Olive oil spray

Directions:

1. Unwrap the string cheese and place the pieces in the freezer for 20 minutes.
2. Preheat the air fryer to 400°F.
3. Set up and fill three shallow soup plates or small pie plates on your counter: one for the flour, one for the egg(s), and one for the bread crumbs.
4. Dip a piece of cold string cheese in the flour until well coated. Gently tap off any excess flour, then set the stick in the egg(s). Roll it around to coat, let any excess egg mixture slip back into the rest, and set the stick in the bread crumbs. Gently roll it around to coat it evenly, even the ends. Now dip it back in the egg(s), then again in the bread crumbs, rolling it to coat well and evenly. Set the stick aside on a cutting board and coat the remaining pieces of string cheese in the same way.
5. Lightly coat the sticks all over with olive oil spray. Place them in the basket in one layer and air-fry undisturbed for 5 minutes, or until golden brown and crisp.
6. Remove the basket from the machine and cool for 5 minutes. Use a nonstick-safe spatula to transfer the mozzarella sticks to a serving platter. Serve hot.

Air-fried Sweet Potato Bites

Servings: 2
Cooking Time: 15 Minutes
Ingredients:
- 2 sweet potatoes, diced into 1-inch cubes
- ½ teaspoon red chili flakes
- 1½ teaspoon cinnamon
- 1 tablespoon olive oil
- 1½ tablespoon honey
- ½ cup fresh parsley, chopped

Directions:
1. Heat your Air Fryer at 350 degrees F/ 175 degrees C ahead of time.
2. In a bowl, stir all of the ingredients well and then coat the sweet potato cubes entirely.
3. Put the sweet potato mixture into the basket.
4. Cook for 15 minutes at 350 degrees F/ 175 degrees C.
5. Serve and enjoy.

Hot Nachos With Chile Salsa

Servings: 4
Cooking Time: 20 Minutes
Ingredients:
- ½ chile de árbol pepper, seeds removed
- 1 tbsp olive oil
- Salt to taste
- 1 shallot, chopped
- 2 garlic cloves
- 1 can diced tomatoes
- 2 tbsp fresh cilantro
- Juice of 1 lime
- ¼ tsp chili-lime seasoning
- 6 corn tortillas

Directions:

1. Add the shallot, garlic, chile de árbol, tomatoes, cilantro, lime juice and salt in a food processor. Pulse until combined and chunky. Pour the salsa into a serving bowl and set aside. Drizzle olive oil on both sides of the tortillas. Stack the tortilla and cut them in half with a sharp knife. Continue to cut into quarters, then cut again so that each tortilla is cut into 8 equal wedges. Season both sides of each wedge with chile-lime seasoning.
2. Preheat air fryer to 400°F. Place the tortilla wedges in the greased frying basket and Air Fry for 4-7 minutes, shaking once until the chips are golden and crisp. Allow to cool slightly and serve with previously prepared salsa.

Curried Sweet Potato Fries

Servings:4
Cooking Time: 8 To 12 Minutes
Ingredients:
- ½ cup sour cream
- ½ cup mango chutney
- 3 teaspoons curry powder, divided
- 4 cups frozen sweet potato fries
- 1 tablespoon olive oil
- Pinch salt
- Freshly ground black pepper

Directions:
1. In a small bowl, combine sour cream, chutney, and 1½ teaspoons of the curry powder. Mix well and set aside.
2. Put the sweet potatoes in a medium bowl. Drizzle with the olive oil and sprinkle with remaining 1½ teaspoons curry powder, salt, and pepper.
3. Put the potatoes in the air fryer basket. Cook for 8 to 12 minutes or until crisp, hot, and golden brown, shaking the basket once during cooking time.
4. Place the fries in a serving basket and serve with the chutney dip.

Cajun-spiced Pickle Chips

Servings: 4
Cooking Time: 20 Minutes
Ingredients:
- 16 oz canned pickle slices
- ½ cup flour
- 2 tbsp cornmeal
- 3 tsp Cajun seasoning
- 1 tbsp dried parsley
- 1 egg, beaten
- ¼ tsp hot sauce
- ½ cup buttermilk
- 3 tbsp light mayonnaise
- 3 tbsp chopped chives
- ⅛ tsp garlic powder
- ⅛ tsp onion powder
- Salt and pepper to taste

Directions:
1. Preheat air fryer to 350°F. Mix flour, cornmeal, Cajun seasoning, and parsley in a bowl. Put the beaten egg in a small bowl nearby. One at a time, dip a pickle

slice in the egg, then roll in the crumb mixture. Gently press the crumbs, so they stick to the pickle. Place the chips in the greased frying basket and Air Fry for 7-9 minutes, flipping once until golden and crispy. In a bowl, whisk hot sauce, buttermilk, mayonnaise, chives, garlic and onion powder, salt, and pepper. Serve with pickles.

Spicy Chicken And Pepper Jack Cheese Bites

Servings: 8
Cooking Time: 8 Minutes
Ingredients:
- 8 ounces cream cheese, softened
- 2 cups grated pepper jack cheese
- 1 Jalapeño pepper, diced
- 2 scallions, minced
- 1 teaspoon paprika
- 2 teaspoons salt, divided
- 3 cups shredded cooked chicken
- ¼ cup all-purpose flour*
- 2 eggs, lightly beaten
- 1 cup panko breadcrumbs*
- olive oil, in a spray bottle
- salsa

Directions:
1. Beat the cream cheese in a bowl until it is smooth and easy to stir. Add the pepper jack cheese, Jalapeño pepper, scallions, paprika and 1 teaspoon of salt. Fold in the shredded cooked chicken and combine well. Roll this mixture into 1-inch balls.
2. Set up a dredging station with three shallow dishes. Place the flour into one shallow dish. Place the eggs into a second shallow dish. Finally, combine the panko breadcrumbs and remaining teaspoon of salt in a third dish.
3. Coat the chicken cheese balls by rolling each ball in the flour first, then dip them into the eggs and finally roll them in the panko breadcrumbs to coat all sides. Refrigerate for at least 30 minutes.
4. Preheat the air fryer to 400°F.
5. Spray the chicken cheese balls with oil and air-fry in batches for 8 minutes. Shake the basket a few times throughout the cooking process to help the balls brown evenly.
6. Serve hot with salsa on the side.

Fried Wontons

Servings: 24
Cooking Time: 6 Minutes
Ingredients:
- 6 ounces Lean ground beef, pork, or turkey
- 1 tablespoon Regular or reduced-sodium soy sauce or tamari sauce
- 1½ teaspoons Minced garlic
- ¾ teaspoon Ground dried ginger
- ½ teaspoon Ground white pepper
- 24 Wonton wrappers (thawed, if necessary)
- Vegetable oil spray

Directions:
1. Preheat the air fryer to 350°F .
2. Stir the ground meat, soy or tamari sauce, garlic, ginger, and white pepper in a bowl until the spices are uniformly distributed in the mixture.
3. Set a small bowl of water on a clean, dry surface or next to a clean, dry cutting board. Set one wonton wrapper on the surface. Dip your clean finger in the water, then run it along the edges of the wrapper. Set 1 teaspoon of the ground meat mixture in the center of the wrapper. Fold it over, corner to corner, to create a filled triangle. Press to seal the edges, then pull the corners on the longest side up and together over the filling to create the classic wonton shape. Press the corners together to seal. Set aside and continue filling and making more filled wontons.
4. Generously coat the filled wontons on all sides with vegetable oil spray. Arrange them in the basket in one layer and air-fry for 6 minutes, shaking the basket gently at the 2- and 4-minute marks to rearrange the wontons (but always making sure they're still in one layer), until golden brown and crisp.
5. Pour the wontons in the basket onto a wire rack or even into a serving bowl. Cool for 2 or 3 minutes (but not much longer) and serve hot.

Spicy Cocktail Wieners

Servings: 4
Cooking Time: 15 Minutes
Ingredients:
- 1 lb. pork cocktail sausages
- For the Sauce:
- ¼ cup mayonnaise
- ¼ cup cream cheese
- 1 whole grain mustard
- ¼- ½ teaspoon balsamic vinegar
- 1 garlic clove, finely minced
- ¼ teaspoon chili powder

Directions:
1. Pork the sausages a few times with a fork, them place them on the cooking pan of your air fryer.
2. Cook the sausages at 390 degrees F/ 200 degrees C for 15 minutes;
3. After 8 minutes of cooking, turn the sausages over and resume cooking.
4. Check for doneness and take the sausages out of the machine.
5. At the same time, thoroughly combine all the ingredients for the sauce.
6. Serve with warm sausages and enjoy!

Mozzarella En Carrozza With Puttanesca Sauce

Servings: 6
Cooking Time: 8 Minutes
Ingredients:
- Puttanesca Sauce
- 2 teaspoons olive oil

- 1 anchovy, chopped (optional)
- 2 cloves garlic, minced
- 1 (14-ounce) can petite diced tomatoes
- ½ cup chicken stock or water
- ⅓ cup Kalamata olives, chopped
- 2 tablespoons capers
- ½ teaspoon dried oregano
- ¼ teaspoon crushed red pepper flakes
- salt and freshly ground black pepper
- 1 tablespoon fresh parsley, chopped
- 8 slices of thinly sliced white bread (Pepperidge Farm®)
- 8 ounces mozzarella cheese, cut into ¼-inch slices
- ½ cup all-purpose flour
- 3 eggs, beaten
- 1½ cups seasoned panko breadcrumbs
- ½ teaspoon garlic powder
- ½ teaspoon salt
- freshly ground black pepper
- olive oil, in a spray bottle

Directions:
1. Start by making the puttanesca sauce. Heat the olive oil in a medium saucepan on the stovetop. Add the anchovies (if using, and I really think you should!) and garlic and sauté for 3 minutes, or until the anchovies have "melted" into the oil. Add the tomatoes, chicken stock, olives, capers, oregano and crushed red pepper flakes and simmer the sauce for 20 minutes. Season with salt and freshly ground black pepper and stir in the fresh parsley.
2. Cut the crusts off the slices of bread. Place four slices of the bread on a cutting board. Divide the cheese between the four slices of bread. Top the cheese with the remaining four slices of bread to make little sandwiches and cut each sandwich into 4 triangles.
3. Set up a dredging station using three shallow dishes. Place the flour in the first shallow dish, the eggs in the second dish and in the third dish, combine the panko breadcrumbs, garlic powder, salt and black pepper. Dredge each little triangle in the flour first (you might think this is redundant, but it helps to get the coating to adhere to the edges of the sandwiches) and then dip them into the egg, making sure both the sides and the edges are coated. Let the excess egg drip off and then press the triangles into the breadcrumb mixture, pressing the crumbs on with your hands so they adhere. Place the coated triangles in the freezer for 2 hours, until the cheese is frozen.
4. Preheat the air fryer to 390°F. Spray all sides of the mozzarella triangles with oil and transfer a single layer of triangles to the air fryer basket. Air-fry in batches at 390°F for 5 minutes. Turn the triangles over and air-fry for an additional 3 minutes.
5. Serve mozzarella triangles immediately with the warm puttanesca sauce.

Pita Chips

Servings: 4

Cooking Time: 10 Minutes

Ingredients:
- 2 rounds Pocketless pita bread
- Olive oil spray or any flavor spray you prefer, even coconut oil spray
- Up to 1 teaspoon Fine sea salt, garlic salt, onion salt, or other flavored salt

Directions:
1. Preheat the air fryer to 400°F.
2. Lightly coat the pita round(s) on both sides with olive oil spray, then lightly sprinkle each side with salt.
3. Cut each coated pita round into 8 even wedges. Lay these in the basket in as close to a single even layer as possible. Many will overlap or even be on top of each other, depending on the exact size of your machine.
4. Air-fry for 6 minutes, shaking the basket and rearranging the wedges at the 4-minute marks, until the wedges are crisp and brown. Turn them out onto a wire rack to cool a few minutes or to room temperature before digging in.

Fried Ranch Pickles

Servings:4

Cooking Time: 10 Minutes

Ingredients:
- 4 dill pickle spears, halved lengthwise
- ¼ cup ranch dressing
- ½ cup blanched finely ground almond flour
- ½ cup grated Parmesan cheese
- 2 tablespoons dry ranch seasoning

Directions:
1. Wrap spears in a kitchen towel 30 minutes to soak up excess pickle juice.
2. Pour ranch dressing into a medium bowl and add pickle spears. In a separate medium bowl, mix flour, Parmesan, and ranch seasoning.
3. Remove each spear from ranch dressing and shake off excess. Press gently into dry mixture to coat all sides. Place spears into ungreased air fryer basket. Adjust the temperature to 400°F and set the timer for 10 minutes, turning spears three times during cooking. Serve warm.

Cocktail Chicken Meatballs

Servings: 4

Cooking Time: 30 Minutes

Ingredients:
- 2 tsp olive oil
- ¼ cup onion, minced
- ¼ red bell pepper, minced
- 3 tsp grated Parmesan cheese
- 1 egg white
- ½ tsp cayenne pepper
- ½ tsp dried thyme
- ½ lb ground chicken

Directions:
1. Preheat air fryer to 370°F. Combine the olive oil, onion, and red bell pepper in a baking pan, then transfer to the air fryer. Bake for 3-5 minutes until tender. Add

the cooked vegetables, Parmesan cheese, egg white, ground chicken, cayenne pepper, and thyme to a bowl and stir. Form the mixture into small meatballs and put them in the frying basket. Air Fry for 10-15 minutes, shaking the basket once until the meatballs are crispy and brown on all sides. Serve warm.

Turkey Spring Rolls

Servings: 4
Cooking Time: 20 Minutes
Ingredients:
- 1 lb turkey breast, grilled, cut into chunks
- 1 celery stalk, julienned
- 1 carrot, grated
- 1 tsp fresh ginger, minced
- 1 tsp sugar
- 1 tsp chicken stock powder
- 1 egg
- 1 tsp corn starch
- 6 spring roll wrappers

Directions:
1. Preheat the air fryer to 360°F. Mix the turkey, celery, carrot, ginger, sugar, and chicken stock powder in a large bowl. Combine thoroughly and set aside. In another bowl, beat the egg, and stir in the cornstarch. On a clean surface, spoon the turkey filling into each spring roll, roll up and seal the seams with the egg-cornstarch mixture. Put each roll in the greased frying basket and Air Fry for 7-8 minutes, flipping once until golden brown. Serve hot.

Breaded Mozzarella Sticks

Servings:6
Cooking Time: 25 Minutes
Ingredients:
- 2 tbsp flour
- 1 egg
- 1 tbsp milk
- ½ cup bread crumbs
- ¼ tsp salt
- ¼ tsp Italian seasoning
- 10 mozzarella sticks
- 2 tsp olive oil
- ½ cup warm marinara sauce

Directions:
1. Place the flour in a bowl. In another bowl, beat the egg and milk. In a third bowl, combine the crumbs, salt, and Italian seasoning. Cut the mozzarella sticks into thirds. Roll each piece in flour, then dredge in egg mixture, and finally roll in breadcrumb mixture. Shake off the excess between each step. Place them in the freezer for 10 minutes.
2. Preheat air fryer to 400°F. Place mozzarella sticks in the frying basket and Air Fry for 5 minutes, shake twice and brush with olive oil. Serve the mozzarella sticks immediately with marinara sauce.

Grilled Ham & Muenster Cheese On Raisin Bread

Servings: 1
Cooking Time: 10 Minutes
Ingredients:
- 2 slices raisin bread
- 2 tablespoons butter, softened
- 2 teaspoons honey mustard
- 3 slices thinly sliced honey ham (about 3 ounces)
- 4 slices Muenster cheese (about 3 ounces)
- 2 toothpicks

Directions:
1. Preheat the air fryer to 370°F.
2. Spread the softened butter on one side of both slices of raisin bread and place the bread, buttered side down on the counter. Spread the honey mustard on the other side of each slice of bread. Layer 2 slices of cheese, the ham and the remaining 2 slices of cheese on one slice of bread and top with the other slice of bread. Remember to leave the buttered side of the bread on the outside.
3. Transfer the sandwich to the air fryer basket and secure the sandwich with toothpicks.
4. Air-fry at 370°F for 5 minutes. Flip the sandwich over, remove the toothpicks and air-fry for another 5 minutes. Cut the sandwich in half and enjoy!!

Smoked Salmon Puffs

Servings: 2
Cooking Time: 8 Minutes
Ingredients:
- Two quarters of one thawed sheet (that is, a half of the sheet; wrap and refreeze the remainder) A 17.25-ounce box frozen puff pastry
- 4 ½-ounce smoked salmon slices
- 2 tablespoons Softened regular or low-fat cream cheese (not fat-free)
- Up to 2 teaspoons Drained and rinsed capers, minced
- Up to 2 teaspoons Minced red onion
- 1 Large egg white
- 1 tablespoon Water

Directions:
1. Preheat the air fryer to 400°F.
2. For a small air fryer, roll the piece of puff pastry into a 6 x 6-inch square on a clean, dry work surface.
3. For a medium or larger air fryer, roll each piece of puff pastry into a 6 x 6-inch square.
4. Set 2 salmon slices on the diagonal, corner to corner, on each rolled-out sheet. Smear the salmon with cream cheese, then sprinkle with capers and red onion. Fold the sheet closed by picking up one corner that does not have an edge of salmon near it and folding the dough across the salmon to its opposite corner. Seal the edges closed by pressing the tines of a flatware fork into them.
5. Whisk the egg white and water in a small bowl until uniform. Brush this mixture over the top(s) of the packet(s).

6. Set the packet(s) in the basket (if you're working with more than one, they cannot touch). Air-fry undisturbed for 8 minutes, or until golden brown and flaky.

7. Use a nonstick-safe spatula to transfer the packet(s) to a wire rack. Cool for 5 minutes before serving.

Popcorn Chicken Bites

Servings: 2
Cooking Time: 8 Minutes
Ingredients:

- 1 pound chicken breasts, cutlets or tenders
- 1 cup buttermilk
- 3 to 6 dashes hot sauce (optional)
- 8 cups cornflakes (or 2 cups cornflake crumbs)
- ½ teaspoon salt
- 1 tablespoon butter, melted
- 2 tablespoons chopped fresh parsley

Directions:

1. Cut the chicken into bite-sized pieces (about 1-inch) and place them in a bowl with the buttermilk and hot sauce (if using). Cover and let the chicken marinate in the buttermilk for 1 to 3 hours in the refrigerator.

2. Preheat the air fryer to 380°F.

3. Crush the cornflakes into fine crumbs by either crushing them with your hands in a bowl, rolling them with a rolling pin in a plastic bag or processing them in a food processor. Place the crumbs in a bowl, add the salt, melted butter and parsley and mix well. Working in batches, remove the chicken from the buttermilk marinade, letting any excess drip off and transfer the chicken to the cornflakes. Toss the chicken pieces in the cornflake mixture to coat evenly, pressing the crumbs onto the chicken.

4. Air-fry the chicken in two batches for 8 minutes per batch, shaking the basket halfway through the cooking process. Re-heat the first batch with the second batch for a couple of minutes if desired.

5. Serve the popcorn chicken bites warm with BBQ sauce or honey mustard for dipping.

Ranch Kale Chips

Servings: 4
Cooking Time: 5 Minutes
Ingredients:

- 4 cups kale, stemmed
- 1 tablespoon nutritional yeast flakes
- 2 teaspoons ranch seasoning
- 2 tablespoons olive oil
- ¼ teaspoon salt

Directions:

1. Add all the recipe ingredients into the suitable mixing bowl and toss well.

2. Grease its air fryer basket with cooking spray.

3. Add kale in air fryer basket and cook for 4 to 5 minutes at 370 degrees F/ 185 degrees C. Shake halfway through.

4. Serve and enjoy.

Cinnamon Honeyed Pretzel Bites

Servings: 6
Cooking Time: 40 Minutes
Ingredients:

- 1 ½ tsp quick-rise yeast
- 2 tsp light brown sugar
- 1 tsp vanilla extract
- ½ tsp lemon zest
- 2 ¼ cups flour
- ½ tsp salt
- ½ tbsp honey
- 1 tbsp cinnamon powder

Directions:

1. Preheat air fryer to 380°F. Stir ¾ cup warm water and yeast in a medium bowl. Sit for 5 minutes. Combine yeast water with 2 cups of flour, brown sugar, vanilla, lemon zest, cinnamon, salt, and honey. Stir until sticky dough forms. Sprinkle the rest of the flour on a flat work surface, then place the dough on the surface. Knead the dough for 2-3 minutes or until it comes together in a smooth ball. Divide the dough into 4 pieces. Roll each section into a log. Cut each log into 5 pieces. Arrange the dough pieces on the greased basket. Bake for 3 minutes, then use tongs to flip the pretzels. Cook for another 3-4 until pretzels have browned. Serve warm and enjoy.

Simple Curried Sweet Potato Fries

Servings: 3
Cooking Time: 20 Minutes
Ingredients:

- 2 small sweet potatoes, peel and cut into fry shape
- ¼ teaspoon coriander
- ½ teaspoon curry powder
- 2 tablespoons olive oil
- ¼ teaspoon salt

Directions:

1. Add all the recipe ingredients into the suitable mixing bowl and toss well.

2. Grease its air fryer basket with cooking spray.

3. Transfer sweet potato fries in the air fryer basket.

4. Cook for 20 minutes at 370 degrees F/ 185 degrees C. Shake halfway through.

5. Serve and enjoy.

Lemon Tofu Cubes

Servings:2
Cooking Time: 7 Minutes
Ingredients:

- ½ teaspoon ground coriander
- 1 tablespoon avocado oil
- 1 teaspoon lemon juice
- ½ teaspoon chili flakes
- 6 oz tofu

Directions:

1. In the shallow bowl mix up ground coriander, avocado oil, lemon juice, and chili flakes. Chop the tofu into cubes and sprinkle with coriander mixture. Shake the tofu. After this, preheat the air fryer to 400°F and put the tofu cubes in it. Cook the tofu for 4 minutes. Then flip the tofu on another side and cook for 3 minutes more.

Garlic Spinach Dip

Servings: 8
Cooking Time: 20 Minutes
Ingredients:
- 8 ounces cream cheese, softened
- ¼ teaspoon garlic powder
- ½ cup onion, minced
- ⅓ cup water chestnuts, drained and chopped
- 1 cup mayonnaise
- 1 cup parmesan cheese, grated
- 1 cup frozen spinach, thawed and squeeze out all liquid
- ½ teaspoon black pepper

Directions:
1. Grease its air fryer basket with cooking spray.
2. Add all the recipe ingredients into the bowl and mix until well combined.
3. Transfer bowl mixture into the prepared baking dish and place dish in air fryer basket.
4. Cook at almost 300 degrees F/ 150 degrees C for 35-40 minutes. After 20 minutes of cooking stir dip.
5. Serve and enjoy.

Veggie Shrimp Toast

Servings:4
Cooking Time: 3 To 6 Minutes
Ingredients:
- 8 large raw shrimp, peeled and finely chopped
- 1 egg white
- 2 garlic cloves, minced
- 3 tablespoons minced red bell pepper
- 1 medium celery stalk, minced
- 2 tablespoons cornstarch
- ¼ teaspoon Chinese five-spice powder
- 3 slices firm thin-sliced no-sodium whole-wheat bread

Directions:
1. Preheat the air fryer to 350ºF (177ºC).
2. In a small bowl, stir together the shrimp, egg white, garlic, red bell pepper, celery, cornstarch, and five-spice powder. Top each slice of bread with one-third of the shrimp mixture, spreading it evenly to the edges. With a sharp knife, cut each slice of bread into 4 strips.
3. Place the shrimp toasts in the air fryer basket in a single layer. You may need to cook them in batches. Air fry for 3 to 6 minutes, until crisp and golden brown.
4. Serve hot.

Honey Tater Tots With Bacon

Servings: 4
Cooking Time: 25 Minutes
Ingredients:
- 24 frozen tater tots
- 6 bacon slices
- 1 tbsp honey
- 1 cup grated cheddar

Directions:
1. Preheat air fryer to 400°F. Air Fry the tater tots for 10 minutes, shaking the basket once halfway through cooking. Cut the bacon into pieces. When the tater tots are done, remove them from the fryer to a baking pan. Top them with bacon and drizzle with honey. Air Fry for 5 minutes to crisp up the bacon. Top the tater tots with cheese and cook for 2 minutes to melt the cheese. Serve.

Zucchini And Potato Tots

Servings:4
Cooking Time: 20 Minutes
Ingredients:
- 1 large zucchini, grated
- 1 medium baked potato, skin removed and mashed
- ¼ cup shredded Cheddar cheese
- 1 large egg, beaten
- ½ teaspoon kosher salt
- Cooking spray

Directions:
1. Preheat the air fryer to 390ºF (199ºC).
2. Wrap the grated zucchini in a paper towel and squeeze out any excess liquid, then combine the zucchini, baked potato, shredded Cheddar cheese, egg, and kosher salt in a large bowl.
3. Spray a baking pan with cooking spray, then place individual tablespoons of the zucchini mixture in the pan and air fry for 10 minutes. Repeat this process with the remaining mixture.
4. Remove the tots and allow to cool on a wire rack for 5 minutes before serving.

Phyllo Vegetable Triangles

Servings: 6
Cooking Time:6 To 11 Minutes
Ingredients:
- 3 tablespoons minced onion
- 2 garlic cloves, minced
- 2 tablespoons grated carrot
- 1 teaspoon olive oil
- 3 tablespoons frozen baby peas, thawed (see Tip)
- 2 tablespoons nonfat cream cheese, at room temperature
- 6 sheets frozen phyllo dough, thawed (see Tip)
- Olive oil spray, for coating the dough

Directions:
1. In a 6-by-2-inch pan, combine the onion, garlic, carrot, and olive oil. Air-fry for 2 to 4 minutes, or until the vegetables are crisp-tender. Transfer to a bowl.
2. Stir in the peas and cream cheese to the vegetable mixture. Let cool while you prepare the dough.
3. Lay one sheet of phyllo on a work surface and lightly spray with olive oil spray. Top with another sheet of phyllo. Repeat with the remaining 4 phyllo sheets; you'll have 3 stacks with 2 layers each. Cut each stack lengthwise into 4 strips (12 strips total).
4. Place a scant 2 teaspoons of the filling near the bottom of each strip. Bring one corner up over the filling to make a triangle; continue folding the triangles over, as you would fold a flag. Seal the edge with a bit of water. Repeat with the remaining strips and filling.
5. Air-fry the triangles, in 2 batches, for 4 to 7 minutes, or until golden brown. Serve.

Polenta Fries With Chili-lime Mayo

Servings: 4
Cooking Time: 28 Minutes
Ingredients:
* 2 teaspoons vegetable or olive oil
* ¼ teaspoon paprika
* 1 pound prepared polenta, cut into 3-inch x ½-inch sticks
* salt and freshly ground black pepper
* Chili-Lime Mayo
* ½ cup mayonnaise
* 1 teaspoon chili powder
* ¼ teaspoon ground cumin
* juice of half a lime
* 1 teaspoon chopped fresh cilantro
* salt and freshly ground black pepper

Directions:
1. Preheat the air fryer to 400°F.
2. Combine the oil and paprika and then carefully toss the polenta sticks in the mixture.
3. Air-fry the polenta fries at 400°F for 15 minutes. Gently shake the basket to rotate the fries and continue to air-fry for another 13 minutes or until the fries have browned nicely. Season to taste with salt and freshly ground black pepper.
4. To make the chili-lime mayo, combine all the ingredients in a small bowl and stir well.
5. Serve the polenta fries warm with chili-lime mayo on the side for dipping.

Zucchini Fritters With Olives

Servings: 6
Cooking Time: 12 Minutes
Ingredients:
* Cooking spray
* ½ cup parsley, chopped
* 1 egg
* ½ cup almond flour
* Black pepper and salt to the taste
* 3 spring onions, chopped
* ½ cup Kalamata olives, pitted and minced
* 3 zucchinis, grated

Directions:
1. In a suitable bowl, mix all the recipe ingredients except the cooking spray, stir well and shape medium fritters out of this mixture.
2. Place the fritters in your air fryer basket, grease them with cooking spray and cook at almost 380 degrees F/ 195 degrees C for 6 minutes on each side.
3. Serve them as an appetizer.

Cuban Sliders

Servings: 8
Cooking Time: 8 Minutes
Ingredients:
* 8 slices ciabatta bread, ¼-inch thick
* cooking spray
* 1 tablespoon brown mustard
* 6-8 ounces thin sliced leftover roast pork
* 4 ounces thin deli turkey
* ⅓ cup bread and butter pickle slices
* 2–3 ounces Pepper Jack cheese slices

Directions:
1. Spray one side of each slice of bread with butter or olive oil cooking spray.
2. Spread brown mustard on other side of each slice.
3. Layer pork roast, turkey, pickles, and cheese on 4 of the slices. Top with remaining slices.
4. Cook at 390°F for approximately 8minutes. The sandwiches should be golden brown.
5. Cut each slider in half to make 8 portions.

Root Veggie Chips With Herb Salt

Servings:2
Cooking Time: 8 Minutes
Ingredients:
* 1 parsnip, washed
* 1 small beet, washed
* 1 small turnip, washed
* ½ small sweet potato, washed
* 1 teaspoon olive oil
* Cooking spray
* Herb Salt:
* ¼ teaspoon kosher salt
* 2 teaspoons finely chopped fresh parsley

Directions:
1. Preheat the air fryer to 360ºF (182ºC).
2. Peel and thinly slice the parsnip, beet, turnip, and sweet potato, then place the vegetables in a large bowl, add the olive oil, and toss.
3. Spray the air fryer basket with cooking spray, then place the vegetables in the basket and air fry for 8 minutes, gently shaking the basket halfway through.
4. While the chips cook, make the herb salt in a small bowl by combining the kosher salt and parsley.
5. Remove the chips and place on a serving plate, then sprinkle the herb salt on top and allow to cool for 2 to 3 minutes before serving.

Buffalo Bites

Servings: 16
Cooking Time: 12 Minutes
Ingredients:
* 1 pound ground chicken
* 8 tablespoons buffalo wing sauce
* 2 ounces Gruyère cheese, cut into 16 cubes
* 1 tablespoon maple syrup

Directions:
1. Mix 4 tablespoons buffalo wing sauce into all the ground chicken.
2. Shape chicken into a log and divide into 16 equal portions.
3. With slightly damp hands, mold each chicken portion around a cube of cheese and shape into a firm ball. When you have shaped 8 meatballs, place them in air fryer basket.

4. Cook at 390°F for approximately 5minutes. Shake basket, reduce temperature to 360°F, and cook for 5 minutes longer.

5. While the first batch is cooking, shape remaining chicken and cheese into 8 more meatballs.

6. Repeat step 4 to cook second batch of meatballs.

7. In a medium bowl, mix the remaining 4 tablespoons of buffalo wing sauce with the maple syrup. Add all the cooked meatballs and toss to coat.

8. Place meatballs back into air fryer basket and cook at 390°F for 2 minutes to set the glaze. Skewer each with a toothpick and serve.

Middle Eastern Phyllo Rolls

Servings: 6
Cooking Time: 5 Minutes
Ingredients:
- 6 ounces Lean ground beef or ground lamb
- 3 tablespoons Sliced almonds
- 1 tablespoon Chutney (any variety), finely chopped
- ¼ teaspoon Ground cinnamon
- ¼ teaspoon Ground coriander
- ¼ teaspoon Ground cumin
- ¼ teaspoon Ground dried turmeric
- ¼ teaspoon Table salt
- ¼ teaspoon Ground black pepper
- 6 18 × 14-inch phyllo sheets (thawed, if necessary)
- Olive oil spray

Directions:
1. Set a medium skillet over medium heat for a minute or two, then crumble in the ground meat. Cook for 3 minutes, stirring often, or until well browned. Stir in the almonds, chutney, cinnamon, coriander, cumin, turmeric, salt, and pepper until well combined. Remove from the heat, scrape the cooked ground meat mixture into a bowl, and cool for 15 minutes.

2. Preheat the air fryer to 400°F.

3. Place one sheet of phyllo dough on a clean, dry work surface. (Keep the others covered.) Lightly coat it with olive oil spray, then fold it in half by bringing the short ends together. Place about 3 tablespoons of the ground meat mixture along one of the longer edges, then fold both of the shorter sides of the dough up and over the meat to partially enclose it (and become a border along the sheet of dough). Roll the dough closed, coat it with olive oil spray on all sides, and set it aside seam side down. Repeat this filling and spraying process with the remaining phyllo sheets.

4. Set the rolls seam side down in the basket in one layer with some air space between them. Air-fry undisturbed for 5 minutes, or until very crisp and golden brown.

5. Use kitchen tongs to transfer the rolls to a wire rack. Cool for only 2 or 3 minutes before serving hot.

Crispy Eggplant With Paprika

Servings: 4
Cooking Time: 20 Minutes
Ingredients:
- 1 eggplant, cut into 1-inch pieces
- ½ teaspoon Italian seasoning
- 1 teaspoon paprika
- ½ teaspoon red pepper
- 1 teaspoon garlic powder
- 2 tablespoons olive oil

Directions:
1. Add all the recipe ingredients into the suitable mixing bowl and toss well.

2. Transfer eggplant mixture into the air fryer basket.

3. Cook at almost 375 degrees F/ 190 degrees C for 20 minutes. Shake basket halfway through.

4. Serve and enjoy.

Beef Steak Sliders

Servings: 8
Cooking Time: 22 Minutes
Ingredients:
- 1 pound top sirloin steaks, about ¾-inch thick
- salt and pepper
- 2 large onions, thinly sliced
- 1 tablespoon extra-light olive oil
- 8 slider buns
- Horseradish Mayonnaise
- 1 cup light mayonnaise
- 4 teaspoons prepared horseradish
- 2 teaspoons Worcestershire sauce
- 1 teaspoon coarse brown mustard

Directions:
1. Place steak in air fryer basket and cook at 390°F for 6minutes. Turn and cook 6 more minutes for medium rare. If you prefer your steak medium, continue cooking for 3 minutes.

2. While the steak is cooking, prepare the Horseradish Mayonnaise by mixing all ingredients together.

3. When steak is cooked, remove from air fryer, sprinkle with salt and pepper to taste, and set aside to rest.

4. Toss the onion slices with the oil and place in air fryer basket. Cook at 390°F for 7 minutes, until onion rings are soft and browned.

5. Slice steak into very thin slices.

6. Spread slider buns with the horseradish mayo and pile on the meat and onions. Serve with remaining horseradish dressing for dipping.

Chocolate Bacon Bites

Servings: 4
Cooking Time: 10 Minutes
Ingredients:
- 4 bacon slices, halved
- 1 cup dark chocolate, melted
- A pinch of pink salt

Directions:
1. Dip each bacon slice in some chocolate, sprinkle pink salt over them, put them in your air fryer's basket and cook at 350°F for 10 minutes. Serve as a snack.

Avocado Fries, Vegan

Servings: 4
Cooking Time: 10 Minutes
Ingredients:
- ¼ cup almond or coconut milk
- 1 tablespoon lime juice
- ⅛ teaspoon hot sauce
- 2 tablespoons flour
- ¾ cup panko breadcrumbs
- ¼ cup cornmeal
- ¼ teaspoon salt
- 1 large avocado
- oil for misting or cooking spray

Directions:
1. In a small bowl, whisk together the almond or coconut milk, lime juice, and hot sauce.
2. Place flour on a sheet of wax paper.
3. Mix panko, cornmeal, and salt and place on another sheet of wax paper.
4. Split avocado in half and remove pit. Peel or use a spoon to lift avocado halves out of the skin.
5. Cut avocado lengthwise into ½-inch slices. Dip each in flour, then milk mixture, then roll in panko mixture.
6. Mist with oil or cooking spray and cook at 390°F for 10minutes, until crust is brown and crispy.

Thai-style Crabwontons

Servings: 4
Cooking Time: 20 Minutes
Ingredients:
- 4 oz cottage cheese, softened
- 2 ½ oz lump crabmeat
- 2 scallions, chopped
- 2 garlic cloves, minced
- 2 tsp tamari sauce
- 12 wonton wrappers
- 1 egg white, beaten
- 5 tbsp Thai sweet chili sauce

Directions:
1. Using a fork, mix together cottage cheese, crabmeat, scallions, garlic, and tamari sauce in a bowl. Set it near your workspace along with a small bowl of water. Place one wonton wrapper on a clean surface. The points should be facing so that it looks like a diamond. Put 1 level tbsp of the crab and cheese mix onto the center of the wonton wrapper. Dip your finger into the water and run the moist finger along the edges of the wrapper.
2. Fold one corner of the wrapper to the opposite side and make a triangle. From the center out, press out any air and seal the edges. Continue this process until all of the wontons have been filled and sealed. Brush both sides of the wontons with beaten egg white.
3. Preheat air fryer to 340°F. Place the wontons on the bottom of the greased frying basket in a single layer. Bake for 8 minutes, flipping the wontons once until golden brown and crispy. Serve hot and enjoy!

Cheese Bacon Jalapeno Poppers

Servings: 5
Cooking Time: 5 Minutes

Ingredients:
- 10 fresh jalapeno peppers, cut in half and remove seeds
- 2 bacon slices, cooked and crumbled
- 1/4 cup cheddar cheese, shredded
- 6 oz cream cheese, softened

Directions:
1. In a bowl, combine together bacon, cream cheese, and cheddar cheese.
2. Stuff each jalapeno half with bacon cheese mixture.
3. Spray air fryer basket with cooking spray.
4. Place stuffed jalapeno halved in air fryer basket and cook at 370°F for 5 minutes.
5. Serve and enjoy.

Chili Corn On The Cob

Servings: 4
Cooking Time: 30 Minutes
Ingredients:
- Salt and pepper to taste
- ½ tsp smoked paprika
- ¼ tsp chili powder
- 4 ears corn, halved
- 1 tbsp butter, melted
- ¼ cup lime juice
- 1 tsp lime zest
- 1 lime, quartered

Directions:
1. Preheat air fryer to 400°F. Combine salt, pepper, lime juice, lime zest, paprika, and chili powder in a small bowl. Toss corn and butter in a large bowl, then add the seasonings from the small bowl. Toss until coated. Arrange the corn in a single layer in the frying basket. Air Fry for 10 minutes, then turn the corn. Air Fry for another 8 minutes. Squeeze lime over the corn and serve.

Brie-currant & Bacon Spread

Servings: 6
Cooking Time: 30 Minutes
Ingredients:
- 4 oz cream cheese, softened
- 3 tbsp mayonnaise
- 1 cup diced Brie cheese
- ½ tsp dried thyme
- 4 oz cooked bacon, crumbled
- 1/3 cup dried currants

Directions:
1. Preheat the air fryer to 350°F. Beat the cream cheese with the mayo until well blended. Stir in the Brie, thyme, bacon, and currants and pour the dip mix in a 6-inch round pan. Put the pan in the fryer and Air Fry for 10-12 minutes, stirring once until the dip is melting and bubbling. Serve warm.

Baked Ricotta With Lemon And Capers

Servings: 4
Cooking Time: 10 Minutes
Ingredients:
- 7-inch pie dish or cake pan

- 1½ cups whole milk ricotta cheese
- zest of 1 lemon, plus more for garnish
- 1 teaspoon finely chopped fresh rosemary
- pinch crushed red pepper flakes
- 2 tablespoons capers, rinsed
- 2 tablespoons extra-virgin olive oil
- salt and freshly ground black pepper
- 1 tablespoon grated Parmesan cheese

Directions:
1. Preheat the air fryer to 380°F.
2. Combine the ricotta cheese, lemon zest, rosemary, red pepper flakes, capers, olive oil, salt and pepper in a bowl and whisk together well. Transfer the cheese mixture to a 7-inch pie dish and place the pie dish in the air fryer basket. You can use an aluminum foil sling to help with this by taking a long piece of aluminum foil, folding it in half lengthwise twice until it is roughly 26 inches by 3 inches. Place this under the pie dish and hold the ends of the foil to move the pie dish in and out of the air fryer basket. Tuck the ends of the foil beside the pie dish while it cooks in the air fryer.
3. Air-fry the ricotta at 380°F for 10 minutes, or until the top is nicely browned in spots.
4. Remove the pie dish from the air fryer and immediately sprinkle the Parmesan cheese on top. Drizzle with a little olive oil and add some freshly ground black pepper and lemon zest as garnish. Serve warm.

Salsa And Cheese Stuffed Mushrooms

Servings: 5
Cooking Time: 10 Minutes
Ingredients:
- 8 ounces large portobello mushrooms
- ⅓ cup salsa
- ½ cup shredded Cheddar cheese
- Cooking oil

Directions:
1. Cut the stem out of the mushrooms: First, chop off the end of the stem, and then make a circular cut around the area where the stem was. Continue to cut until you have removed the rest of the stem.
2. Stuff the mushrooms with the salsa. Sprinkle the shredded cheese on top.
3. Place the mushrooms in the air fryer. Cook for 8 minutes.
4. Cool before serving.

Cheesy Hash Brown Bruschetta

Servings:4
Cooking Time: 6 To 8 Minutes
Ingredients:
- 4 frozen hash brown patties
- 1 tablespoon olive oil
- ⅓ cup chopped cherry tomatoes
- 3 tablespoons diced fresh Mozzarella
- 2 tablespoons grated Parmesan cheese
- 1 tablespoon balsamic vinegar
- 1 tablespoon minced fresh basil

Directions:
1. Preheat the air fryer to 400°F (204°C).
2. Place the hash brown patties in the air fryer in a single layer. Air fry for 6 to 8 minutes, or until the potatoes are crisp, hot, and golden brown.
3. Meanwhile, combine the olive oil, tomatoes, Mozzarella, Parmesan, vinegar, and basil in a small bowl.
4. When the potatoes are done, carefully remove from the basket and arrange on a serving plate. Top with the tomato mixture and serve.

Hash Brown Bruschetta

Servings:4
Cooking Time: 6 To 8 Minutes
Ingredients:
- 4 frozen hash brown patties
- 1 tablespoon olive oil
- ⅓ cup chopped cherry tomatoes
- 3 tablespoons diced fresh mozzarella
- 2 tablespoons grated Parmesan cheese
- 1 tablespoon balsamic vinegar
- 1 tablespoon minced fresh basil

Directions:
1. Place the hash brown patties in the air fryer in a single layer. Air-fry for 6 to 8 minutes or until the potatoes are crisp, hot, and golden brown.
2. Meanwhile, combine the olive oil, tomatoes, mozzarella, Parmesan, vinegar, and basil in a small bowl.
3. When the potatoes are done, carefully remove from the basket and arrange on a serving plate. Top with the tomato mixture and serve.
4. Did You Know? Bruschetta comes from the word that means "to roast over coals," and refers to the toasted bread. It has many incarnations, including a recipe made by simply rubbing the warm little toasts with a cut clove of fresh garlic.

Herbed Pita Chips

Servings:4
Cooking Time: 5 To 6 Minutes
Ingredients:
- ¼ teaspoon dried basil
- ¼ teaspoon marjoram
- ¼ teaspoon ground oregano
- ¼ teaspoon garlic powder
- ¼ teaspoon ground thyme
- ¼ teaspoon salt
- 2 whole 6-inch pitas, whole grain or white
- Cooking spray

Directions:
1. Preheat the air fryer to 330°F (166°C).
2. Mix all the seasonings together.
3. Cut each pita half into 4 wedges. Break apart wedges at the fold.
4. Mist one side of pita wedges with oil. Sprinkle with half of seasoning mix.
5. Turn pita wedges over, mist the other side with oil, and sprinkle with remaining seasonings.
6. Place pita wedges in air fryer basket and bake for 2 minutes.

7. Shake the basket and bake for 2 minutes longer. Shake again, and if needed, bake for 1 or 2 more minutes, or until crisp. Watch carefully because at this point they will cook very quickly.
8. Serve hot.

Prosciutto Polenta Rounds

Servings: 6
Cooking Time: 40 Minutes + 10 Minutes To Cool
Ingredients:
*   1 tube precooked polenta
*   1 tbsp garlic oil
*   4 oz cream cheese, softened
*   3 tbsp mayonnaise
*   2 scallions, sliced
*   1 tbsp minced fresh chives
*   6 prosciutto slices, chopped

Directions:
1. Preheat the air fryer to 400°F. Slice the polenta crosswise into 12 rounds. Brush both sides of each round with garlic oil and put 6 of them in the frying basket. Put a rack in the basket over the polenta and add the other 6 rounds. Bake for 15 minutes, flip, and cook for 10-15 more minutes or until the polenta is crispy and golden. While the polenta is cooking, beat the cream cheese and mayo and stir in the scallions, chives, and prosciutto. When the polenta is cooked, lay out on a wire rack to cool for 15 minutes. Top with the cream cheese mix and serve.

Sweet And Spicy Beef Jerky

Servings:6
Cooking Time: 4 Hours
Ingredients:
*   1 pound eye of round beef, fat trimmed, sliced into ¼"-thick strips
*   ¼ cup soy sauce
*   2 tablespoons sriracha hot chili sauce
*   ½ teaspoon ground black pepper
*   2 tablespoons granular brown erythritol

Directions:
1. Place beef in a large sealable bowl or bag. Pour soy sauce and sriracha into bowl or bag, then sprinkle in pepper and erythritol. Shake or stir to combine ingredients and coat steak. Cover and place in refrigerator to marinate at least 2 hours up to overnight.
2. Once marinated, remove strips from marinade and pat dry. Place into ungreased air fryer basket in a single layer, working in batches if needed. Adjust the temperature to 180°F and set the timer for 4 hours. Jerky will be chewy and dark brown when done. Store in airtight container in a cool, dry place up to 2 weeks.

Yellow Onion Rings

Servings: 3
Cooking Time: 30 Minutes
Ingredients:
*   ½ sweet yellow onion
*   ½ cup buttermilk
*   ¾ cup flour

*   1 tbsp cornstarch
*   Salt and pepper to taste
*   ¾ tsp garlic powder
*   ½ tsp dried oregano
*   1 cup bread crumbs

Directions:
1. Preheat air fryer to 390°F. Cut the onion into ½-inch slices. Separate the onion slices into rings. Place the buttermilk in a bowl and set aside. In another bowl, combine the flour, cornstarch, salt, pepper, and garlic. Stir well and set aside. In a separate bowl, combine the breadcrumbs with oregano and salt.
2. Dip the rings into the buttermilk, dredge in flour, dip into the buttermilk again, and then coat into the crumb mixture. Put in the greased frying basket without overlapping. Spritz them with cooking oil and Air Fry for 13-16 minutes, shaking once or twice until the rings are crunchy and browned. Serve hot.

Panko Crusted Chicken Tenders

Servings: 4
Cooking Time: 10 Minutes
Ingredients:
*   12 ounces chicken breasts, cut into tenders
*   1 egg white
*   ⅛ cup flour
*   ½ cup panko bread crumbs
*   Black pepper and salt, to taste

Directions:
1. At 350 degrees F/ 175 degrees C, preheat your air fryer. and grease its air fryer basket.
2. Season the chicken tenders with some black pepper and salt.
3. Coat the chicken tenders with flour, then dip in egg whites and then dredge in the panko bread crumbs.
4. Arrange the prepared tender in the air fryer basket and cook for about 10 minutes.
5. Dish out in a platter and serve warm.

Za'atar Garbanzo Beans

Servings: 6
Cooking Time: 12 Minutes
Ingredients:
*   One 14.5-ounce can garbanzo beans, drained and rinsed
*   1 tablespoon extra-virgin olive oil
*   6 teaspoons za'atar seasoning mix
*   2 tablespoons chopped parsley
*   Salt and pepper, to taste

Directions:
1. Preheat the air fryer to 390°F.
2. In a medium bowl, toss the garbanzo beans with olive oil and za'atar seasoning.
3. Pour the beans into the air fryer basket and cook for 12 minutes, or until toasted as you like. Stir every 3 minutes while roasting.
4. Remove the beans from the air fryer basket into a serving bowl, top with fresh chopped parsley, and season with salt and pepper.

Chapter 4: Bread And Breakfast Recipes

The Simple Air Fryer Cookbook for Beginners

Nutty Whole Wheat Muffins

Servings: 8
Cooking Time: 11 Minutes
Ingredients:

- ½ cup whole-wheat flour, plus 2 tablespoons
- ¼ cup oat bran
- 2 tablespoons flaxseed meal
- ¼ cup brown sugar
- ½ teaspoon baking soda
- ½ teaspoon baking powder
- ¼ teaspoon salt
- ½ teaspoon cinnamon
- ½ cup buttermilk
- 2 tablespoons melted butter
- 1 egg
- ½ teaspoon pure vanilla extract
- ½ cup grated carrots
- ¼ cup chopped pecans
- ¼ cup chopped walnuts
- 1 tablespoon pumpkin seeds
- 1 tablespoon sunflower seeds
- 16 foil muffin cups, paper liners removed
- cooking spray

Directions:
1. Preheat air fryer to 330°F.
2. In a large bowl, stir together the flour, bran, flaxseed meal, sugar, baking soda, baking powder, salt, and cinnamon.
3. In a medium bowl, beat together the buttermilk, butter, egg, and vanilla. Pour into flour mixture and stir just until dry ingredients moisten. Do not beat.
4. Gently stir in carrots, nuts, and seeds.
5. Double up the foil cups so you have 8 total and spray with cooking spray.
6. Place 4 foil cups in air fryer basket and divide half the batter among them.
7. Cook at 330°F for 11minutes or until toothpick inserted in center comes out clean.
8. Repeat step 7 to cook remaining 4 muffins.

Blueberry French Toast Sticks

Servings: 4
Cooking Time: 20 Minutes
Ingredients:

- 3 bread slices, cut into strips
- 1 tbsp butter, melted
- 2 eggs
- 1 tbsp milk
- 1 tbsp sugar
- ½ tsp vanilla extract
- 1 cup fresh blueberries
- 1 tbsp lemon juice

Directions:
1. Preheat air fryer to 380°F. After laying the bread strips on a plate, sprinkle some melted butter over each piece. Whisk the eggs, milk, vanilla, and sugar, then dip

the bread in the mix. Place on a wire rack to let the batter drip. Put the bread strips in the air fryer and Air Fry for 5-7 minutes. Use tongs to flip them once and cook until golden. With a fork, smash the blueberries and lemon juice together. Spoon the blueberries sauce over the French sticks. Serve immediately.

Baked Pancakes With Caramelized Apples

Servings: 2
Cooking Time: 4 Minutes
Ingredients:

- 1 tablespoon milk
- 1 cup flour
- 1 ½ tablespoons of sugar
- 1 egg
- ½ teaspoon salt
- ½ teaspoon baking soda
- 1 tablespoon olive oil or another

Directions:
1. Mix all dry ingredients. And mix all the liquid ingredients separately.
2. Add rest of the liquid ingredients to dry ingredients and mix well with a whisk.
3. At 370 degrees F/ 185 degrees C, preheat your air fryer.
4. Grease its air fryer basket or special dish with a little olive oil.
5. Cook in portions for 2 minutes on each side.
6. To make the caramelized Apples: peel the apples, cut into cubes and place in the pan. Sprinkle with sugar and cinnamon, cook until the apples are golden and soft.

Huevos Rancheros

Servings: 4
Cooking Time: 45 Minutes + Cooling Time
Ingredients:

- 1 tbsp olive oil
- 20 cherry tomatoes, halved
- 2 chopped plum tomatoes
- ¼ cup tomato sauce
- 2 scallions, sliced
- 2 garlic cloves, minced
- 1 tsp honey
- ½ tsp salt
- ⅛ tsp cayenne pepper
- ¼ tsp grated nutmeg
- ¼ tsp paprika
- 4 eggs

Directions:
1. Preheat the air fryer to 370°F. Combine the olive oil, cherry tomatoes, plum tomatoes, tomato sauce, scallions, garlic, nutmeg, honey, salt, paprika and cayenne in a 7-inch springform pan that has been wrapped in foil to prevent leaks. Put the pan in the frying basket and
2. Bake the mix for 15-20 minutes, stirring twice until the tomatoes are soft. Mash some of the tomatoes in the pan with a fork, then stir them into the sauce. Also, break

the eggs into the sauce, then return the pan to the fryer and Bake for 2 minutes. Remove the pan from the fryer and stir the eggs into the sauce, whisking them through the sauce. Don't mix in completely. Cook for 4-8 minutes more or until the eggs are set. Let cool, then serve.

Hashbrown Potatoes Lyonnaise

Servings: 4
Cooking Time: 33 Minutes
Ingredients:
- 1 Vidalia (or other sweet) onion, sliced
- 1 teaspoon butter, melted
- 1 teaspoon brown sugar
- 2 large russet potatoes, sliced ½-inch thick
- 1 tablespoon vegetable oil
- salt and freshly ground black pepper

Directions:
1. Preheat the air fryer to 370°F.
2. Toss the sliced onions, melted butter and brown sugar together in the air fryer basket. Air-fry for 8 minutes, shaking the basket occasionally to help the onions cook evenly.
3. While the onions are cooking, bring a 3-quart saucepan of salted water to a boil on the stovetop. Par-cook the potatoes in boiling water for 3 minutes. Drain the potatoes and pat them dry with a clean kitchen towel.
4. Add the potatoes to the onions in the air fryer basket and drizzle with vegetable oil. Toss to coat the potatoes with the oil and season with salt and freshly ground black pepper.
5. Increase the air fryer temperature to 400°F and air-fry for 22 minutes tossing the vegetables a few times during the cooking time to help the potatoes brown evenly. Season to taste again with salt and freshly ground black pepper and serve warm.

English Breakfast

Servings: 2
Cooking Time: 30 Minutes
Ingredients:
- 6 bacon strips
- 1 cup cooked white beans
- 1 tbsp melted butter
- ½ tbsp flour
- Salt and pepper to taste
- 2 eggs

Directions:
1. Preheat air fryer to 360°F. In a second bowl, combine the beans, butter, flour, salt, and pepper. Mix well. Put the bacon in the frying basket and Air Fry for 10 minutes, flipping once. Remove the bacon and stir in the beans. Crack the eggs on top and cook for 10-12 minutes until the eggs are set. Serve with bacon.

Chia Seed Banana Bread

Servings: 6
Cooking Time: 35 Minutes
Ingredients:
- 2 bananas, mashed
- 2 tbsp sunflower oil
- 2 tbsp maple syrup
- ½ tsp vanilla
- ½ tbsp chia seeds
- ½ tbsp ground flaxseeds
- 1 cup pastry flour
- ¼ cup sugar
- ½ tsp cinnamon
- 1 orange, zested
- ¼ tsp salt
- ¼ tsp ground nutmeg
- ½ tsp baking powder

Directions:
1. Preheat air fryer to 350°F. Place the bananas, oil, maple syrup, vanilla, chia, and flaxseeds in a bowl and stir to combine. Add the flour, sugar, cinnamon, salt, nutmeg, baking powder, and orange zest. Stir to combine.
2. Pour the batter into a greased baking pan. Smooth the top with a rubber spatula and Bake for 25 minutes or until a knife inserted in the center comes out clean. Remove and let cool for a minute, then cut into wedges and serve. Enjoy warm!

Veggie Frittata

Servings: 4
Cooking Time:8 To 12 Minutes
Ingredients:
- ½ cup chopped red bell pepper
- ⅓ cup minced onion
- ⅓ cup grated carrot
- 1 teaspoon olive oil
- 6 egg whites
- 1 egg
- ⅓ cup 2 percent milk
- 1 tablespoon grated Parmesan cheese

Directions:
1. In a 6-by-2-inch pan, stir together the red bell pepper, onion, carrot, and olive oil. Put the pan into the air fryer. Cook for 4 to 6 minutes, shaking the basket once, until the vegetables are tender.
2. Meanwhile, in a medium bowl, beat the egg whites, egg, and milk until combined.
3. Pour the egg mixture over the vegetables in the pan. Sprinkle with the Parmesan cheese. Return the pan to the air fryer.
4. Bake for 4 to 6 minutes more, or until the frittata is puffy and set.
5. Cut into 4 wedges and serve.

Avocado Toasts With Poached Eggs

Servings: 4
Cooking Time: 15 Minutes
Ingredients:
- 4 eggs
- Salt and pepper to taste
- 4 bread pieces, toasted
- 1 pitted avocado, sliced

- ½ tsp chili powder
- ½ tsp dried rosemary

Directions:

1. Preheat air fryer to 320°F. Crack 1 egg into each greased ramekin and season with salt and black pepper. Place the ramekins into the air frying basket. Bake for 6-8 minutes.

2. Scoop the flesh of the avocado into a small bowl. Season with salt, black pepper, chili powderp and rosemary. Using a fork, smash the avocado lightly. Spread the smashed avocado evenly over toasted bread slices. Remove the eggs from the air fryer and gently spoon one onto each slice of avocado toast. Serve and enjoy!

Seasoned Herbed Sourdough Croutons

Servings: 4
Cooking Time: 7 Minutes

Ingredients:

- 4 cups cubed sourdough bread, 1-inch cubes
- 1 tablespoon olive oil
- 1 teaspoon fresh thyme leaves
- ¼ – ½ teaspoon salt
- freshly ground black pepper

Directions:

1. Combine all ingredients in a bowl and taste to make sure it is seasoned to your liking.

2. Preheat the air fryer to 400°F.

3. Toss the bread cubes into the air fryer and air-fry for 7 minutes, shaking the basket once or twice while they cook.

4. Serve warm or store in an airtight container.

Aromatic Mushroom Omelet

Servings: 4
Cooking Time: 30 Minutes

Ingredients:

- 6 eggs
- 2 tbsp milk
- ½ yellow onion, diced
- ½ cup diced mushrooms
- 2 tbsp chopped parsley
- 1 tsp dried oregano
- 1 tbsp chopped chives
- ½ tbsp chopped dill
- ½ cup grated Gruyère cheese

Directions:

1. Preheat air fryer to 350°F. Beat eggs in a medium bowl, then add the rest of the ingredients, except for the parsley. Stir until completely combined. Pour the mixture into a greased pan and bake in the air fryer for 18-20 minutes until the eggs are set. Top with parsley and serve.

Bacon Muffins

Servings: 8
Cooking Time: 15 Minutes

Ingredients:

- 6 large eggs
- 3 slices of cooked and chopped bacon
- ½ cup of chopped green and red bell pepper
- ½ cup of shredded cheddar cheese
- ¼ cup of shredded mozzarella cheese
- ¼ cup of chopped fresh spinach
- ¼ cup of chopped onions
- 2 tablespoons milk
- Black pepper and salt, to taste

Directions:

1. Put eggs, milk, black pepper, and salt into a suitable mixing bowl.

2. Whisk it until well combined.

3. Add in chopped bell peppers, spinach, black peppers, onions, ½ of shredded cheeses, and crumbled bacon. Mix it well.

4. First, place the silicone cups in the air fryer, then pour the egg mixture into them and add the remaining cheeses.

5. At 300 degrees F/ 150 degrees C, preheat your Air fryer.

6. Cook the prepared egg muffins for almost 12–15 minutes.

7. Serve warm and enjoy your Egg Muffins with Bacon!

Breakfast Chimichangas

Servings: 4
Cooking Time: 8 Minutes

Ingredients:

- Four 8-inch flour tortillas
- ½ cup canned refried beans
- 1 cup scrambled eggs
- ½ cup grated cheddar or Monterey jack cheese
- 1 tablespoon vegetable oil
- 1 cup salsa

Directions:

1. Lay the flour tortillas out flat on a cutting board. In the center of each tortilla, spread 2 tablespoons refried beans. Next, add ¼ cup eggs and 2 tablespoons cheese to each tortilla.

2. To fold the tortillas, begin on the left side and fold to the center. Then fold the right side into the center. Next fold the bottom and top down and roll over to completely seal the chimichanga. Using a pastry brush or oil mister, brush the tops of the tortilla packages with oil.

3. Preheat the air fryer to 400°F for 4 minutes. Place the chimichangas into the air fryer basket, seam side down, and air fry for 4 minutes. Using tongs, turn over the chimichangas and cook for an additional 2 to 3 minutes or until light golden brown.

Easy Egg Soufflé

Servings: 2
Cooking Time: 8 Minutes

Ingredients:

- 2 eggs
- ¼ teaspoon chili black pepper

- 2 tablespoons heavy cream
- ¼ teaspoon black pepper
- 1 tablespoon parsley, chopped
- Salt

Directions:

1. In a suitable bowl, whisk eggs with remaining gradients.
2. Spray 2 ramekins with cooking spray.
3. Pour egg mixture into the prepared ramekins and place into the air fryer basket.
4. Cook soufflé at 390 degrees F/ 200 degrees C for 8 minutes
5. Serve and enjoy.

Whisked Egg In Bell Pepper

Servings: 2
Cooking Time: 13 Minutes
Ingredients:

- 4 eggs
- 1 bell pepper, halved and remove seeds
- 4 small tomatoes finely slice.
- oregano
- black pepper
- garlic powder
- olive oil
- Salt

Directions:

1. Cut and peel the black peppers. Put a mixture of vegetables and seasonings in each half. Whisk 1 egg into each ½ of the black pepper.
2. Place bell pepper halves into the air fryer basket and cook at almost 390 degrees F/ 200 degrees C for 13 minutes.
3. Serve and enjoy.

Grilled Butter Sandwich

Servings: 1
Cooking Time: 10 Minutes
Ingredients:

- 2 slices of bread
- 3 slices of any cheese
- 1 tablespoon of melted butter

Directions:

1. At 350 degrees F/ 175 degrees C, preheat your air fryer.
2. Spread the melted butter over 1 side of each piece of bread.
3. Arrange the cheese slices over the bread and make a sandwich.
4. Put it in the air fryer and fry at 350 degrees F/ 175 degrees C for almost 10 minutes almost.
5. Serve warm and enjoy your Grilled Butter Sandwich!
6. Sandwich Fillings: Spread some pesto inside the sandwich and use just mozzarella cheese.
7. Put cooked bacon and use only cheddar cheese.

8. Add some fresh spinach with Swiss cheese inside the sandwich.

Healthy Granola

Servings: 4
Cooking Time: 10 Minutes
Ingredients:

- ¼ cup chocolate hazelnut spread
- 1 cup chopped pecans
- 1 cup quick-cooking oats
- 1 tbsp chia seeds
- 1 tbsp flaxseed
- 1 tbsp sesame seeds
- 1 cup coconut shreds
- ¼ cup maple syrup
- 1 tbsp light brown sugar
- ½ tsp vanilla extract
- ¼ cup hazelnut flour
- 2 tbsp cocoa powder
- Salt to taste

Directions:

1. Preheat air fryer at 350ºF. Combine the pecans, oats, chia seeds, flaxseed, sesame seeds, coconut shreds, chocolate hazelnut spread, maple syrup, sugar, vanilla extract, hazelnut flour, cocoa powder, and salt in a bowl. Press mixture into a greased cake pan. Place cake pan in the frying basket and Bake for 5 minutes, stirring once. Let cool completely before crumbling. Store it into an airtight container up to 5 days.

Vodka Basil Muffins With Strawberries

Servings:6
Cooking Time: 20 Minutes
Ingredients:

- ½ cup flour
- ½ cup granular sugar
- ½ tsp baking powder
- ⅛ tsp salt
- ½ cup chopped strawberries
- ¼ tsp vanilla extract
- 3 tbsp butter, melted
- 2 eggs
- ¼ tsp vodka
- 1 tbsp chopped basil

Directions:

1. Preheat air fryer to 375ºF. Combine the dry ingredients in a bowl. Set aside. In another bowl, whisk the wet ingredients. Pour wet ingredients into the bowl with the dry ingredients and gently combine. Add basil and vodka to the batter. Do not overmix and spoon batter into six silicone cupcake liners lightly greased with olive oil. Place liners in the frying basket and Bake for 7 minutes. Let cool for 5 minutes onto a cooling rack before serving.

Avocado Parsley Omelet

Servings: 4
Cooking Time: 15 Minutes
Ingredients:
- 4 eggs, whisked
- 1 tablespoon parsley, chopped
- ½ teaspoon cheddar cheese, shredded
- 1 avocado, peeled, pitted and cubed
- Cooking spray

Directions:
1. Mix the whisked eggs, chopped parsley, shredded cheddar cheese, and avocado cubes together in a bowl.
2. Grease a suitable baking pan with cooking spray.
3. Pour the egg mixture into the baking pan and spread.
4. Insert the baking pan inside your air fryer and cook at 370 degrees F/ 185 degrees C for 15 minutes.
5. When cooked, serve warm.

Tasty English Breakfast

Servings: 8
Cooking Time: 20 Minutes
Ingredients:
- 8 sausages
- 8 bacon slices
- 4 eggs
- 1 16-ounce can have baked beans
- 8 slices of toast

Directions:
1. Spread the sausages and bacon slices in your air fryer and air fry for almost 10 minutes at a 320 degrees F/ 160 degrees C.
2. Add the baked beans to a ramekin, then place another ramekin and add the eggs and whisk.
3. Increase the temperature to 290 degrees F/ 145 degrees C.
4. Place it in your air fryer and cook it for 10 minutes more.
5. Serve and enjoy!

Easy Vanilla Muffins

Servings: 6
Cooking Time: 35 Minutes + Cooling Time
Ingredients:
- 1 1/3 cups flour
- 5 tbsp butter, melted
- ¼ cup brown sugar
- 2 tbsp raisins
- ½ tsp ground cinnamon
- 1/3 cup granulated sugar
- ¼ cup milk
- 1 large egg
- 1 tsp vanilla extract
- 1 tsp baking powder
- Pinch of salt

Directions:
1. Preheat the air fryer to 330°F. Combine 1/3 cup of flour, 2 ½ tbsp of butter, brown sugar, and cinnamon in a bowl and mix until crumbly. Set aside. In another bowl, combine the remaining butter, granulated sugar, milk, egg, and vanilla and stir well. Add the remaining flour, baking powder, raisins, and salt and stir until combined.
2. Spray 6 silicone muffin cups with baking spray and spoon half the batter into them. Add a tsp of the cinnamon mixture, then add the rest of the batter and sprinkle with the remaining cinnamon mixture, pressing into the batter. Put the muffin cups in the frying basket and Bake for 14-18 minutes or until a toothpick inserted into the center comes out clean. Cool for 10 minutes, then remove the muffins from the cups. Serve and enjoy!

Orange Rolls

Servings: 8
Cooking Time: 10 Minutes
Ingredients:
- parchment paper
- 3 ounces low-fat cream cheese
- 1 tablespoon low-fat sour cream or plain yogurt (not Greek yogurt)
- 2 teaspoons sugar
- ¼ teaspoon pure vanilla extract
- ¼ teaspoon orange extract
- 1 can (8 count) organic crescent roll dough
- ¼ cup chopped walnuts
- ¼ cup dried cranberries
- ¼ cup shredded, sweetened coconut
- butter-flavored cooking spray
- Orange Glaze
- ½ cup powdered sugar
- 1 tablespoon orange juice
- ¼ teaspoon orange extract
- dash of salt

Directions:
1. Cut a circular piece of parchment paper slightly smaller than the bottom of your air fryer basket. Set aside.
2. In a small bowl, combine the cream cheese, sour cream or yogurt, sugar, and vanilla and orange extracts. Stir until smooth.
3. Preheat air fryer to 300°F.
4. Separate crescent roll dough into 8 triangles and divide cream cheese mixture among them. Starting at wide end, spread cheese mixture to within 1 inch of point.
5. Sprinkle nuts and cranberries evenly over cheese mixture.
6. Starting at wide end, roll up triangles, then sprinkle with coconut, pressing in lightly to make it stick. Spray tops of rolls with butter-flavored cooking spray.
7. Place parchment paper in air fryer basket, and place 4 rolls on top, spaced evenly.
8. Cook for 10minutes, until rolls are golden brown and cooked through.
9. Repeat steps 7 and 8 to cook remaining 4 rolls. You should be able to use the same piece of parchment paper twice.
10. In a small bowl, stir together ingredients for glaze and drizzle over warm rolls.

Apple French Toast Sandwich

Servings: 1
Cooking Time: 30 Minutes
Ingredients:
- 2 white bread slices
- 2 eggs
- 1 tsp cinnamon
- ½ peeled apple, sliced
- 1 tbsp brown sugar
- ¼ cup whipped cream

Directions:
1. Preheat air fryer to 350°F. Coat the apple slices with brown sugar in a small bowl. Whisk the eggs and cinnamon into a separate bowl until fluffy and completely blended. Coat the bread slices with the egg mixture, then place them on the greased frying basket. Top with apple slices and Air Fry for 20 minutes, flipping once until the bread is brown nicely and the apple is crispy.
2. Place one French toast slice onto a serving plate, then spoon the whipped cream on top and spread evenly. Scoop the caramelized apple slices onto the whipped cream, and cover with the second toast slice. Serve.

Simple Cinnamon Toasts

Servings:4
Cooking Time: 4 Minutes
Ingredients:
- 1 tablespoon salted butter
- 2 teaspoons ground cinnamon
- 4 tablespoons sugar
- ½ teaspoon vanilla extract
- 10 bread slices

Directions:
1. Preheat the air fryer to 380°F (193ºC).
2. In a bowl, combine the butter, cinnamon, sugar, and vanilla extract. Spread onto the slices of bread.
3. Put the bread inside the air fryer and bake for 4 minutes or until golden brown.
4. Serve warm.

French Toast Sticks

Servings: 4
Cooking Time: 7 Minutes
Ingredients:
- 2 eggs
- ½ cup milk
- ⅛ teaspoon salt
- ½ teaspoon pure vanilla extract
- ¾ cup crushed cornflakes
- 6 slices sandwich bread, each slice cut into 4 strips
- oil for misting or cooking spray
- maple syrup or honey

Directions:
1. In a small bowl, beat together eggs, milk, salt, and vanilla.
2. Place crushed cornflakes on a plate or in a shallow dish.
3. Dip bread strips in egg mixture, shake off excess, and roll in cornflake crumbs.
4. Spray both sides of bread strips with oil.
5. Place bread strips in air fryer basket in single layer.
6. Cook at 390°F for 7minutes or until they're dark golden brown.
7. Repeat steps 5 and 6 to cook remaining French toast sticks.
8. Serve with maple syrup or honey for dipping.

Tasty Hash Browns With Radish

Servings: 4
Cooking Time: 13 Minutes
Ingredients:
- 1-pound radishes, washed and cut off roots
- 1 tablespoon olive oil
- ½ teaspoon paprika
- ½ teaspoon onion powder
- ½ teaspoon garlic powder
- 1 medium onion
- ¼ teaspoon black pepper
- ¾ teaspoon salt

Directions:
1. Slice onion and radishes using a mandolin slicer.
2. Add sliced onion and radishes in a suitable mixing bowl and toss with olive oil.
3. Transfer onion and radish slices in air fryer basket and cook at almost 360 degrees F/ 180 degrees C for 8 minutes. Shake basket twice.
4. Return onion and radish slices in a suitable mixing bowl and toss with seasonings.
5. Again, cook onion and radish slices in air fryer basket for 5 minutes at 400 degrees F/ 205 degrees C. Shake the basket halfway through.
6. Serve and enjoy.

Jalapeño Egg Cups

Servings:4
Cooking Time: 14 Minutes
Ingredients:
- 4 large eggs
- ½ teaspoon salt
- ¼ teaspoon ground black pepper
- ¼ cup chopped pickled jalapeños
- 2 ounces cream cheese, softened
- ¼ teaspoon garlic powder
- ½ cup shredded sharp Cheddar cheese

Directions:
1. In a medium bowl, beat eggs together with salt and pepper, then pour evenly into four 4" ramekins greased with cooking spray.
2. In a separate large bowl, mix jalapeños, cream cheese, garlic powder, and Cheddar. Spoon ¼ of the mixture into the center of one ramekin. Repeat with remaining mixture and ramekins.
3. Place ramekins in air fryer basket. Adjust the temperature to 320°F and set the timer for 14 minutes. Eggs will be set when done. Serve warm.

Hard-cooked Eggs

Servings:6
Cooking Time: 15 Minutes
Ingredients:
- 6 large eggs

Directions:
1. Carefully put the eggs in a single layer in the air fryer basket.
2. Bake for at least 8 minutes for a slightly runny yolk, or 12 to 15 minutes for a firmer yolk. You may need to experiment with your air fryer to find the best time.
3. Remove the eggs from the air fryer carefully, using tongs, and immediately place them in a bowl of very cold water.
4. Let the eggs stand in the cold water for 5 minutes, then gently crack the shell under water. Let the eggs stand for another minute or two, then peel and eat.

Thyme Beef & Eggs

Servings: 1
Cooking Time: 25 Minutes
Ingredients:
- 2 tbsp butter
- 1 rosemary sprig
- 2 garlic cloves, pressed
- 8 oz sirloin steak
- Salt and pepper to taste
- ⅛ tsp cayenne pepper
- 2 eggs
- 1 tsp dried thyme

Directions:
1. Preheat air fryer to 400°F. On a clean cutting board, place butter and half of the rosemary spring in the center. Set aside. Season both sides of the steak with salt, black pepper, thyme, pressed garlic, and cayenne pepper. Transfer the steak to the frying basket and top with the other half of the rosemary sprig. Cook for 4 minutes, then flip the steak. Cook for another 3 minutes.
2. Remove the steak and set it on top of the butter and rosemary sprig on the cutter board. Tent with foil and let it rest. Grease ramekin and crack both eggs into it. Season with salt and pepper. Transfer the ramekin to the frying basket and bake for 4-5 minutes until the egg white is cooked and set. Remove the foil from the steak and slice. Serve with eggs and enjoy.

Mushroom & Cavolo Nero Egg Muffins

Servings: 6
Cooking Time: 20 Minutes
Ingredients:
- 8 oz baby Bella mushrooms, sliced
- 6 eggs, beaten
- 1 garlic clove, minced
- Salt and pepper to taste
- ½ tsp chili powder
- 1 cup cavolo nero
- 2 scallions, diced

Directions:
1. Preheat air fryer to 320°F. Place the eggs, garlic, salt, pepper, and chili powder in a bowl and beat until well combined. Fold in the mushrooms, cavolo nero, and scallions. Divide the mixture between greased muffin cups. Place into the air fryer and Bake for 12-15 minutes, or until the eggs are set. Cool for 5 minutes. Enjoy!

Quesadillas

Servings: 4
Cooking Time: 12 Minutes
Ingredients:
- 4 eggs
- 2 tablespoons skim milk
- salt and pepper
- oil for misting or cooking spray
- 4 flour tortillas
- 4 tablespoons salsa
- 2 ounces Cheddar cheese, grated
- ½ small avocado, peeled and thinly sliced

Directions:
1. Preheat air fryer to 270°F.
2. Beat together eggs, milk, salt, and pepper.
3. Spray a 6 x 6-inch air fryer baking pan lightly with cooking spray and add egg mixture.
4. Cook 9minutes, stirring every 1 to 2minutes, until eggs are scrambled to your liking. Remove and set aside.
5. Spray one side of each tortilla with oil or cooking spray. Flip over.
6. Divide eggs, salsa, cheese, and avocado among the tortillas, covering only half of each tortilla.
7. Fold each tortilla in half and press down lightly.
8. Place 2 tortillas in air fryer basket and cook at 390°F for 3minutes or until cheese melts and outside feels slightly crispy. Repeat with remaining two tortillas.
9. Cut each cooked tortilla into halves or thirds.

Oregano And Coconut Scramble

Servings: 4
Cooking Time: 20 Minutes
Ingredients:
- 8 eggs, whisked
- 2 tablespoons oregano, chopped
- Salt and black pepper to the taste
- 2 tablespoons parmesan, grated
- ¼ cup coconut cream

Directions:
1. In a bowl, mix the eggs with all the ingredients and whisk. Pour this into a pan that fits your air fryer, introduce it in the preheated fryer and cook at 350°F for 20 minutes, stirring often. Divide the scramble between plates and serve for breakfast.

Chicken Sausages

Servings:8
Cooking Time:8 To 12 Minutes
Ingredients:
- 1 Granny Smith apple, peeled and finely chopped
- ⅓ cup minced onion

- 3 tablespoons ground almonds
- 2 garlic cloves, minced
- 1 egg white
- 2 tablespoons apple juice
- ⅛ teaspoon freshly ground black pepper
- 1 pound ground chicken breast

Directions:

1. In a medium bowl, thoroughly mix the apple, onion, almonds, garlic, egg white, apple juice, and pepper.
2. With your hands, gently work the chicken breast into the apple mixture until combined.
3. Form the mixture into 8 patties. Put the patties into the air fryer basket. You may need to cook them in batches. Air-fry for 8 to 12 minutes, or until the patties reach an internal temperature of 165°F on a meat thermometer (see Tip). Serve.

Super Easy Bacon Cups

Servings:2
Cooking Time: 20 Minutes

Ingredients:

- 3 slices bacon, cooked, sliced in half
- 2 slices ham
- 1 slice tomato
- 2 eggs
- 2 teaspoons grated Parmesan cheese
- Salt and ground black pepper, to taste

Directions:

1. Preheat the air fryer to 375ºF (191ºC). Line 2 greased muffin tins with 3 half-strips of bacon
2. Put one slice of ham and half slice of tomato in each muffin tin on top of the bacon
3. Crack one egg on top of the tomato in each muffin tin and sprinkle each with half a teaspoon of grated Parmesan cheese. Sprinkle with salt and ground black pepper, if desired.
4. Bake in the preheated air fryer for 20 minutes. Remove from the air fryer and let cool.
5. Serve warm.

Meaty Omelet

Servings: 4
Cooking Time: 20 Minutes

Ingredients:

- 6 eggs
- ½ cup grated Swiss cheese
- 3 breakfast sausages, sliced
- 8 bacon strips, sliced
- Salt and pepper to taste

Directions:

1. Preheat air fryer to 360°F. In a bowl, beat the eggs and stir in Swiss cheese, sausages and bacon. Transfer the mixture to a baking dish and set in the fryer. Bake for 15 minutes or until golden and crisp. Season and serve.

Chapter 5: Vegetarians Recipes

Cheddar-bean Flautas

Servings: 4
Cooking Time: 15 Minutes
Ingredients:
- 8 corn tortillas
- 1 can refried beans
- 1 cup shredded cheddar
- 1 cup guacamole

Directions:
1. Preheat air fryer to 390°F. Wet the tortillas with water. Spray the frying basket with oil and stack the tortillas inside. Air Fry for 1 minute. Remove to a flat surface, laying them out individually. Scoop an equal amount of beans in a line down the center of each tortilla. Top with cheddar cheese. Roll the tortilla sides over the filling and put seam-side down in the greased frying basket. Air Fry for 7 minutes or until the tortillas are golden and crispy. Serve immediately topped with guacamole.

Almond Asparagus

Servings:3
Cooking Time:6 Minutes
Ingredients:
- 1 pound asparagus
- 1/3 cup almonds, sliced
- 2 tablespoons olive oil
- 2 tablespoons balsamic vinegar
- Salt and black pepper, to taste

Directions:
1. Preheat the Air fryer to 400°F and grease an Air fryer basket.
2. Mix asparagus, oil, vinegar, salt, and black pepper in a bowl and toss to coat well.
3. Arrange asparagus into the Air fryer basket and sprinkle with the almond slices.
4. Cook for about 6 minutes and dish out to serve hot.

Mediterranean Pan Pizza

Servings:2
Cooking Time: 8 Minutes
Ingredients:
- 1 cup shredded mozzarella cheese
- ¼ medium red bell pepper, seeded and chopped
- ½ cup chopped fresh spinach leaves
- 2 tablespoons chopped black olives
- 2 tablespoons crumbled feta cheese

Directions:
1. Sprinkle mozzarella into an ungreased 6" round nonstick baking dish in an even layer. Add remaining ingredients on top.
2. Place dish into air fryer basket. Adjust the temperature to 350°F and set the timer for 8 minutes, checking halfway through to avoid burning. Top of pizza will be golden brown and the cheese melted when done.
3. Remove dish from fryer and let cool 5 minutes before slicing and serving.

Twice-baked Broccoli-cheddar Potatoes

Servings:4
Cooking Time: 35 Minutes
Ingredients:
- 4 large russet potatoes
- 2 tablespoons plus 2 teaspoons ranch dressing
- 1 teaspoon salt
- ½ teaspoon ground black pepper
- ¼ cup chopped cooked broccoli florets
- 1 cup shredded sharp Cheddar cheese

Directions:
1. Preheat the air fryer to 400°F.
2. Using a fork, poke several holes in potatoes. Place in the air fryer basket and cook 30 minutes until fork-tender.
3. Once potatoes are cool enough to handle, slice lengthwise and scoop out the cooked potato into a large bowl, being careful to maintain the structural integrity of potato skins. Add ranch dressing, salt, pepper, broccoli, and Cheddar to potato flesh and stir until well combined.
4. Scoop potato mixture back into potato skins and return to the air fryer basket. Cook an additional 5 minutes until cheese is melted. Serve warm.

Spring Veggie Empanadas

Servings: 4
Cooking Time: 75 Minutes
Ingredients:
- 10 empanada pastry discs
- 1 tbsp olive oil
- 1 shallot, minced
- 1 garlic clove, minced
- ½ cup whole milk
- 1 cup chopped broccoli
- ½ cup chopped cauliflower
- ½ cup diced carrots
- ¼ cup diced celery
- ⅛ tsp ground nutmeg
- 1 tsp cumin powder
- 1 tsp minced ginger
- 1 egg

Directions:
1. Melt the olive oil in a pot over medium heat. Stir in shallot and garlic and cook through for 1 minute. Next, add 1 tablespoon of flour and continue stirring. Whisk in milk, then lower the heat. After that, add broccoli, cauliflower, carrots, celery, cumin powder, pepper, ginger, and nutmeg. Cook for 2 minutes then remove from the heat. Allow to cool for 5 minutes.
2. Preheat air fryer to 350°F. Lightly flour a flat work surface and turn out the pastry discs. Scoop ¼ of the vegetables in the center of each circle. Whisk the egg and 1 teaspoon of water in a small bowl and brush the entire edge of the circle with the egg wash and fold the dough over the filling into a half-moon shape. Crimp the edge with a fork to seal. Arrange the patties in a single layer in the frying basket and bake for 12 minutes. Flip the patties and bake for another 10 to 12 minutes until the outside crust is golden. Serve immediately and enjoy.

Cheesy Brussel Sprouts

Servings:3
Cooking Time:10 Minutes
Ingredients:

- 1 pound Brussels sprouts, trimmed and halved
- ¼ cup whole wheat breadcrumbs
- ¼ cup Parmesan cheese, shredded
- 1 tablespoon balsamic vinegar
- 1 tablespoon extra-virgin olive oil
- Salt and black pepper, to taste

Directions:
1. Preheat the Air fryer to 400°F and grease an Air fryer basket.
2. Mix Brussel sprouts, vinegar, oil, salt, and black pepper in a bowl and toss to coat well.
3. Arrange the Brussel sprouts in the Air fryer basket and cook for about 5 minutes.
4. Sprinkle with breadcrumbs and cheese and cook for about 5 more minutes.
5. Dish out and serve hot.

Healthy Living Mushroom Enchiladas

Servings: 4
Cooking Time: 40 Minutes
Ingredients:

- 2 cups sliced mushrooms
- ½ onion, thinly sliced
- 2 garlic cloves, minced
- 1 tbsp olive oil
- 10 oz spinach, chopped
- ½ tsp ground cumin
- 1 tbsp dried oregano
- 1 tsp chili powder
- ¼ cup grated feta cheese
- ¼ tsp red pepper flakes
- 1 cup grated mozzarella cheese
- 1 cup sour cream
- 2 tbsp mayonnaise
- Juice of 1 lime
- Salt and pepper to taste
- 8 corn tortillas
- 1 jalapeño pepper, diced
- ¼ cup chopped cilantro

Directions:
1. Preheat air fryer to 400°F. Combine mushrooms, onion, oregano, garlic, chili powder, olive oil, and salt in a small bowl until well coated. Transfer to the greased frying basket. Cook for 5 minutes, then shake the basket. Cook for another 3 to 4 minutes, then transfer to a medium bowl. Wipe out the frying basket. Take the garlic cloves from the mushroom mixture and finely mince them. Return half of the garlic to the bowl with the mushrooms. Stir in spinach, cumin, red pepper flakes, and ½ cup of mozzarella. Place the other half of the minced garlic in a small bowl along with sour cream, mayonnaise, feta, the rest of the mozzarella, lime juice, and black pepper.
2. To prepare the enchiladas, spoon 2 tablespoons of mushroom mixture in the center of each tortilla. Roll the tortilla and place it seam-side down in the baking dish. Repeat for the rest of the tortillas. Top with sour cream mixture and garnish with jalapenos. Place the dish in the frying basket and bake for 20 minutes until heated through and just brown on top. Top with cilantro. Serve.

Broccoli With Olives

Servings:4
Cooking Time:19 Minutes
Ingredients:

- 2 pounds broccoli, stemmed and cut into 1-inch florets
- 1/3 cup Kalamata olives, halved and pitted
- ¼ cup Parmesan cheese, grated
- 2 tablespoons olive oil
- Salt and ground black pepper, as required
- 2 teaspoons fresh lemon zest, grated

Directions:
1. Preheat the Air fryer to 400°F and grease an Air fryer basket.
2. Boil the broccoli for about 4 minutes and drain well.
3. Mix broccoli, oil, salt, and black pepper in a bowl and toss to coat well.
4. Arrange broccoli into the Air fryer basket and cook for about 15 minutes.
5. Stir in the olives, lemon zest and cheese and dish out to serve.

Pesto Vegetable Kebabs

Servings:4
Cooking Time: 8 Minutes
Ingredients:

- 12 ounces button mushrooms
- 12 ounces cherry tomatoes
- 2 medium zucchini, cut into ¼" slices
- 1 medium red onion, peeled and cut into 1" cubes
- 1 cup pesto, divided
- ½ teaspoon salt
- ¼ teaspoon ground black pepper

Directions:
1. Soak eight 6" skewers in water 10 minutes to avoid burning. Preheat the air fryer to 350°F.
2. Place a mushroom on a skewer, followed by a tomato, zucchini slice, and red onion piece. Repeat to fill up the skewer, then follow the same pattern for remaining skewers.
3. Brush each skewer evenly using ½ cup pesto. Sprinkle kebabs with salt and pepper. Place in the air fryer basket and cook 10 minutes, turning halfway through cooking time, until vegetables are tender. Brush kebabs with remaining ½ cup pesto before serving.

Corn And Pepper Jack Chile Rellenos With Roasted Tomato Sauce

Servings: 3
Cooking Time: 30 Minutes
Ingredients:
- 3 Poblano peppers
- 1 cup all-purpose flour*
- salt and freshly ground black pepper
- 2 eggs, lightly beaten
- 1 cup plain breadcrumbs*
- olive oil, in a spray bottle
- Sauce
- 2 cups cherry tomatoes
- 1 Jalapeño pepper, halved and seeded
- 1 clove garlic
- ¼ red onion, broken into large pieces
- 1 tablespoon olive oil
- salt, to taste
- 2 tablespoons chopped fresh cilantro
- Filling
- olive oil
- ¼ red onion, finely chopped
- 1 teaspoon minced garlic
- 1 cup corn kernels, fresh or frozen
- 2 cups grated pepper jack cheese

Directions:
1. Start by roasting the peppers. Preheat the air fryer to 400°F. Place the peppers into the air fryer basket and air-fry at 400°F for 10 minutes, turning them over halfway through the cooking time. Remove the peppers from the basket and cover loosely with foil.
2. While the peppers are cooling, make the roasted tomato sauce. Place all sauce Ingredients except for the cilantro into the air fryer basket and air-fry at 400°F for 10 minutes, shaking the basket once or twice. When the sauce Ingredients have finished air-frying, transfer everything to a blender or food processor and blend or process to a smooth sauce, adding a little warm water to get the desired consistency. Season to taste with salt, add the cilantro and set aside.
3. While the sauce Ingredients are cooking in the air fryer, make the filling. Heat a skillet on the stovetop over medium heat. Add the olive oil and sauté the red onion and garlic for 4 to 5 minutes. Transfer the onion and garlic to a bowl, stir in the corn and cheese, and set aside.
4. Set up a dredging station with three shallow dishes. Place the flour, seasoned with salt and pepper, in the first shallow dish. Place the eggs in the second dish, and fill the third shallow dish with the breadcrumbs. When the peppers have cooled, carefully slice into one side of the pepper to create an opening. Pull the seeds out of the peppers and peel away the skins, trying not to tear the pepper. Fill each pepper with some of the corn and cheese filling and close the pepper up again by folding one side of the opening over the other. Carefully roll each pepper in the seasoned flour, then into the egg and finally into the breadcrumbs to coat on all sides, trying not to let the pepper fall open. Spray the peppers on all sides with a little olive oil.

5. Air-fry two peppers at a time at 350°F for 6 minutes. Turn the peppers over and air-fry for another 4 minutes. Serve the peppers warm on a bed of the roasted tomato sauce.

Garlicky Brussel Sprouts With Saffron Aioli

Servings: 4
Cooking Time: 20 Minutes
Ingredients:
- 1 lb Brussels sprouts, halved
- 1 tsp garlic powder
- Salt and pepper to taste
- ½ cup mayonnaise
- ½ tbsp olive oil
- 1 tbsp Dijon mustard
- 1 tsp minced garlic
- Salt and pepper to taste
- ½ tsp liquid saffron

Directions:
1. Preheat air fryer to 380°F. Combine the Brussels sprouts, garlic powder, salt and pepper in a large bowl. Place in the fryer and spray with cooking oil. Bake for 12-14 minutes, shaking once, until just brown.
2. Meanwhile, in a small bowl, mix mayonnaise, olive oil, mustard, garlic, saffron, salt and pepper. When the Brussels sprouts are slightly cool, serve with aioli. Enjoy!

Quick-to-make Quesadillas

Servings: 4
Cooking Time: 30 Minutes
Ingredients:
- 12 oz goat cheese
- 2 tbsp vinegar
- 1 tbsp Taco seasoning
- 1 ripe avocado, pitted
- 4 scallions, finely sliced
- 2 tbsp lemon juice
- 4 flour tortillas
- ¼ cup hot sauce
- ½ cup Alfredo sauce
- 16 cherry tomatoes, halved

Directions:
1. Preheat air fryer to 400°F. Slice goat cheese into 4 pieces. Set aside. In a bowl, whisk vinegar and taco seasoning until combined. Submerge each slice into the vinegar and Air Fry for 12 minutes until crisp, turning once. Let cool slightly before cutting into 1/2-inch thick strips.
2. Using a fork, mash the avocado in a bowl. Stir in scallions and lemon juice and set aside. Lay one tortilla on a flat surface, cut from one edge to the center, then spread ¼ of the avocado mixture on one quadrant, 1 tbsp of hot sauce on the next quadrant, and finally 2 tbsp of Alfredo sauce on the other half. Top the non-sauce half with ¼ of cherry tomatoes and ¼ of goat cheese strips.
3. To fold, start with the avocado quadrant, folding each over the next one until you create a stacked triangle. Repeat the process with the remaining tortillas. Air Fry for 5 minutes until crispy, turning once. Serve warm.

Crispy Cabbage Steaks

Servings:4
Cooking Time: 10 Minutes

Ingredients:

- 1 small head green cabbage, cored and cut into ½"-thick slices
- ¼ teaspoon salt
- ¼ teaspoon ground black pepper
- 2 tablespoons olive oil
- 1 clove garlic, peeled and finely minced
- ½ teaspoon dried thyme
- ½ teaspoon dried parsley

Directions:

1. Sprinkle each side of cabbage with salt and pepper, then place into ungreased air fryer basket, working in batches if needed.
2. Drizzle each side of cabbage with olive oil, then sprinkle with remaining ingredients on both sides. Adjust the temperature to 350°F and set the timer for 10 minutes, turning "steaks" halfway through cooking. Cabbage will be browned at the edges and tender when done. Serve warm.

Sweet And Sour Brussel Sprouts

Servings:2
Cooking Time:10 Minutes

Ingredients:

- 2 cups Brussels sprouts, trimmed and halved lengthwise
- 1 tablespoon balsamic vinegar
- 1 tablespoon maple syrup
- Salt, as required

Directions:

1. Preheat the Air fryer to 400°F and grease an Air fryer basket.
2. Mix all the ingredients in a bowl and toss to coat well.
3. Arrange the Brussel sprouts in the Air fryer basket and cook for about 10 minutes, shaking once halfway through.
4. Dish out in a bowl and serve hot.

Fried Potatoes With Bell Peppers

Servings: 4
Cooking Time: 30 Minutes

Ingredients:

- 3 russet potatoes, cubed
- 1 tbsp canola oil
- 1 tbsp olive oil
- 1 tsp paprika
- Salt and pepper to taste
- 1 chopped shallot
- ½ chopped red bell peppers
- ½ diced yellow bell peppers

Directions:

1. Preheat air fryer to 370°F. Whisk the canola oil, olive oil, paprika, salt, and pepper in a bowl. Toss in the potatoes to coat. Place the potatoes in the air fryer and Bake for 20 minutes, shaking the basket periodically. Top the potatoes with shallot and bell peppers and cook for an additional 3-4 minutes or until the potatoes are cooked through and the peppers are soft. Serve warm.

Hellenic Zucchini Bites

Servings:4
Cooking Time: 20 Minutes

Ingredients:

- 8 pitted Kalamata olives, halved
- 2 tsp olive oil
- 1 zucchini, sliced
- ½ tsp salt
- ½ tsp Greek oregano
- ½ cup marinara sauce
- ½ cup feta cheese crumbles
- 2 tbsp chopped dill

Directions:

1. Preheat air fryer to 350ºF. Brush olive oil over both sides of the zucchini circles. Lay out slices on a large plate and sprinkle with salt. Then, top with marinara sauce, feta crumbles, Greek oregano and olives. Place the topped circles in the frying basket and Air Fry for 5 minutes. Garnish with chopped dill to serve.

Rainbow Quinoa Patties

Servings: 4
Cooking Time: 20 Minutes

Ingredients:

- 1 cup canned tri-bean blend, drained and rinsed
- 2 tbsp olive oil
- ½ tsp ground cumin
- ½ tsp garlic salt
- 1 tbsp paprika
- 1/3 cup uncooked quinoa
- 2 tbsp chopped onion
- ¼ cup shredded carrot
- 2 tbsp chopped cilantro
- 1 tsp chili powder
- ½ tsp salt
- 2 tbsp mascarpone cheese

Directions:

1. Place 1/3 cup of water, 1 tbsp of olive oil, cumin, and salt in a saucepan over medium heat and bring it to a boil. Remove from the heat and stir in quinoa. Let rest covered for 5 minutes.
2. Preheat air fryer at 350ºF. Using the back of a fork, mash beans until smooth. Toss in cooked quinoa and the remaining ingredients. Form mixture into 4 patties. Place patties in the greased frying basket and Air Fry for 6 minutes, turning once, and brush with the remaining olive oil. Serve immediately.

Bengali Samosa With Mango Chutney

Servings: 4
Cooking Time: 65 Minutes

Ingredients:

- ¼ tsp ground fenugreek seeds

- 1 cup diced mango
- 1 tbsp minced red onion
- 2 tsp honey
- 1 tsp minced ginger
- 1 tsp apple cider vinegar
- 1 phyllo dough sheet
- 2 tbsp olive oil
- 1 potato, mashed
- ½ tsp garam masala
- ¼ tsp ground turmeric
- ⅛ tsp chili powder
- ¼ tsp ground cumin
- ½ cup green peas
- 2 scallions, chopped

Directions:

1. Mash mango in a small bowl until chunky. Stir in onion, ginger, honey, and vinegar. Save in the fridge until ready to use. Place the mashed potato in a bowl. Add half of the olive oil, garam masala, turmeric, chili powder, ground fenugreek seeds, cumin, and salt and stir until mostly smooth. Stir in peas and scallions.

2. Preheat air fryer to 425°F. Lightly flour a flat work surface and transfer the phyllo dough. Cut into 8 equal portions and roll each portion to ¼-inch thick rounds. Divide the potato filling between the dough rounds. Fold in three sides and pinch at the meeting point, almost like a pyramid. Arrange the samosas in the frying basket and brush with the remaining olive oil. Bake for 10 minutes, then flip the samosas. Bake for another 4-6 minutes until the crust is crisp and golden. Serve with mango chutney.

Pesto Pepperoni Pizza Bread

Servings:4
Cooking Time: 25 Minutes
Ingredients:

- 2 eggs, beaten
- 2 tbsp flour
- 2 tbsp cassava flour
- 1/3 cup whipping cream
- ¼ cup chopped pepperoni
- 1/3 cup grated mozzarella
- 2 tsp Italian seasoning
- ½ tsp baking powder
- ⅛ tsp salt
- 3 tsp grated Parmesan cheese
- ½ cup pesto

Directions:

1. Preheat air fryer to 300ºF. Combine all ingredients, except for the Parmesan and pesto sauce, in a bowl until mixed. Pour the batter into a pizza pan. Place it in the frying basket and Bake for 20 minutes. After, sprinkle Parmesan on top and cook for 1 minute. Let chill for 5 minutes before slicing. Serve with warmed pesto sauce.

Mushroom-rice Stuffed Bell Peppers

Servings: 4
Cooking Time: 30 Minutes
Ingredients:

- 4 red bell peppers, tops sliced
- 1 ½ cups cooked rice
- ¼ cup chopped leeks
- ¼ cup sliced mushrooms
- ¾ cup tomato sauce
- Salt and pepper to taste
- ¾ cup shredded mozzarella
- 2 tbsp parsley, chopped

Directions:

1. Fill a large pot of water and heat on high until it boils. Remove seeds and membranes from the peppers. Carefully place peppers into the boiling water for 5 minutes. Remove and set aside to cool. Mix together rice, leeks, mushrooms, tomato sauce, parsley, salt, and pepper in a large bowl. Stuff each pepper with the rice mixture. Top with mozzarella.

2. Preheat air fryer to 350°F. Arrange the peppers on the greased frying basket and Bake for 10 minutes. Serve.

Breaded Avocado Tacos

Servings: 3
Cooking Time: 20 Minutes
Ingredients:

- 2 tomatoes, diced
- ¼ cup diced red onion
- 1 jalapeño, finely diced
- 1 tbsp lime juice
- 1 tsp lime zest
- ¼ cup chopped cilantro
- 1 tsp salt
- 1 egg
- 2 tbsp milk
- 1 cup crumbs
- ¼ cup of almond flour
- 1 avocado, sliced into fries
- 6 flour tortillas
- 1 cup coleslaw mix

Directions:

1. In a bowl, combine the tomatoes, jalapeño, red onion, lime juice, lime zest, cilantro, and salt. Let chill the pico de gallo covered in the fridge until ready to use.

2. Preheat air fryer at 375ºF. In a small bowl, beat egg and milk. In another bowl, add breadcrumbs. Dip avocado slices in the egg mixture, then dredge them in the mixed almond flour and breadcrumbs. Place avocado slices in the greased frying basket and Air Fry for 5 minutes. Add 2 avocado fries to each tortilla. Top each with coleslaw mix. Serve immediately.

Easy Roasted Cauliflower

Servings: 2 Servings
Cooking Time: 15 Minutes
Ingredients:

- 3 cups of cauliflower
- 1 tablespoon of pine nuts
- 1 tablespoon of chopped fresh parsley
- ¾ teaspoon of dried oregano

- ½ teaspoon of fresh lime juice
- 1 ½ teaspoons of olive oil
- Pinch of black pepper and salt, to taste

Directions:
1. Preheat your air fryer to 375ºF. Spray some oil inside the air fryer basket.
2. Put cauliflower in a medium bowl, add in oil, pepper, oregano, and salt. Toss gently to coat evenly.
3. Transfer into the air fryer basket. Cook at 375ºF for 10 minutes.
4. Remove from the air fryer and put in a serving bowl. Top with pine nuts, chopped fresh parsley, and lemon juice.
5. Serve and enjoy your Easy Roasted Cauliflower!

Cheese And Bean Enchiladas

Servings:4
Cooking Time: 9 Minutes

Ingredients:
- 1 can pinto beans, drained and rinsed
- 1 ½ tablespoons taco seasoning
- 1 cup red enchilada sauce, divided
- 1 ½ cups shredded Mexican-blend cheese, divided
- 4 fajita-size flour tortillas

Directions:
1. Preheat the air fryer to 320°F.
2. In a large microwave-safe bowl, microwave beans for 1 minute. Mash half the beans and fold into whole beans. Mix in taco seasoning, ¼ cup enchilada sauce, and 1 cup cheese until well combined.
3. Place ¼ cup bean mixture onto each tortilla. Fold up one end about 1", then roll to close.
4. Place enchiladas into a 3-quart baking pan, pushing together as needed to make them fit. Pour remaining ¾ cup enchilada sauce over enchiladas and top with remaining ½ cup cheese.
5. Place pan in the air fryer basket and cook 8 minutes until cheese is brown and bubbling and the edges of tortillas are brown. Serve warm.

Sweet Corn Bread

Servings: 6
Cooking Time: 35 Minutes

Ingredients:
- 2 eggs, beaten
- ½ cup cornmeal
- ½ cup pastry flour
- 1/3 cup sugar
- 1 tsp lemon zest
- ½ tbsp baking powder
- ¼ tsp salt
- ¼ tsp baking soda
- ½ tbsp lemon juice
- ½ cup milk
- ¼ cup sunflower oil

Directions:
1. Preheat air fryer to 350°F. Add the cornmeal, flour, sugar, lemon zest, baking powder, salt, and baking soda in a bowl. Stir with a whisk until combined. Add the eggs, lemon juice, milk, and oil to another bowl and stir well. Add the wet mixture to the dry mixture and stir gently until combined. Spray a baking pan with oil. Pour the batter in and Bake in the fryer for 25 minutes or until golden and a knife inserted in the center comes out clean. Cut into wedges and serve.

Parmesan Artichokes

Servings: 4
Cooking Time: 35 Minutes

Ingredients:
- 2 medium artichokes, trimmed and quartered, with the centers removed
- 2 tbsp. coconut oil, melted
- 1 egg, beaten
- ½ cup parmesan cheese, grated
- ¼ cup blanched, finely ground flour

Directions:
1. Place the artichokes in a bowl with the coconut oil and toss to coat, then dip the artichokes into a bowl of beaten egg.
2. In a separate bowl, mix together the parmesan cheese and the flour. Combine with the pieces of artichoke, making sure to coat each piece well. Transfer the artichoke to the fryer.
3. Cook at 400°F for ten minutes, shaking occasionally throughout the cooking time. Serve hot.

Chapter 6: Beef, pork & Lamb Recipes

Lemon Pork Escalopes

Servings: 4
Cooking Time: 45 Minutes
Ingredients:
- 4 pork loin chops
- 1 cup breadcrumbs
- 2 eggs, beaten
- Salt and pepper to taste
- ½ tbsp thyme, chopped
- ½ tsp smoked paprika
- ½ tsp ground cumin
- 1 lemon, zested

Directions:
1. Preheat air fryer to 350°F. Mix the breadcrumbs, thyme, smoked paprika, cumin, lemon zest, salt, and pepper in a bowl. Add the pork chops and toss to coat. Dip in the beaten eggs, then dip again into the dry ingredients. Place the coated chops in the greased frying basket and Air Fry for 16-18 minutes, turning once. Serve and enjoy!

Ritzy Skirt Steak Fajitas

Servings:4
Cooking Time: 30 Minutes
Ingredients:
- 2 tablespoons olive oil
- ¼ cup lime juice
- 1 clove garlic, minced
- ½ teaspoon ground cumin
- ½ teaspoon hot sauce
- ½ teaspoon salt
- 2 tablespoons chopped fresh cilantro
- 1 pound (454 g) skirt steak
- 1 onion, sliced
- 1 teaspoon chili powder
- 1 red pepper, sliced
- 1 green pepper, sliced
- Salt and freshly ground black pepper, to taste
- 8 flour tortillas
- Toppings:
- Shredded lettuce
- Crumbled Queso Fresco (or grated Cheddar cheese)
- Sliced black olives
- Diced tomatoes
- Sour cream
- Guacamole

Directions:
1. Combine the olive oil, lime juice, garlic, cumin, hot sauce, salt and cilantro in a shallow dish. Add the skirt steak and turn it over several times to coat all sides. Pierce the steak with a needle-style meat tenderizer or paring knife. Marinate the steak in the refrigerator for at least 3 hours, or overnight. When you are ready to cook, remove the steak from the refrigerator and let it sit at room temperature for 30 minutes.
2. Preheat the air fryer to 400°F (204°C).

3. Toss the onion slices with the chili powder and a little olive oil and transfer them to the air fryer basket. Air fry for 5 minutes. Add the red and green peppers to the air fryer basket with the onions, season with salt and pepper and air fry for 8 more minutes, until the onions and peppers are soft. Transfer the vegetables to a dish and cover with aluminum foil to keep warm.
4. Put the skirt steak in the air fryer basket and pour the marinade over the top. Air fry at 400°F (204°C) for 12 minutes. Flip the steak over and air fry for an additional 5 minutes. Transfer the cooked steak to a cutting board and let the steak rest for a few minutes. If the peppers and onions need to be heated, return them to the air fryer for just 1 to 2 minutes.
5. Thinly slice the steak at an angle, cutting against the grain of the steak. Serve the steak with the onions and peppers, the warm tortillas and the fajita toppings on the side.
6. Serve immediately.

Sweet And Spicy Spare Ribs

Servings:6
Cooking Time: 30 Minutes
Ingredients:
- ¼ cup granular brown erythritol
- 2 teaspoons paprika
- 2 teaspoons chili powder
- 1 teaspoon garlic powder
- ½ teaspoon cayenne pepper
- 2 teaspoons salt
- 1 teaspoon ground black pepper
- 1 rack pork spare ribs

Directions:
1. In a small bowl, mix erythritol, paprika, chili powder, garlic powder, cayenne pepper, salt, and black pepper. Rub spice mix over ribs on both sides. Place ribs on ungreased aluminum foil sheet and wrap to cover.
2. Place ribs into ungreased air fryer basket. Adjust the temperature to 400°F and set the timer for 25 minutes.
3. When timer beeps, remove ribs from foil, then place back into air fryer basket to cook an additional 5 minutes, turning halfway through cooking. Ribs will be browned and have an internal temperature of at least 180°F when done. Serve warm.

Moroccan-style Steak With Salad

Servings: 4
Cooking Time: 20 Minutes
Ingredients:
- 2 lbs. flank steak
- ¼ cup soy sauce
- 1 cup dry red wine
- Salt, to taste
- ½-teaspoon ground black pepper
- 2 parsnips, peeled and sliced lengthways
- 1 tablespoon paprika
- ½ teaspoon onion powder
- ½ teaspoon garlic powder

- ½-teaspoon ground coriander
- ¼-teaspoon ground allspice
- 1 tablespoon olive oil
- ½ tablespoon lime juice
- 1 teaspoon honey
- 1 cup lettuce leaves, shredded
- ½ cup pomegranate seeds

Directions:
1. In a suitable bowl, add the soy sauce, wine, salt, black pepper and flank steak, then refrigerate the mixture for 2 hours to marinate the steak completely.
2. Spray the cooking basket with cooking spray and then transfer the marinated steak on it.
3. Sprinkle the parsnips on the top, add the paprika, onion powder, garlic powder, coriander, and allspice.
4. Cook at 400 degrees F/ 205 degrees C for 7 minutes, then turn the steak over and cook for 5 minutes more.
5. To make the dressing, mix up the olive oil, lime juice and honey. In a salad bowl, add the lettuce leaves and roasted parsnip, then toss with the dressing.
6. When the steak cook, slice and place on top of the salad.
7. Sprinkle over the pomegranate seeds and serve. Enjoy!

Barbecued Baby Back Ribs

Servings: 4
Cooking Time: 30 Minutes
Ingredients:
- 1 rack baby back ribs
- 1 teaspoon onion powder
- 1 teaspoon garlic powder
- 1 teaspoon brown sugar
- 1 teaspoon dried oregano
- Salt
- Pepper
- ½ cup barbecue sauce

Directions:
1. Use a sharp knife to remove the thin membrane from the back of the ribs. Cut the rack in half or as needed so that the ribs are able to fit in the air fryer.
2. In a small bowl, combine the onion powder, garlic powder, brown sugar, oregano, and salt and pepper to taste. Rub the seasoning onto the front and back of the ribs.
3. Cover the ribs with plastic wrap or foil and allow them to sit at room temperature for 30 minutes.
4. Place the ribs in the air fryer. It is okay to stack them. Cook for 15 minutes.
5. Open the air fryer. Flip the ribs. Cook for an additional 15 minutes.
6. Transfer the ribs to a serving dish. Drizzle the ribs with the barbecue sauce and serve.

Mushroom & Quinoa-stuffed Pork Loins

Servings: 3
Cooking Time: 25 Minutes
Ingredients:

- 3 boneless center-cut pork loins, pocket cut in each loin
- ½ cup diced white mushrooms
- 1 tsp vegetable oil
- 3 bacon slices, diced
- ½ onion, peeled and diced
- 1 cup baby spinach
- Salt and pepper to taste
- ½ cup cooked quinoa
- ½ cup mozzarella cheese

Directions:
1. Warm the oil in a skillet over medium heat. Add the bacon and cook for 3 minutes until the fat is rendered but not crispy. Add in onion and mushrooms and stir-fry for 3 minutes until the onions are translucent. Stir in spinach, salt, and pepper and cook for 1 minute until the spinach wilts. Set aside and toss in quinoa.
2. Preheat air fryer at 350ºF. Stuff quinoa mixture into each pork loin and sprinkle with mozzarella cheese. Place them in the frying basket and Air Fry for 11 minutes. Let rest onto a cutting board for 5 minutes before serving.

T-bone Steak With Roasted Tomato, Corn And Asparagus Salsa

Servings: 2
Cooking Time: 15-20 Minutes
Ingredients:
- 1 (20-ounce) T-bone steak
- salt and freshly ground black pepper
- Salsa
- 1½ cups cherry tomatoes
- ¾ cup corn kernels (fresh, or frozen and thawed)
- 1½ cups sliced asparagus (1-inch slices) (about ½ bunch)
- 1 tablespoon + 1 teaspoon olive oil, divided
- salt and freshly ground black pepper
- 1½ teaspoons red wine vinegar
- 3 tablespoons chopped fresh basil
- 1 tablespoon chopped fresh chives

Directions:
1. Preheat the air fryer to 400°F.
2. Season the steak with salt and pepper and air-fry at 400°F for 10 minutes (medium-rare), 12 minutes (medium), or 15 minutes (well-done), flipping the steak once halfway through the cooking time.
3. In the meantime, toss the tomatoes, corn and asparagus in a bowl with a teaspoon or so of olive oil, salt and freshly ground black pepper.
4. When the steak has finished cooking, remove it to a cutting board, tent loosely with foil and let it rest. Transfer the vegetables to the air fryer and air-fry at 400°F for 5 minutes, shaking the basket once or twice during the cooking process. Transfer the cooked vegetables back into the bowl and toss with the red wine vinegar, remaining olive oil and fresh herbs.
5. To serve, slice the steak on the bias and serve with some of the salsa on top.

Simple Pulled Pork

Servings:1
Cooking Time: 24 Minutes
Ingredients:
- 2 tablespoons barbecue dry rub
- 1 pound (454 g) pork tenderloin
- ⅓ cup heavy cream
- 1 teaspoon butter

Directions:
1. Preheat the air fryer to 370ºF (188ºC).
2. Massage the dry rub into the tenderloin, coating it well.
3. Air fry the tenderloin in the air fryer for 20 minutes. When air fried, shred with two forks.
4. Add the heavy cream and butter into the air fryer along with the shredded pork and stir well. Air fry for a further 4 minutes.
5. Allow to cool, then serve.

Pork Meatballs

Servings:18
Cooking Time: 12 Minutes
Ingredients:
- 1 pound ground pork
- 1 large egg, whisked
- ½ teaspoon garlic powder
- ½ teaspoon salt
- ½ teaspoon ground ginger
- ¼ teaspoon crushed red pepper flakes
- 1 medium scallion, trimmed and sliced

Directions:
1. Combine all ingredients in a large bowl. Spoon out 2 tablespoons mixture and roll into a ball. Repeat to form eighteen meatballs total.
2. Place meatballs into ungreased air fryer basket. Adjust the temperature to 400°F and set the timer for 12 minutes, shaking the basket three times throughout cooking. Meatballs will be browned and have an internal temperature of at least 145°F when done. Serve warm.

Beer Corned Beef

Servings: 3
Cooking Time: 50 Minutes
Ingredients:
- 1 whole onion, chopped
- 4 carrots, chopped
- 12 oz. bottle beer
- 1½ cups chicken broth
- 4 pounds corned beef

Directions:
1. At 380 degrees F/ 195 degrees C, preheat your air fryer.
2. Cover beef with beer and set aside for 20 minutes.
3. Place carrots, onion and beef in a pot and heat over high heat.
4. Add in broth and bring to a boil. Drain the meat and veggies.
5. Top with beef spice.
6. Place the meat and veggies in air fryer's cooking basket and cook for 30 minutes.

7. Serve.

Montreal Steak

Servings: 2
Cooking Time: 7 Minutes
Ingredients:
- 12 oz. steak
- ½-teaspoon liquid smoke
- 1 tablespoon soy sauce
- ½-tablespoon cocoa powder
- 1 tablespoon Montreal steak seasoning
- Pepper
- Salt

Directions:
1. In a large zip-lock bag, coat the steak well with the liquid smoke, soy sauce, and steak seasonings, then refrigerate the mixture for overnight.
2. Coat the cooking basket of your air fryer with cooking spray.
3. Arrange the marinated steak to the air fryer and cook at 375 degrees F/ 190 degrees C for 7 minutes.
4. After that, turn the steak and cook another side for 5 minutes more.
5. Serve and enjoy.

Beef With Spanish Rice Casserole

Servings: 3
Cooking Time: 50 Minutes
Ingredients:
- ½-pound lean ground beef
- 2 tablespoons chopped green bell pepper
- 1 tablespoon chopped fresh cilantro
- ¼ cup shredded Cheddar cheese
- ½ teaspoon brown sugar
- ½ pinch ground pepper
- ⅓ cup uncooked long grain rice
- ¼ cup finely chopped onion
- ¼ cup chile sauce
- ¼ teaspoon ground cumin
- ¼ teaspoon Worcestershire sauce
- ½ (14.5 ounce) can canned tomatoes
- ½ cup water
- ½ teaspoon salt

Directions:
1. Spray the cooking pan of your air fryer with cooking spray.
2. Transfer the ground beef to the pan and cook at 360 degrees F/ 180 degrees C for 10 minutes.
3. After 5 minutes of cooking time, mix the crumble beef.
4. After discarding the excess fat, stir in pepper, Worcestershire sauce, salt, chile sauce, rice, cumin, brown sugar, water, tomatoes, green bell pepper, and onion.
5. Use the aluminum foil to cover the pan and cook for 25 minutes more, stirring regularly.
6. Stir at the end, press hard and sprinkle with cheese, then cook at 390 degrees F/ 200 degrees C for 15 minutes more or until the tops are lightly browned.
7. when done, serve with cilantro.

French-style Pork Medallions

Servings: 4
Cooking Time: 25 Minutes
Ingredients:

- 1 lb pork medallions
- Salt and pepper to taste
- ½ tsp dried marjoram
- 2 tbsp butter
- 1 tbsp olive oil
- 1 tsp garlic powder
- 1 shallot, diced
- 1cup chicken stock
- 2 tbsp Dijon mustard
- 2 tbsp grainy mustard
- 1/3 cup heavy cream

Directions:

1. Preheat the air fryer to 350°F. Pound the pork medallions with a rolling pin to about ¼ inch thickness. Rub them with salt, pepper, garlic, and marjoram. Place into the greased frying basket and Bake for 7 minutes or until almost done. Remove and wipe the basket clean. Combine the butter, olive oil, shallot, and stock in a baking pan, and set it in the frying basket. Bake for 5 minutes or until the shallot is crispy and tender. Add the mustard and heavy cream and cook for 4 more minutes or until the mix starts to thicken. Then add the pork to the sauce and cook for 5 more minutes, or until the sauce simmers. Remove and serve warm.

Italian Meatballs

Servings: 4
Cooking Time: 12 Minutes
Ingredients:

- 12 ounces lean ground beef
- 4 ounces Italian sausage, casing removed
- ½ cup breadcrumbs
- 1 cup grated Parmesan cheese
- 1 egg
- 2 tablespoons milk
- 2 teaspoons Italian seasoning
- ½ teaspoon onion powder
- ½ teaspoon garlic powder
- Pinch of red pepper flakes

Directions:

1. In a large bowl, place all the ingredients and mix well. Roll out 24 meatballs.
2. Preheat the air fryer to 360°F.
3. Place the meatballs in the air fryer basket and cook for 12 minutes, tossing every 4 minutes. Using a food thermometer, check to ensure the internal temperature of the meatballs is 165°F.

Italian-style Cheeseburgers With Cheese Slices

Servings: 4
Cooking Time: 12 Minutes
Ingredients:

- 1-pound ground beef
- 4 cheddar cheese slices
- ½ teaspoon Italian seasoning
- Black pepper
- Salt

Directions:

1. Grease its air fryer basket with cooking spray.
2. In a suitable bowl, mix together ground beef, Italian seasoning, black pepper, and salt.
3. Make 4 equal shapes of patties from meat mixture and place into the air fryer basket.
4. Cook at almost 375 degrees F/ 190 degrees C for 5 minutes. Turn patties to another side and cook for 5 minutes more.
5. Place cheese slices on top of each patty and cook for 2 minutes more.
6. Serve and enjoy.

Sweet And Spicy Pork Ribs

Servings:4
Cooking Time: 20 Minutes Per Batch
Ingredients:

- 1 rack pork spareribs, white membrane removed
- ¼ cup brown sugar
- 2 teaspoons salt
- 2 teaspoons ground black pepper
- 1 tablespoon chili powder
- 1 teaspoon garlic powder
- ½ teaspoon cayenne pepper

Directions:

1. Preheat the air fryer to 400°F.
2. Place ribs on a work surface and cut the rack into two pieces to fit in the air fryer basket.
3. In a medium bowl, whisk together brown sugar, salt, black pepper, chili powder, garlic powder, and cayenne to make a dry rub.
4. Massage dry rub onto both sides of ribs until well coated. Place a portion of ribs in the air fryer basket, working in batches as necessary.
5. Cook 20 minutes until internal temperature reaches at least 190°F and no pink remains. Let rest 5 minutes before cutting and serving.

Flank Steak With Chimichurri Sauce

Servings: 4
Cooking Time: 25 Minutes + Chilling Time
Ingredients:

- For Marinade
- 2/3 cup olive oil
- 1 tbsp Dijon mustard
- 1 orange, juiced and zested
- 1 lime, juiced and zested
- 1/3 cup tamari sauce
- 2 tbsp red wine vinegar
- 4 cloves garlic, minced
- 1 flank steak
- For Chimichurri Sauce
- 2 red jalapeños, minced
- 1 cup Italian parsley leaves

- ¼ cup cilantro leaves
- ¼ cup oregano leaves
- ¼ cup olive oil
- ½ onion, diced
- 4 cloves garlic, minced
- 2 tbsp lime juice
- 2 tsp lime zest
- 2 tbsp red wine vinegar
- ½ tsp ground cumin
- ½ tsp salt

Directions:

1. Whisk all the marinade ingredients in a large bowl. Toss in flank steak and let marinate covered for at least 1 hour. In a food processor, blend parsley, cilantro, oregano, red jalapeños, olive oil, onion, garlic, lime juice, lime zest, vinegar, cumin, and salt until you reach your desired consistency. Let chill in the fridge until ready to use.

2. Preheat air fryer at 325ºF. Place flank steak in the greased frying basket and Bake for 18-20 minutes until rare, turning once. Let rest onto a cutting board for 5 minutes before slicing thinly against the grain. Serve with chimichurri sauce on the side.

Baharat Lamb Kebab With Mint Sauce

Servings: 6
Cooking Time: 50 Minutes

Ingredients:

- 1 lb ground lamb
- ¼ cup parsley, chopped
- 3 garlic cloves, minced
- 1 shallot, diced
- Salt and pepper to taste
- 1 tsp ground cumin
- ¼ tsp ground cinnamon
- ¼ tsp baharat seasoning
- ¼ tsp chili powder
- ¼ tsp ground ginger
- 3 tbsp olive oil
- 1 cup Greek yogurt
- ½ cup mint, chopped
- 2 tbsp lemon juice
- ¼ tsp hot paprika

Directions:

1. Preheat air fryer to 360°F. Mix the ground lamb, parsley, 2 garlic cloves, shallot, 2 tbsp olive oil, salt, black pepper, cumin, cinnamon, baharat seasoning, chili powder, and ginger in a bowl. Divide the mixture into 4 equal quantities, and roll each into a long oval. Drizzle with the remaining olive oil, place them in a single layer in the frying basket and Air Fry for 10 minutes. While the kofta is cooking, mix together the Greek yogurt, mint, remaining garlic, lemon juice, hot paprika, salt, and pepper in a bowl. Serve the kofta with mint sauce.

Kochukaru Pork Lettuce Cups

Servings: 4
Cooking Time: 25 Minutes

Ingredients:

- 1 tsp kochukaru (chili pepper flakes)
- 12 baby romaine lettuce leaves
- 1 lb pork tenderloin, sliced
- Salt and pepper to taste
- 3 scallions, chopped
- 3 garlic cloves, crushed
- ¼ cup soy sauce
- 2 tbsp gochujang
- ½ tbsp light brown sugar
- ½ tbsp honey
- 1 tbsp grated fresh ginger
- 2 tbsp rice vinegar
- 1 tsp toasted sesame oil
- 2 ¼ cups cooked brown rice
- ½ tbsp sesame seeds
- 2 spring onions, sliced

Directions:

1. Mix the scallions, garlic, soy sauce, kochukaru, honey, brown sugar, and ginger in a small bowl. Mix well. Place the pork in a large bowl. Season with salt and pepper. Pour the marinade over the pork, tossing the meat in the marinade until coated. Cover the bowl with plastic wrap and allow to marinate overnight. When ready to cook,

2. Preheat air fryer to 400°F. Remove the pork from the bowl and discard the marinade. Place the pork in the greased frying basket and Air Fry for 10 minutes, flipping once until browned and cooked through. Meanwhile, prepare the gochujang sauce. Mix the gochujang, rice vinegar, and sesame oil until smooth. To make the cup, add 3 tbsp of brown rice on the lettuce leaf. Place a slice of pork on top, drizzle a tsp of gochujang sauce and sprinkle with some sesame seeds and spring onions. Wrap the lettuce over the mixture similar to a burrito. Serve warm.

Pepperoni Bagel Pizzas

Servings: 4
Cooking Time: 20 Minutes

Ingredients:

- 2 bagels, halved horizontally
- 2 cups shredded mozzarella
- ¼ cup grated Parmesan
- 1 cup passata
- 1/3 cup sliced pepperoni
- 2 scallions, chopped
- 2 tbsp minced fresh chives
- 1 tsp red chili flakes

Directions:

1. Preheat the air fryer to 375°F. Put the bagel halves, cut side up, in the frying basket. Bake for 2-3 minutes until golden. Remove and top them with passata, pepperoni, scallions, and cheeses. Put the bagels topping-side up to the frying basket and cook for 8-12 more minutes or until the bagels are hot and the cheese has melted and is bubbling. Top with the chives and chili flakes and serve.

Corn Dogs

Servings:4
Cooking Time: 8 Minutes
Ingredients:
- 1½ cups shredded mozzarella cheese
- 1 ounce cream cheese
- ½ cup blanched finely ground almond flour
- 4 beef hot dogs

Directions:
1. Place mozzarella, cream cheese, and flour in a large microwave-safe bowl. Microwave on high 45 seconds, then stir with a fork until a soft ball of dough forms.
2. Press dough out into a 12" × 6" rectangle, then use a knife to separate into four smaller rectangles.
3. Wrap each hot dog in one rectangle of dough and place into ungreased air fryer basket. Adjust the temperature to 400°F and set the timer for 8 minutes, turning corn dogs halfway through cooking. Corn dogs will be golden brown when done. Serve warm.

Pork With Aloha Salsa

Servings:4
Cooking Time: 8 Minutes
Ingredients:
- 2 eggs
- 2 tablespoons milk
- ¼ cup flour
- ¼ cup panko bread crumbs
- 4 teaspoons sesame seeds
- 1 pound (454 g) boneless, thin pork cutlets (⅜- to ½-inch thick)
- Lemon pepper and salt, to taste
- ¼ cup cornstarch
- Cooking spray
- Aloha Salsa:
- 1 cup fresh pineapple, chopped in small pieces
- ¼ cup red onion, finely chopped
- ¼ cup green or red bell pepper, chopped
- ½ teaspoon ground cinnamon
- 1 teaspoon low-sodium soy sauce
- ⅛ teaspoon crushed red pepper
- ⅛ teaspoon ground black pepper

Directions:
1. In a medium bowl, stir together all ingredients for salsa. Cover and refrigerate while cooking the pork.
2. Preheat the air fryer to 390ºF (199ºC).
3. Beat the eggs and milk in a shallow dish.
4. In another shallow dish, mix the flour, panko, and sesame seeds.
5. Sprinkle pork cutlets with lemon pepper and salt.
6. Dip pork cutlets in cornstarch, egg mixture, and then panko coating. Spray both sides with cooking spray.
7. Air fry the cutlets for 3 minutes. Turn cutlets over, spraying both sides, and continue air frying for 5 minutes or until well done.
8. Serve fried cutlets with salsa on the side.

Beef And Mushroom Meatballs

Servings:6
Cooking Time: 15 Minutes
Ingredients:
- Olive oil
- 2 pounds lean ground beef
- ⅔ cups finely chopped mushrooms
- 4 tablespoons chopped parsley
- 2 eggs, beaten
- 2 teaspoons salt
- 1 teaspoon freshly ground black pepper
- 1 cup whole-wheat bread crumbs

Directions:
1. Spray a fryer basket lightly with olive oil.
2. In a large bowl, mix together the beef, mushrooms, and parsley. Add the eggs, salt, and pepper and mix gently. Add the bread crumbs and mix until the bread crumbs are no longer dry. Be careful not to overmix.
3. Using a small cookie scoop, form 24 meatballs.
4. Place the meatballs in the fryer basket in a single layer and spray lightly with olive oil. You may need to cook the meatballs in batches.
5. Air fry until the internal temperature reaches at least 160°F, 10 to 15 minutes, shaking the basket every 5 minutes for even cooking.

Empanadas

Servings:4
Cooking Time: 28 Minutes
Ingredients:
- 1 pound 80/20 ground beef
- ¼ cup taco seasoning
- ⅓ cup salsa
- 2 refrigerated piecrusts
- 1 cup shredded Colby-jack cheese

Directions:
1. In a medium skillet over medium heat, brown beef about 10 minutes until cooked through. Drain fat, then add taco seasoning and salsa to the pan. Bring to a boil, then cook 30 seconds. Reduce heat and simmer 5 minutes. Remove from heat.
2. Preheat the air fryer to 370°F.
3. Cut three 5" circles from each piecrust, forming six total. Reroll scraps out to ½" thickness. Cut out two more 5" circles to make eight circles total.
4. For each empanada, place ¼ cup meat mixture onto the lower half of a pastry circle and top with 2 tablespoons cheese. Dab a little water along the edge of pastry and fold circle in half to fully cover meat and cheese, pressing the edges together. Use a fork to gently seal the edges. Repeat with remaining pastry, meat, and cheese.
5. Spritz empanadas with cooking spray. Place in the air fryer basket and cook 12 minutes, turning halfway through cooking time, until crust is golden. Serve warm.

Lemon Pork Tenderloin

Servings: 4
Cooking Time: 12 Minutes
Ingredients:

- ⅓ cup apricot jam
- 2 tablespoons lemon juice
- 2 teaspoons olive oil
- ½ teaspoon dried tarragon
- 1 (1-pound) pork tenderloin, diced
- 4 plums, pitted and quartered
- 4 small apricots, pitted and halved

Directions:

1. In a suitable bowl, mix the jam, lemon juice, olive oil, and tarragon.
2. Add the pork and stir to coat. Let stand for almost 10 minutes at room temperature.
3. Alternating the items, thread the pork, plums, and apricots onto 4 metal skewers that fit into the air fryer.
4. Brush with any remaining jam mixture. Discard any remaining marinade.
5. Cook the kebabs in the preheated Air Fryer for 9 to 12 minutes, or until the pork reaches 145 degrees F/ 60 degrees C on a meat thermometer and the fruit is tender.
6. Serve immediately.

Apple Cornbread Stuffed Pork Loin With Apple Gravy

Servings: 4
Cooking Time: 61 Minutes
Ingredients:

- 4 strips of bacon, chopped
- 1 Granny Smith apple, peeled, cored and finely chopped
- 2 teaspoons fresh thyme leaves
- ¼ cup chopped fresh parsley
- 2 cups cubed cornbread
- ½ cup chicken stock
- salt and freshly ground black pepper
- 1 (2-pound) boneless pork loin
- kitchen twine
- Apple Gravy:
- 2 tablespoons butter
- 1 shallot, minced
- 1 Granny Smith apple, peeled, cored and finely chopped
- 3 sprigs fresh thyme
- 2 tablespoons flour
- 1 cup chicken stock
- ½ cup apple cider
- salt and freshly ground black pepper, to taste

Directions:

1. Preheat the air fryer to 400°F.
2. Add the bacon to the air fryer and air-fry for 6 minutes until crispy. While the bacon is cooking, combine the apple, fresh thyme, parsley and cornbread in a bowl and toss well. Moisten the mixture with the chicken stock and season to taste with salt and freshly

ground black pepper. Add the cooked bacon to the mixture.
3. Butterfly the pork loin by holding it flat on the cutting board with one hand, while slicing into the pork loin parallel to the cutting board with the other. Slice into the longest side of the pork loin, but stop before you cut all the way through. You should then be able to open the pork loin up like a book, making it twice as wide as it was when you started. Season the inside of the pork with salt and freshly ground black pepper.
4. Spread the cornbread mixture onto the butterflied pork loin, leaving a one-inch border around the edge of the pork. Roll the pork loin up around the stuffing to enclose the stuffing, and tie the rolled pork in several places with kitchen twine or secure with toothpicks. Try to replace any stuffing that falls out of the roast as you roll it, by stuffing it into the ends of the rolled pork. Season the outside of the pork with salt and freshly ground black pepper.
5. Preheat the air fryer to 360°F.
6. Place the stuffed pork loin into the air fryer, seam side down. Air-fry the pork loin for 15 minutes at 360°F. Turn the pork loin over and air-fry for an additional 15 minutes. Turn the pork loin a quarter turn and air-fry for an additional 15 minutes. Turn the pork loin over again to expose the fourth side, and air-fry for an additional 10 minutes. The pork loin should register 155°F on an instant read thermometer when it is finished.
7. While the pork is cooking, make the apple gravy. Preheat a saucepan over medium heat on the stovetop and melt the butter. Add the shallot, apple and thyme sprigs and sauté until the apple starts to soften and brown a little. Add the flour and stir for a minute or two. Whisk in the stock and apple cider vigorously to prevent the flour from forming lumps. Bring the mixture to a boil to thicken and season to taste with salt and pepper.
8. Transfer the pork loin to a resting plate and loosely tent with foil, letting the pork rest for at least 5 minutes before slicing and serving with the apple gravy poured over the top.

Beef Tenderloin Steaks With Marjoram

Servings: 4
Cooking Time: 11 Minutes
Ingredients:

- 4 beef tenderloin steaks
- Salt and pepper, to your taste
- 1 teaspoon dried oregano
- 1 teaspoon dried thyme
- 1 teaspoon marjoram
- 1 teaspoon dried sage
- 1 teaspoon garlic powder
- 1 teaspoon dried coriander
- 2 tablespoons olive oil
- 2 eggs, well-whisked
- ½ cup seasoned breadcrumbs

Directions:

1. Mix up the olive oil, salt, pepper, thyme, oregano, sage, marjoram, garlic powder, oregano, and coriander in

a large-size bowl, then use the spice mixture to season the beef tenderloin steaks.

2. In a shallow bowl, add the whisked egg; in another bowl, add the breadcrumbs.

3. Coat the seasoned beef tenderloin steak with the egg mixture and breadcrumbs in order; coat the left steaks with the same steps.

4. Cook the steaks in your air fryer at 380 degrees F/ 195 degrees C for 11 minutes.

5. When done, serve and enjoy with the fresh salad and potatoes.

Broccoli & Mushroom Beef

Servings: 4
Cooking Time: 30 Minutes
Ingredients:
- 1 lb sirloin strip steak, cubed
- 1 cup sliced cremini mushrooms
- 2 tbsp potato starch
- ½ cup beef broth
- 1 tsp soy sauce
- 2 ½ cups broccoli florets
- 1 onion, chopped
- 1 tbsp grated fresh ginger
- 1 cup cooked quinoa

Directions:
1. Add potato starch, broth, and soy sauce to a bowl and mix, then add in the beef and coat thoroughly. Marinate for 5 minutes. Preheat air fryer to 400°F. Set aside the broth and move the beef to a bowl. Add broccoli, onion, mushrooms, and ginger and transfer the bowl to the air fryer. Bake for 12-15 minutes until the beef is golden brown and the veggies soft. Pour the reserved broth over the beef and cook for 2-3 more minutes until the sauce is bubbling. Serve warm over cooked quinoa.

Double Cheese & Beef Burgers

Servings: 4
Cooking Time: 30 Minutes
Ingredients:
- 4 toasted onion buns, split
- ¼ cup breadcrumbs
- 2 tbsp milk
- 1 tp smoked paprika
- 6 tbsp salsa
- 2 tsp cayenne pepper
- 2 tbsp grated Cotija cheese
- 1 ¼ lb ground beef
- 4 Colby Jack cheese slices
- ¼ cup sour cream

Directions:
1. Preheat the air fryer to 375°F. Combine the breadcrumbs, milk, paprika, 2 tbsp of salsa, cayenne, and Cotija cheese in a bowl and mix. Let stand for 5 minutes. Add the ground beef and mix with your hands. Form into 4 patties and lay them on wax paper. Place the patties into the greased frying basket and Air Fry for 11-14 minutes, flipping once during cooking until golden and crunchy on the outside. Put a slice of Colby jack on top

of each and cook for another minute until the cheese melts. Combine the remaining salsa with sour cream. Spread the mix on the bun bottoms, lay the patties on top, and spoon the rest of the mix over. Add the top buns and serve.

Juicy Cheeseburger

Servings: 4 Servings
Cooking Time: 20 Minutes
Ingredients:
- 1 pound of 80/20 ground chuck beef
- 4 buns
- 4 slices of any cheese you like
- 1 ½ tablespoons of burger seasonings
- 1 teaspoon of Worcestershire sauce
- 1 teaspoon of liquid smoke
- Lettuce leaves, slices of tomatoes, onions, ketchup, for serving
- Pinch of salt and black pepper, to taste

Directions:
1. Preheat your air fryer to 360ºF.
2. Add the ground beef, sauce, liquid smoke, seasonings, black pepper, and salt in a large mixing bowl. Mix it until smooth and make 4 patties.
3. Put the formed patties in the air fryer basket and cook at 360ºF for 8 minutes. Flip them and cook for an extra 3–4 minutes.
4. Serve on buns* with ketchup, lettuce leaves, slices of onions, and tomatoes. Enjoy your Juicy Cheeseburger!

Spicy Pork Belly Pieces

Servings: 4
Cooking Time: 50 Minutes
Ingredients:
- 1 ½ lbs. pork belly, cut into 4 pieces
- Kosher salt and ground black pepper, to taste
- 1 teaspoon smoked paprika
- ½-teaspoon turmeric powder
- 1 tablespoon oyster sauce
- 1 tablespoon green onions
- 4 cloves garlic, sliced
- 1 lb. new potatoes, scrubbed

Directions:
1. Heat your Air Fryer to 390 degrees F/ 200 degrees C in advance.
2. Use the kitchen to pat the pork belly pieces dry and season with the remaining spices.
3. Spray the coated pieces with a non-stick spray on all sides and add the oyster sauce.
4. Cook the pork belly pieces in the preheated Air Fryer for 30 minutes.
5. Turn them over every 10 minutes.
6. When the time is over, increase the temperature to 400 degrees F/ 205 degrees C.
7. Add the green onions, garlic, and new potatoes and cook for another 15 minutes, shaking regularly.
8. When done, serve warm and enjoy.

Wasabi-coated Pork Loin Chops

Servings: 3
Cooking Time: 14 Minutes
Ingredients:
- 1½ cups Wasabi peas
- ¼ cup Plain panko bread crumbs
- 1 Large egg white(s)
- 2 tablespoons Water
- 3 5- to 6-ounce boneless center-cut pork loin chops (about ½ inch thick)

Directions:
1. Preheat the air fryer to 375°F.
2. Put the wasabi peas in a food processor. Cover and process until finely ground, about like panko bread crumbs. Add the bread crumbs and pulse a few times to blend.
3. Set up and fill two shallow soup plates or small pie plates on your counter: one for the egg white(s), whisked with the water until uniform; and one for the wasabi pea mixture.
4. Dip a pork chop in the egg white mixture, coating the chop on both sides as well as around the edge. Allow any excess egg white mixture to slip back into the rest, then set the chop in the wasabi pea mixture. Press gently and turn it several times to coat evenly on both sides and around the edge. Set aside, then dip and coat the remaining chop(s).
5. Set the chops in the basket with as much air space between them as possible. Air-fry, turning once at the 6-minute mark, for 12 minutes, or until the chops are crisp and browned and an instant-read meat thermometer inserted into the center of a chop registers 145°F. If the machine is at 360°F, you may need to add 2 minutes to the cooking time.
6. Use kitchen tongs to transfer the chops to a wire rack. Cool for a couple of minutes before serving.

Beef Al Carbon (street Taco Meat)

Servings: 6
Cooking Time: 8 Minutes
Ingredients:
- 1½ pounds sirloin steak, cut into ½-inch cubes
- ¾ cup lime juice
- ½ cup extra-virgin olive oil
- 1 teaspoon ground cumin
- 2 teaspoons garlic powder
- 1 teaspoon salt

Directions:
1. In a large bowl, toss together the steak, lime juice, olive oil, cumin, garlic powder, and salt. Allow the meat to marinate for 30 minutes. Drain off all the marinade and pat the meat dry with paper towels.
2. Preheat the air fryer to 400°F.
3. Place the meat in the air fryer basket and spray with cooking spray. Cook the meat for 5 minutes, toss the meat, and continue cooking another 3 minutes, until slightly crispy.

Mexican-style Shredded Beef

Servings:6
Cooking Time: 35 Minutes
Ingredients:
- 1 beef chuck roast, cut into 2" cubes
- 1 teaspoon salt
- ½ teaspoon ground black pepper
- ½ cup no-sugar-added chipotle sauce

Directions:
1. In a large bowl, sprinkle beef cubes with salt and pepper and toss to coat. Place beef into ungreased air fryer basket. Adjust the temperature to 400°F and set the timer for 30 minutes, shaking the basket halfway through cooking. Beef will be done when internal temperature is at least 160°F.
2. Place cooked beef into a large bowl and shred with two forks. Pour in chipotle sauce and toss to coat.
3. Return beef to air fryer basket for an additional 5 minutes at 400°F to crisp with sauce. Serve warm.

Chili-lime Pork Loin

Servings:4
Cooking Time: 30 Minutes
Ingredients:
- 1 tablespoon lime juice
- 1 tablespoon olive oil, plus more for spraying
- ½ tablespoon soy sauce
- ½ tablespoon chili powder
- ¼ tablespoon minced garlic
- 1 pound boneless pork tenderloin

Directions:
1. In a large zip-top plastic bag, mix together the lime juice, olive oil, soy sauce, chili powder, and garlic and mix well. Add the pork, seal, and refrigerate for at least 1 hour or overnight.
2. Spray a fryer basket lightly with olive oil.
3. Shake off any excess marinade from the pork and place it in the fryer basket.
4. Air fry for 15 minutes. Flip the tenderloin over and cook until the pork reaches an internal temperature of at least 145°F an additional 5 minutes. If necessary, continue to cook in 2- to 3-minute intervals until it reaches the proper temperature.
5. Let the tenderloin rest for 10 minutes before cutting into slices and serving.

Provolone Stuffed Beef And Pork Meatballs

Servings:6
Cooking Time: 12 Minutes
Ingredients:
- 1 tablespoon olive oil
- 1 small onion, finely chopped
- 1 to 2 cloves garlic, minced
- ¾ pound (340 g) ground beef
- ¾ pound (340 g) ground pork
- ¾ cup bread crumbs
- ¼ cup grated Parmesan cheese

- ¼ cup finely chopped fresh parsley
- ½ teaspoon dried oregano
- 1½ teaspoons salt
- Freshly ground black pepper, to taste
- 2 eggs, lightly beaten
- 5 ounces (142 g) sharp or aged provolone cheese, cut into 1-inch cubes

Directions:
1. Preheat a skillet over medium-high heat. Add the oil and cook the onion and garlic until tender, but not browned.
2. Transfer the onion and garlic to a large bowl and add the beef, pork, bread crumbs, Parmesan cheese, parsley, oregano, salt, pepper and eggs. Mix well until all the ingredients are combined. Divide the mixture into 12 evenly sized balls. Make one meatball at a time, by pressing a hole in the meatball mixture with the finger and pushing a piece of provolone cheese into the hole. Mold the meat back into a ball, enclosing the cheese.
3. Preheat the air fryer to 380°F (193ºC).
4. Working in two batches, transfer six of the meatballs to the air fryer basket and air fry for 12 minutes, shaking the basket and turning the meatballs twice during the cooking process. Repeat with the remaining 6 meatballs. Serve warm.

Tender Pork Ribs With Bbq Sauce

Servings: 4
Cooking Time: 25 Minutes
Ingredients:
- 1 lb. baby back ribs
- 3 tablespoons olive oil
- ½ teaspoon pepper
- ½ teaspoon smoked salt
- 1 tablespoon Dijon mustard
- ⅓ cup soy sauce
- 2 cloves garlic, minced
- ½ cup BBQ sauce

Directions:
1. Cut the ribs in half after removing their back membrane.
2. To marinate the ribs completely, prepare a large dish, add the olive oil, pepper, salt, Dijon mustard, soy sauce, garlic and ribs, then cover and refrigerate for 2 hours.
3. When ready, cook the pork ribs in your air fryer at 370 degrees F/ 185 degrees C for 25 minutes.
4. With the BBQ sauce on the top, serve and enjoy!

Simple Lamb Chops

Servings:2
Cooking Time:6 Minutes
Ingredients:
- 4 lamb chops
- Salt and black pepper, to taste
- 1 tablespoon olive oil

Directions:
1. Preheat the Air fryer to 390°F and grease an Air fryer basket.

2. Mix the olive oil, salt, and black pepper in a large bowl and add chops.
3. Arrange the chops in the Air fryer basket and cook for about 6 minutes.
4. Dish out the lamb chops and serve hot.

Barbecue-style London Broil

Servings: 5
Cooking Time: 17 Minutes
Ingredients:
- ¾ teaspoon Mild smoked paprika
- ¾ teaspoon Dried oregano
- ¾ teaspoon Table salt
- ¾ teaspoon Ground black pepper
- ¼ teaspoon Garlic powder
- ¼ teaspoon Onion powder
- 1½ pounds Beef London broil (in one piece)
- Olive oil spray

Directions:
1. Preheat the air fryer to 400°F.
2. Mix the smoked paprika, oregano, salt, pepper, garlic powder, and onion powder in a small bowl until uniform.
3. Pat and rub this mixture across all surfaces of the beef. Lightly coat the beef on all sides with olive oil spray.
4. When the machine is at temperature, lay the London broil flat in the basket and air-fry undisturbed for 8 minutes for the small batch, 10 minutes for the medium batch, or 12 minutes for the large batch for medium-rare, until an instant-read meat thermometer inserted into the center of the meat registers 130°F. Add 1, 2, or 3 minutes, respectively for medium, until an instant-read meat thermometer registers 135°F. Or add 3, 4, or 5 minutes respectively for medium, until an instant-read meat thermometer registers 145°F.
5. Use kitchen tongs to transfer the London broil to a cutting board. Let the meat rest for 10 minutes. It needs a long time for the juices to be reincorporated into the meat's fibers. Carve it against the grain into very thin slices to serve.

Fast Lamb Satay

Servings:2
Cooking Time: 8 Minutes
Ingredients:
- ¼ teaspoon cumin
- 1 teaspoon ginger
- ½ teaspoons nutmeg
- Salt and ground black pepper, to taste
- 2 boneless lamb steaks
- Cooking spray

Directions:
1. Combine the cumin, ginger, nutmeg, salt and pepper in a bowl.
2. Cube the lamb steaks and massage the spice mixture into each one.

3. Leave to marinate for 10 minutes, then transfer onto metal skewers.
4. Preheat the air fryer to 400°F (204°C).
5. Spritz the skewers with the cooking spray, then air fry them in the air fryer for 8 minutes.
6. Take care when removing them from the air fryer and serve.

Beef Burgers With Worcestershire Sauce

Servings: 4
Cooking Time: 15 Minutes
Ingredients:
- 1 ½ pound ground beef
- Black pepper and salt to season
- ¼ teaspoon liquid smoke
- 2 teaspoons onion powder
- 1 teaspoon garlic powder
- 1 ½ tablespoon Worcestershire sauce
- Burgers:
- 4 buns
- 4 trimmed lettuce leaves
- 4 tablespoons mayonnaise
- 1 large tomato, sliced
- 4 slices Cheddar cheese

Directions:
1. At 370 degrees F/ 185 degrees C, preheat your air fryer.
2. In a suitable bowl, combine the beef, salt, black pepper, liquid smoke, onion powder, garlic powder and Worcestershire sauce using your hands.
3. Form 3 to 4 patties out of the mixture.
4. Place the patties in the fryer basket making sure to leave enough space between them.
5. Ideally, work with 2 patties at a time.
6. Close the air fryer and cook for 10 minutes.
7. Turn the beef with kitchen tongs, reduce the temperature to 350 degrees F/ 175 degrees C, and cook further for 5 minutes.
8. Remove the patties onto a plate.
9. Assemble burgers with the lettuce, mayonnaise, sliced cheese, and sliced tomato.

Crispy Pork Belly

Servings:4
Cooking Time: 20 Minutes
Ingredients:
- 1 pound pork belly, cut into 1" cubes
- ¼ cup soy sauce
- 1 tablespoon Worcestershire sauce
- 2 teaspoons sriracha hot chili sauce
- ½ teaspoon salt
- ¼ teaspoon ground black pepper

Directions:
1. Place pork belly into a medium sealable bowl or bag and pour in soy sauce, Worcestershire sauce, and sriracha. Seal and let marinate 30 minutes in the refrigerator.

2. Remove pork from marinade, pat dry with a paper towel, and sprinkle with salt and pepper.
3. Place pork in ungreased air fryer basket. Adjust the temperature to 360°F and set the timer for 20 minutes, shaking the basket halfway through cooking. Pork belly will be done when it has an internal temperature of at least 145°F and is golden brown.
4. Let pork belly rest on a large plate 10 minutes. Serve warm.

Elegant Pork Chops

Servings: 4
Cooking Time: 25 Minutes
Ingredients:
- 4 pork chops, bone-in
- Salt and black pepper, to taste
- ½ teaspoon onion powder
- ½ teaspoon paprika
- ½ teaspoon celery seeds
- 2 cooking apples, peeled and sliced
- 1 tablespoon honey
- 1 tablespoon peanut oil

Directions:
1. Place the pork in a suitable greased baking pan.
2. Season with black pepper and salt, and transfer the pan to the cooking basket.
3. Cook the pork chops in the preheated air fryer at about 370 degrees F/ 185 degrees C for almost 10 minutes.
4. Meanwhile, in a suitable saucepan, simmer the remaining ingredients over medium heat for about 8 minutes or until the apples are softened.
5. Pour the applesauce over the prepared pork chops.
6. Add to the preheated Air Fryer and air fry for 5 minutes more.
7. Serve

Garlic Fillets

Servings: 4
Cooking Time: 15 Minutes
Ingredients:
- 1-pound beef filet mignon
- 1 teaspoon minced garlic
- 1 tablespoon peanut oil
- ½ teaspoon salt
- 1 teaspoon dried oregano

Directions:
1. Chop the beef into the medium size pieces and sprinkle with salt and dried oregano. Then add minced garlic and peanut oil and mix up the meat well. Place the bowl with meat in the fridge for 10 minutes to marinate. Meanwhile, preheat the air fryer to 400°F. Put the marinated beef pieces in the air fryer and cook them for 10 minutes Then flip the beef on another side and cook for 5 minutes more.

Seedy Rib Eye Steak Bites

Servings: 4
Cooking Time: 20 Minutes
Ingredients:
- 1 lb rib eye steak, cubed
- 2 garlic cloves, minced
- 2 tbsp olive oil
- 1 tbsp thyme, chopped
- 1 tsp ground fennel seeds
- Salt and pepper to taste
- 1 onion, thinly sliced

Directions:
1. Preheat air fryer to 380°F. Place the steak, garlic, olive oil, thyme, fennel seeds, salt, pepper, and onion in a bowl. Mix until all of the beef and onion are well coated. Put the seasoned steak mixture into the frying basket. Roast for 10 minutes, stirring once. Let sit for 5 minutes. Serve.

Pesto-rubbed Veal Chops

Servings: 2
Cooking Time: 12-15 Minutes
Ingredients:
- ¼ cup Purchased pesto
- 2 10-ounce bone-in veal loin or rib chop(s)
- ½ teaspoon Ground black pepper

Directions:
1. Preheat the air fryer to 400°F.
2. Rub the pesto onto both sides of the veal chop(s). Sprinkle one side of the chop(s) with the ground black pepper. Set aside at room temperature as the machine comes up to temperature.
3. Set the chop(s) in the basket. If you're cooking more than one chop, leave as much air space between them as possible. Air-fry undisturbed for 12 minutes for medium-rare, or until an instant-read meat thermometer inserted into the center of a chop registers 135°F. Or air-fry undisturbed for 15 minutes for medium-well, or until an instant-read meat thermometer registers 145°F.
4. Use kitchen tongs to transfer the chops to a cutting board or a wire rack. Cool for 5 minutes before serving.

Friday Night Cheeseburgers

Servings: 4
Cooking Time: 20 Minutes
Ingredients:
- 1 lb ground beef
- 1 tsp Worcestershire sauce
- 1 tbsp allspice
- Salt and pepper to taste
- 4 cheddar cheese slices
- 4 buns

Directions:
1. Preheat air fryer to 360°F. Combine beef, Worcestershire sauce, allspice, salt and pepper in a large bowl. Divide into 4 equal portions and shape into patties. Place the burgers in the greased frying basket and Air Fry for 8 minutes. Flip and cook for another 3-4 minutes.

Top each burger with cheddar cheese and cook for another minute so the cheese melts. Transfer to a bun and serve.

Cajun Pork

Servings: 3
Cooking Time: 12 Minutes
Ingredients:
- 1 lb. pork loin, sliced into 1-inch cubes
- 2 tablespoons Cajun seasoning
- 3 tablespoons brown sugar
- ¼ cup cider vinegar

Directions:
1. Coat the pork loin well with Cajun seasoning and 3 tablespoons of brown sugar in a suitable dish. Let the pork loin marinate for 3 hours.
2. To baste, mix the brown sugar and vinegar well in a bowl.
3. Thread pork pieces onto skewers, then baste with sauce.
4. Cook at 360 degrees F/ 180 degrees C for 12 minutes, flipping and basting with sauce halfway through.
5. Cooking in batches is suggested.
6. When done, serve and enjoy.

Citrus Pork Loin Roast

Servings:8
Cooking Time: 45 Minutes
Ingredients:
- 1 tablespoon lime juice
- 1 tablespoon orange marmalade
- 1 teaspoon coarse brown mustard
- 1 teaspoon curry powder
- 1 teaspoon dried lemongrass
- 2 pound (907 g) boneless pork loin roast
- Salt and ground black pepper, to taste
- Cooking spray

Directions:
1. Preheat the air fryer to 360ºF (182ºC).
2. Mix the lime juice, marmalade, mustard, curry powder, and lemongrass.
3. Rub mixture all over the surface of the pork loin. Season with salt and pepper.
4. Spray air fryer basket with cooking spray and place pork roast diagonally in the basket.
5. Air fry for approximately 45 minutes, until the internal temperature reaches at least 145ºF (63ºC).
6. Wrap roast in foil and let rest for 10 minutes before slicing.
7. Serve immediately.

Easy-peasy Beef Sliders

Servings:4
Cooking Time: 25 Minutes
Ingredients:
- 1 lb ground beef
- ¼ tsp cumin
- ¼ tsp mustard power

- 1/3 cup grated yellow onion
- ½ tsp smoked paprika
- Salt and pepper to taste

Directions:
1. Preheat air fryer to 350°F. Combine the ground beef, cumin, mustard, onion, paprika, salt, and black pepper in a bowl. Form mixture into 8 patties and make a slight indentation in the middle of each. Place beef patties in the greased frying basket and Air Fry for 8-10 minutes, flipping once. Serve right away and enjoy!

Panko-breaded Pork Chops

Servings: 5
Cooking Time: 15 Minutes

Ingredients:
- 5 (3½- to 5-ounce) pork chops (bone-in or boneless)
- Seasoning salt
- Pepper
- ¼ cup all-purpose flour
- 2 tablespoons panko bread crumbs
- Cooking oil

Directions:
1. Season the pork chops with the seasoning salt and pepper to taste.
2. Sprinkle the flour on both sides of the pork chops, then coat both sides with panko bread crumbs.
3. Place the pork chops in the air fryer. Stacking them is okay. (See Air fryer cooking tip.) Spray the pork chops with cooking oil. Cook for 6 minutes.
4. Open the air fryer and flip the pork chops. Cook for an additional 6 minutes
5. Cool before serving.

Pork Tenderloins

Servings: 3
Cooking Time: 30 Minutes

Ingredients:
- 1 teaspoon salt
- ½ teaspoon pepper
- 1 lb. pork tenderloin
- 2 tablespoons minced fresh rosemary
- 2 tablespoons olive oil, divided
- 1 garlic cloves, minced
- Apricot Glaze Ingredients:
- 1 cup apricot preserves
- 3 garlic cloves, minced
- 4 tablespoons lemon juice

Directions:
1. After mixing the pepper, salt, garlic, oil, and rosemary well, brush the pork with them on all sides.
2. If needed, you can cut pork crosswise in half.
3. Arrange the pork to the sprayed cooking pan and cook at 390 degrees F/ 200 degrees C for 3 minutes on each side.
4. While cooking the pork, mix all of the glaze ingredients well.

5. Baste the pork every 5 minutes.
6. Cook at 330 degrees F/ 165 degrees C and cook for 20 minutes more.
7. When done, serve and enjoy.

Homemade Ham Cheese Sandwiches

Servings: 4
Cooking Time: 10 Minutes

Ingredients:
- 4 slices lean pork ham
- 4 slices cheese
- 8 slices tomato

Directions:
1. At 360 degrees F/ 180 degrees C, preheat your Air fryer.
2. Spread 4 slices of bread on a flat surface.
3. Spread the slices with cheese, tomato, turkey and ham.
4. Cover with the remaining pork slices to form sandwiches.
5. Add the sandwiches to the air fryer basket and cook for almost 10 minutes.
6. Serve.

Beef And Cheddar Burgers

Servings:4
Cooking Time: 25 Minutes

Ingredients:
- 1 tablespoon olive oil
- 1 onion, sliced into rings
- 1 teaspoon garlic, minced or puréed
- 1 teaspoon mustard
- 1 teaspoon basil
- 1 teaspoon mixed herbs
- Salt and ground black pepper, to taste
- 1 teaspoon tomato, puréed
- 4 buns
- 1 ounce (28 g) Cheddar cheese, sliced
- 10.5 ounces (298 g) beef, minced
- Salad leaves

Directions:
1. Preheat the air fryer to 390°F (199°C).
2. Grease the air fryer with olive oil and allow it to warm up.
3. Put the diced onion in the air fryer and air fry until they turn golden brown.
4. Mix in the garlic, mustard, basil, herbs, salt, and pepper, and air fry for 25 minutes.
5. Lay 2 to 3 onion rings and puréed tomato on two of the buns. Put one slice of cheese and the layer of beef on top. Top with salad leaves before closing off the sandwich with the other buns.
6. Serve immediately.

Peppered Steak Bites

Servings: 4
Cooking Time: 14 Minutes
Ingredients:
- 1 pound sirloin steak, cut into 1-inch cubes
- ½ teaspoon coarse sea salt
- 1 teaspoon coarse black pepper
- 2 teaspoons Worcestershire sauce
- ½ teaspoon garlic powder
- ¼ teaspoon red pepper flakes
- ¼ cup chopped parsley

Directions:
1. Preheat the air fryer to 390°F.
2. In a large bowl, place the steak cubes and toss with the salt, pepper, Worcestershire sauce, garlic powder, and red pepper flakes.
3. Pour the steak into the air fryer basket and cook for 10 to 14 minutes, depending on how well done you prefer your bites. Starting at the 8-minute mark, toss the steak bites every 2 minutes to check for doneness.
4. When the steak is cooked, remove it from the basket to a serving bowl and top with the chopped parsley. Allow the steak to rest for 5 minutes before serving.

Chapter 7: Fish And Seafood Recipes

Chili Blackened Shrimp

Servings: 4
Cooking Time: 15 Minutes
Ingredients:
- 1 lb peeled shrimp, deveined
- 1 tsp paprika
- ½ tsp dried dill
- ½ tsp red chili flakes
- ½ lemon, juiced
- Salt and pepper to taste

Directions:
1. Preheat air fryer to 400°F. In a resealable bag, add shrimp, paprika, dill, red chili flakes, lemon juice, salt and pepper. Seal and shake well. Place the shrimp in the greased frying basket and Air Fry for 7-8 minutes, shaking the basket once until blackened. Let cool slightly and serve.

Homemade Fish Sticks

Servings:4
Cooking Time: 15 Minutes
Ingredients:
- Olive oil
- 4 fish fillets (cod, tilapia or pollock)
- ½ cup whole-wheat flour
- 1 teaspoon seasoned salt
- 2 eggs
- 1½ cups whole-wheat panko bread crumbs
- ½ tablespoon dried parsley flakes

Directions:
1. Spray a fryer basket lightly with olive oil.
2. Cut the fish fillets lengthwise into "sticks."
3. In a shallow bowl, mix together the whole-wheat flour and seasoned salt.
4. In a small bowl whisk the eggs with 1 teaspoon of water.
5. In another shallow bowl, mix together the panko bread crumbs and parsley flakes.
6. Coat each fish stick in the seasoned flour, then in the egg mixture, and dredge them in the panko bread crumbs.
7. Place the fish sticks in the fryer basket in a single layer and lightly spray the fish sticks with olive oil. You may need to cook them in batches.
8. Air fry for 5 to 8 minutes. Flip the fish sticks over and lightly spray with the olive oil. Cook until golden brown and crispy, 5 to 7 more minutes.

Easy Marinated Salmon Fillets

Servings:4
Cooking Time: 20 Minutes
Ingredients:
- 1 tablespoon olive oil, plus more for spraying
- ¼ cup soy sauce
- ¼ cup rice wine vinegar
- 1 tablespoon brown sugar
- 1 teaspoon mustard powder
- 1 teaspoon ground ginger
- ½ teaspoon freshly ground black pepper
- ½ teaspoon minced garlic
- 4 (6 ounce) salmon fillets, skin-on

Directions:
1. Spray a fryer basket lightly with olive oil.
2. In a small bowl combine the soy sauce, rice wine vinegar, brown sugar, 1 tablespoon of olive oil, mustard powder, ginger, black pepper, and garlic to make a marinade.
3. Place the fillets in a shallow baking dish and pour the marinade over them. Cover the baking dish and marinate for at least 1 hour in the refrigerator, turning the fillets occasionally to keep them coated in the marinade.
4. Shake off as much marinade as possible from the fillets and place them, skin side down, in the fryer basket in a single layer. You may need to cook the fillets in batches.
5. Air fry for 10 to 15 minutes for medium-rare to medium done salmon or 15 to 20 minutes for well done. The minimum internal temperature should be 145°F at the thickest part of the fillet.

Southern Shrimp With Cocktail Sauce

Servings: 2
Cooking Time: 20 Minutes
Ingredients:
- ½ lb raw shrimp, tail on, deveined and shelled
- 1 cup ketchup
- 2 tbsp prepared horseradish
- 1 tbsp lemon juice
- ½ tsp Worcestershire sauce
- 1/8 tsp chili powder
- Salt and pepper to taste
- 1/3 cup flour
- 2 tbsp cornstarch
- ¼ cup milk
- 1 egg
- ½ cup bread crumbs
- 1 tbsp Cajun seasoning
- 1 lemon, cut into pieces

Directions:
1. In a small bowl, whisk the ketchup, horseradish, lemon juice, Worcestershire sauce, chili powder, salt, and pepper. Let chill covered in the fridge until ready to use. Preheat air fryer at 375ºF. In a bowl, mix the flour, cornstarch, and salt. In another bowl, beat the milk and egg and in a third bowl, combine breadcrumbs and Cajun seasoning.
2. Roll the shrimp in the flour mixture, shake off excess flour. Then, dip in the egg, shake off excess egg. Finally, dredge in the breadcrumbs mixture. Place shrimp in the greased frying basket and Air Fry for 8 minutes, flipping once. Serve with cocktail sauce and lemon slices.

Pollock Fillets With Rosemary & Oregano

Servings: 3
Cooking Time: 15 Minutes
Ingredients:
- 1 tablespoon olive oil
- 1 red onion, sliced
- 2 cloves garlic, chopped
- 1 Florina pepper, deveined and minced
- 3 pollock fillets, skinless
- 2 ripe tomatoes, diced
- 12 Kalamata olives, pitted and chopped
- 1 tablespoon capers
- 1 teaspoon oregano
- 1 teaspoon rosemary
- Sea salt, to taste
- ½ cup white wine

Directions:
1. Start by preheating your Air Fryer to 360 degrees F/ 180 degrees C.
2. Heat the oil in a baking pan. Once hot, sauté the onion, garlic, and pepper for 2 to 3 minutes or until fragrant.
3. Add the fish fillets to the baking pan, then top with the tomatoes, olives, and capers.
4. After sprinkling with the oregano, rosemary and salt, pour in white wine and transfer to the pan.
5. Cook for 10 minutes at 395 degrees F/ 200 degrees C.
6. Taste for seasoning and serve on individual plates, garnished with some extra Mediterranean herbs if desired.
7. Enjoy!

Snapper With Fruit

Servings: 4
Cooking Time:9 To 13 Minutes
Ingredients:
- 4 (4-ounce) red snapper fillets (see Tip)
- 2 teaspoons olive oil
- 3 nectarines, halved and pitted
- 3 plums, halved and pitted
- 1 cup red grapes
- 1 tablespoon freshly squeezed lemon juice
- 1 tablespoon honey
- ½ teaspoon dried thyme

Directions:
1. Put the red snapper in the air fryer basket and drizzle with the olive oil. Air-fry for 4 minutes.
2. Remove the basket and add the nectarines and plums. Scatter the grapes over all.
3. Drizzle with the lemon juice and honey and sprinkle with the thyme.
4. Return the basket to the air fryer and air-fry for 5 to 9 minutes more, or until the fish flakes when tested with a fork and the fruit is tender. Serve immediately.

Tilapia Al Pesto

Servings:4
Cooking Time: 25 Minutes
Ingredients:
- 4 tilapia fillets
- 1 egg
- 2 tbsp buttermilk
- 1 cup crushed cornflakes
- Salt and pepper to taste
- 4 tsp pesto
- 2 tbsp butter, melted
- 4 lemon wedges

Directions:
1. Preheat air fryer to 350ºF. Whisk egg and buttermilk in a bowl. In another bowl, combine cornflakes, salt, and pepper. Spread 1 tsp of pesto on each tilapia fillet, then tightly roll the fillet from one short end to the other. Secure with a toothpick. Dip each fillet in the egg mixture and dredge in the cornflake mixture. Place fillets in the greased frying basket, drizzle with melted butter, and Air Fry for 6 minutes. Let rest onto a serving dish for 5 minutes before removing the toothpicks. Serve with lemon wedges.

Lobster Tails With Lemon Garlic Butter

Servings: 2
Cooking Time: 5 Minutes
Ingredients:
- 4 ounces unsalted butter
- 1 tablespoon finely chopped lemon zest
- 1 clove garlic, thinly sliced
- 2 (6-ounce) lobster tails
- salt and freshly ground black pepper
- ½ cup white wine
- ½ lemon, sliced
- vegetable oil

Directions:
1. Start by making the lemon garlic butter. Combine the butter, lemon zest and garlic in a small saucepan. Melt and simmer the butter on the stovetop over the lowest possible heat while you prepare the lobster tails.
2. Prepare the lobster tails by cutting down the middle of the top of the shell. Crack the bottom shell by squeezing the sides of the lobster together so that you can access the lobster meat inside. Pull the lobster tail up out of the shell, but leave it attached at the base of the tail. Lay the lobster meat on top of the shell and season with salt and freshly ground black pepper. Pour a little of the lemon garlic butter on top of the lobster meat and transfer the lobster to the refrigerator so that the butter solidifies a little.
3. Pour the white wine into the air fryer drawer and add the lemon slices. Preheat the air fryer to 400°F for 5 minutes.
4. Transfer the lobster tails to the air fryer basket. Air-fry at 370° for 5 minutes, brushing more butter on halfway through cooking. (Add a minute or two if your lobster tail is more than 6-ounces.) Remove and serve with more butter for dipping or drizzling.

Sesame-glazed Salmon

Servings:4
Cooking Time: 16 Minutes
Ingredients:
- 3 tablespoons soy sauce
- 1 tablespoon rice wine or dry sherry
- 1 tablespoon brown sugar
- 1 tablespoon toasted sesame oil
- 1 teaspoon minced garlic
- ¼ teaspoon minced ginger
- 4 (6 ounce) salmon fillets, skin-on
- Olive oil
- ½ tablespoon sesame seeds

Directions:
1. In a small bowl, mix together the soy sauce, rice wine, brown sugar, toasted sesame oil, garlic, and ginger.
2. Place the salmon in a shallow baking dish and pour the marinade over the fillets. Cover and refrigerate for at least 1 hour, turning the fillets occasionally to coat in the marinade.
3. Spray a fryer basket lightly with olive oil.
4. Shake off as much marinade as possible and place the fillets, skin side down, in the fryer basket in a single layer. Reserve the marinade. You may need to cook them in batches.
5. Air fry for 8 to 10 minutes. Brush the tops of the salmon fillets with the reserved marinade and sprinkle with sesame seeds.
6. Increase the fryer temperature to 400°F and cook for 2 to 5 more minutes for medium, 1 to 3 minutes for medium rare, or 4 to 6 minutes for well done.

Buttery Shrimp Scampi

Servings: 4
Cooking Time: 10 Minutes
Ingredients:
- 1 pound shrimp, peeled and deveined
- 10 garlic cloves, peeled
- 2 tablespoons olive oil
- 1 fresh lemon, cut into wedges
- ¼ cup parmesan cheese, grated
- 2 tablespoons butter, melted

Directions:
1. At 370 degrees F/ 185 degrees C, preheat your air fryer.
2. Mix together shrimp, lemon wedges, olive oil, and garlic cloves in a suitable bowl.
3. Pour shrimp mixture into the air fryer basket and place into the air fryer and cook for almost 10 minutes.
4. Drizzle melted butter and parmesan cheese.
5. Serve and enjoy.

Caribbean Jerk Cod Fillets

Servings:2
Cooking Time: 20 Minutes
Ingredients:
- ¼ cup chopped cooked shrimp
- ¼ cup diced mango
- 1 tomato, diced
- 2 tbsp diced red onion
- 1 tbsp chopped parsley
- ¼ tsp ginger powder
- 2 tsp lime juice
- Salt and pepper to taste
- 2 cod fillets
- 2 tsp Jerk seasoning

Directions:
1. In a bowl, combine the shrimp, mango, tomato, red onion, parsley, ginger powder, lime juice, salt, and black pepper. Let chill the salsa in the fridge until ready to use.
2. Preheat air fryer to 350ºF. Sprinkle cod fillets with Jerk seasoning. Place them in the greased frying basket and Air Fry for 10 minutes or until the cod is opaque and flakes easily with a fork. Divide between 2 medium plates. Serve topped with the Caribbean salsa.

Perfect Soft-shelled Crabs

Servings:2
Cooking Time: 12 Minutes
Ingredients:
- ½ cup All-purpose flour
- 1 tablespoon Old Bay seasoning
- 1 Large egg(s), well beaten
- 1 cup Ground oyster crackers
- 2 2½-ounce cleaned soft-shelled crab(s), about 4 inches across
- Vegetable oil spray

Directions:
1. Preheat the air fryer to 375°F.
2. Set up and fill three shallow soup plates or small pie plates on your counter: one for the flour, whisked with the Old Bay until well combined; one for the beaten egg(s); and one for the cracker crumbs.
3. Set a soft-shelled crab in the flour mixture and turn to coat evenly and well on all sides, even inside the legs. Dip the crab into the egg(s) and coat well, turning at least once, again getting some of the egg between the legs. Let any excess egg slip back into the rest, then set the crab in the cracker crumbs. Turn several times, pressing very gently to get the crab evenly coated with crumbs, even between the legs. Generously coat the crab on all sides with vegetable oil spray. Set it aside if you're making more than one and coat these in the same way.
4. Set the crab(s) in the basket with as much air space between them as possible. They may overlap slightly, particularly at the ends of their legs, depending on the basket's size. Air-fry undisturbed for 12 minutes, or until very crisp and golden brown. If the machine is at 390°F, the crabs may be done in only 10 minutes.
5. Use kitchen tongs to gently transfer the crab(s) to a wire rack. Cool for a couple of minutes before serving.

Fish And Vegetable Tacos

Servings: 4
Cooking Time:9 To 12 Minutes
Ingredients:
- 1 pound white fish fillets, such as sole or cod (see Tip)
- 2 teaspoons olive oil
- 3 tablespoons freshly squeezed lemon juice, divided
- 1½ cups chopped red cabbage
- 1 large carrot, grated
- ½ cup low-sodium salsa
- ⅓ cup low-fat Greek yogurt
- 4 soft low-sodium whole-wheat tortillas

Directions:
1. Brush the fish with the olive oil and sprinkle with 1 tablespoon of lemon juice. Air-fry in the air fryer basket for 9 to 12 minutes, or until the fish just flakes when tested with a fork.
2. Meanwhile, in a medium bowl, stir together the remaining 2 tablespoons of lemon juice, the red cabbage, carrot, salsa, and yogurt.
3. When the fish is cooked, remove it from the air fryer basket and break it up into large pieces.
4. Offer the fish, tortillas, and the cabbage mixture, and let each person assemble a taco.

Herbed Catfish

Servings: 4
Cooking Time: 12 Minutes
Ingredients:
- 20 ounces catfish fillet, 4 ounces each fillet
- 2 eggs, beaten
- 1 teaspoon dried thyme
- ½ teaspoon salt
- 1 teaspoon apple cider vinegar
- 1 teaspoon avocado oil
- ¼ teaspoon cayenne pepper
- ⅓ cup coconut flour

Directions:
1. Sprinkle the catfish fillets with dried thyme, salt, apple cider vinegar, cayenne pepper, and coconut flour.
2. Then sprinkle the fish fillets with avocado oil.
3. At 385 degrees F/ 195 degrees C, preheat your air fryer.
4. Put the catfish fillets in the air fryer basket and cook them for almost 8 minutes.
5. Then flip the fish on another side and cook for 4 minutes more.

Crumbs Crusted Shrimp

Servings: 8
Cooking Time: 8 Minutes
Ingredients:
- 2-pound shrimp, peeled and deveined
- 4 egg whites
- 2 tablespoons olive oil
- 1 cup flour
- ½ teaspoon cayenne pepper
- 1 cup bread crumbs
- Black pepper and salt to taste

Directions:
1. Combine together the flour, black pepper, and salt in a shallow bowl.
2. In a separate bowl, mix the egg whites using a whisk.
3. In a third bowl, combine the bread crumbs, cayenne pepper, and salt.
4. At 400 degrees F/ 205 degrees C, preheat your air fryer.
5. Cover the shrimp with the flour mixture before dipping it in the egg white and lastly rolling in the bread crumbs.
6. Put the coated shrimp in the fryer's basket and top with a light drizzle of olive oil.
7. Air fry the shrimp at almost 400 degrees F/ 205 degrees C for 8 minutes, in multiple batches if necessary.

Shrimp "scampi"

Servings:4
Cooking Time: 5 Minutes
Ingredients:
- 1½ pounds Large shrimp, peeled and deveined
- ¼ cup Olive oil
- 2 tablespoons Minced garlic
- 1 teaspoon Dried oregano
- Up to 1 teaspoon Red pepper flakes
- ½ teaspoon Table salt
- 2 tablespoons White balsamic vinegar

Directions:
1. Preheat the air fryer to 400°F.
2. Stir the shrimp, olive oil, garlic, oregano, red pepper flakes, and salt in a large bowl until the shrimp are well coated.
3. When the machine is at temperature, transfer the shrimp to the basket. They will overlap and even sit on top of each other. Air-fry for 5 minutes, tossing and rearranging the shrimp twice to make sure the covered surfaces are exposed, until pink and firm.
4. Pour the contents of the basket into a serving bowl. Pour the vinegar over the shrimp while hot and toss to coat.

Blackened Shrimp

Servings: 4
Cooking Time: 10 Minutes
Ingredients:
- 1 pound raw shrimp, peeled and deveined (see Prep tip, here)
- 1 teaspoon paprika
- ½ teaspoon dried oregano
- ½ teaspoon cayenne pepper
- Juice of ½ lemon
- Salt
- Pepper
- Cooking oil

Directions:

1. Place the shrimp in a sealable plastic bag and add the paprika, oregano, cayenne pepper, lemon juice, and salt and pepper to taste. Seal the bag and shake well to combine.
2. Spray a grill pan or the air fryer basket with cooking oil.
3. Place the shrimp in the air fryer. It is okay to stack the shrimp. Cook for 4 minutes.
4. Open the air fryer and shake the basket. Cook for an additional 3 to 4 minutes, or until the shrimp has blackened.
5. Cool before serving.

Stuffed Shrimp

Servings: 4
Cooking Time: 12 Minutes Per Batch
Ingredients:
- 16 tail-on shrimp, peeled and deveined (last tail section intact)
- ¾ cup crushed panko breadcrumbs
- oil for misting or cooking spray
- Stuffing
- 2 6-ounce cans lump crabmeat
- 2 tablespoons chopped shallots
- 2 tablespoons chopped green onions
- 2 tablespoons chopped celery
- 2 tablespoons chopped green bell pepper
- ½ cup crushed saltine crackers
- 1 teaspoon Old Bay Seasoning
- 1 teaspoon garlic powder
- ¼ teaspoon ground thyme
- 2 teaspoons dried parsley flakes
- 2 teaspoons fresh lemon juice
- 2 teaspoons Worcestershire sauce
- 1 egg, beaten

Directions:
1. Rinse shrimp. Remove tail section (shell) from 4 shrimp, discard, and chop the meat finely.
2. To prepare the remaining 12 shrimp, cut a deep slit down the back side so that the meat lies open flat. Do not cut all the way through.
3. Preheat air fryer to 360°F.
4. Place chopped shrimp in a large bowl with all of the stuffing ingredients and stir to combine.
5. Divide stuffing into 12 portions, about 2 tablespoons each.
6. Place one stuffing portion onto the back of each shrimp and form into a ball or oblong shape. Press firmly so that stuffing sticks together and adheres to shrimp.
7. Gently roll each stuffed shrimp in panko crumbs and mist with oil or cooking spray.
8. Place 6 shrimp in air fryer basket and cook at 360°F for 10minutes. Mist with oil or spray and cook 2 minutes longer or until stuffing cooks through inside and is crispy outside.
9. Repeat step 8 to cook remaining shrimp.

Sea Bream Fillet With Tomato Sauce

Servings: 4
Cooking Time: 8 Minutes
Ingredients:
- 1 tablespoon keto tomato sauce
- 1 tablespoon avocado oil
- 1 teaspoon ground black pepper
- ½-teaspoon salt
- 12 oz. sea bream fillet

Directions:
1. Cut the sea bream fillet on 4 servings.
2. After that, mix up tomato sauce, avocado oil, salt, and ground black pepper in a mixing bowl.
3. Rub the fish fillets with tomato mixture on both sides.
4. Line the air fryer basket with foil.
5. Put the sea bream fillets on the foil and cook them for 8 minutes at 390 degrees F/ 200 degrees C.

Tuna Veggie Stir-fry

Servings:4
Cooking Time: 7 To 12 Minutes
Ingredients:
- 1 tablespoon olive oil
- 1 red bell pepper, chopped
- 1 cup green beans, cut into 2-inch pieces
- 1 onion, sliced
- 2 cloves garlic, sliced
- 2 tablespoons low-sodium soy sauce
- 1 tablespoon honey
- ½ pound fresh tuna, cubed

Directions:
1. In a 6-inch metal bowl, combine the olive oil, pepper, green beans, onion, and garlic.
2. Cook in the air fryer for 4 to 6 minutes, stirring once, until crisp and tender. Add soy sauce, honey, and tuna, and stir.
3. Cook for another 3 to 6 minutes, stirring once, until the tuna is cooked as desired. Tuna can be served rare or medium-rare, or you can cook it until well done.

Cheesy Salmon-stuffed Avocados

Servings:2
Cooking Time: 20 Minutes
Ingredients:
- ¼ cup apple cider vinegar
- 1 tsp granular sugar
- ¼ cup sliced red onions
- 2 oz cream cheese, softened
- 1 tbsp capers
- 2 halved avocados, pitted
- 4 oz smoked salmon
- ¼ tsp dried dill
- 2 cherry tomatoes, halved
- 1 tbsp cilantro, chopped

Directions:
1. Warm apple vinegar and sugar in a saucepan over medium heat and simmer for 4 minutes until boiling.

Add in onion and turn the heat off. Let sit until ready to use. Drain before using. In a small bowl, combine cream cheese and capers. Let chill in the fridge until ready to use.

2. Preheat air fryer to 350ºF. Place avocado halves, cut sides-up, in the frying basket, and Air Fry for 4 minutes. Transfer avocado halves to 2 plates. Top with cream cheese mixture, smoked salmon, dill, red onions, tomato halves and cilantro. Serve immediately.

Typical Cod Nuggets

Servings: 4
Cooking Time: 10 Minutes
Ingredients:
- 16-ounce cod
- To make the breading:
- 1 cup all-purpose flour
- 2 tablespoons olive oil
- 2 eggs, beaten
- 1 pinch salt
- ¾ cup panko breadcrumbs, finely processed

Directions:
1. Thoroughly mix the oil, salt and crumbs in a medium-size bowl.
2. Take the cod, make pieces from it of about 5 inches by 1 inch.
3. In a bowl of medium size, thoroughly mix the salt, oil and crumbs.
4. Side by side place three bowls; add the flour in the first bowl, crumb mixture in the second and eggs in the third. Dip the fish in the flour, one by one, and then mix in the egg mix.
5. Lastly coat with the crumb mixture completely.
6. Place the fish pieces in the basket that has been coated with cooking oil or spray.
7. Arrange the basket to the air fryer and cook at 390 degrees F/ 200 degrees C for 10 minutes or until turn pink.
8. Serve the crispy fish!

Creamy Savory Salmon

Servings: 4
Cooking Time: 25 Minutes
Ingredients:
- For salmon:
- 2 teaspoons olive oil
- 24-ounce (4 pieces) salmon
- 1 pinch salt
- For the sauce:
- ½ cup sour cream
- ½ cup non-fat: Greek yogurt
- 1 pinch salt
- 2 tablespoons dill, finely chopped

Directions:
1. Make the salmon pieces of 6 ounces each, brush the pieces with olive oil and then top them with salt.
2. Place the pieces in the basket that has been coated with cooking oil or spray.

3. Arrange the basket to the air fryer and cook at 270 degrees F/ 130 degrees C for 20-25 minutes.
4. In a bowl of medium size, thoroughly mix the sauce ingredients.
5. When the pieces has finished, serve warm with the sauce!

Tuna Cakes

Servings:4
Cooking Time: 10 Minutes
Ingredients:
- 4 pouches tuna, drained
- 1 large egg, whisked
- 2 tablespoons peeled and chopped white onion
- ½ teaspoon Old Bay Seasoning

Directions:
1. In a large bowl, mix all ingredients together and form into four patties.
2. Place patties into ungreased air fryer basket. Adjust the temperature to 400°F and set the timer for 10 minutes. Patties will be browned and crispy when done. Let cool 5 minutes before serving.

Black Olive & Shrimp Salad

Servings: 4
Cooking Time: 15 Minutes
Ingredients:
- 1 lb cleaned shrimp, deveined
- ½ cup olive oil
- 4 garlic cloves, minced
- 1 tbsp balsamic vinegar
- ¼ tsp cayenne pepper
- ¼ tsp dried basil
- ¼ tsp salt
- ¼ tsp onion powder
- 1 tomato, diced
- ¼ cup black olives

Directions:
1. Preheat air fryer to 380°F. Place the olive oil, garlic, balsamic, cayenne, basil, onion powder and salt in a bowl and stir to combine. Divide the tomatoes and black olives between 4 small ramekins. Top with shrimp and pour a quarter of the oil mixture over the shrimp. Bake for 6-8 minutes until the shrimp are cooked through. Serve.

Garlic-lemon Steamer Clams

Servings:2
Cooking Time: 30 Minutes
Ingredients:
- 25 Manila clams, scrubbed
- 2 tbsp butter, melted
- 1 garlic clove, minced
- 2 lemon wedges

Directions:
1. Add the clams to a large bowl filled with water and let sit for 10 minutes. Drain. Pour more water and let sit for 10 more minutes. Drain. Preheat air fryer to 350°F.

Place clams in the basket and Air Fry for 7 minutes. Discard any clams that don't open. Remove clams from shells and place them into a large serving dish. Drizzle with melted butter and garlic and squeeze lemon on top. Serve.

Tasty Juicy Salmon

Servings: 2
Cooking Time: 13 Minutes
Ingredients:
- 2 salmon fillets
- 4 asparagus stalks
- ¼ cup champagne
- Salt and black pepper, to taste
- ¼ cup white sauce
- 1½ teaspoon olive oil

Directions:
1. Heat the air fryer ahead of time.
2. In a bowl, mix the salmon fillets, asparagus, champagne, salt, black pepper, white sauce, and olive oil together and divide this mixture evenly over 2 foil papers.
3. Arrange the foil papers in the basket of your air fryer and cook for about 13 minutes at 355 degrees F/ 180 degrees C.
4. Dish out in a platter and serve hot.

Buttery Lobster Tails

Servings:4
Cooking Time: 6 Minutes
Ingredients:
- 4 6- to 8-ounce shell-on raw lobster tails
- 2 tablespoons Butter, melted and cooled
- 1 teaspoon Lemon juice
- ½ teaspoon Finely grated lemon zest
- ½ teaspoon Garlic powder
- ½ teaspoon Table salt
- ½ teaspoon Ground black pepper

Directions:
1. Preheat the air fryer to 375°F .
2. To give the tails that restaurant look, you need to butterfly the meat. To do so, place a tail on a cutting board so that the shell is convex. Use kitchen shears to cut a line down the middle of the shell from the larger end to the smaller, cutting only the shell and not the meat below, and stopping before the back fins. Pry open the shell, leaving it intact. Use your clean fingers to separate the meat from the shell's sides and bottom, keeping it attached to the shell at the back near the fins. Pull the meat up and out of the shell through the cut line, laying the meat on top of the shell and closing the shell under the meat. Make two equidistant cuts down the meat from the larger end to near the smaller end, each about ¼ inch deep, for the classic restaurant look on the plate. Repeat this procedure with the remaining tail(s).
3. Stir the butter, lemon juice, zest, garlic powder, salt, and pepper in a small bowl until well combined. Brush this mixture over the lobster meat set atop the shells.

4. When the machine is at temperature, place the tails shell side down in the basket with as much air space between them as possible. Air-fry undisturbed for 6 minutes, or until the lobster meat has pink streaks over it and is firm.
5. Use kitchen tongs to transfer the tails to a wire rack. Cool for only a minute or two before serving.

Lime Flaming Halibut

Servings:2
Cooking Time: 20 Minutes
Ingredients:
- 2 tbsp butter, melted
- ½ tsp chili powder
- ½ cup bread crumbs
- 2 halibut fillets

Directions:
1. Preheat air fryer to 350ºF. In a bowl, mix the butter, chili powder and bread crumbs. Press mixture onto tops of halibut fillets. Place halibut in the greased frying basket and Air Fry for 10 minutes or until the fish is opaque and flake easily with a fork. Serve right away.

Fried Breaded Prawns

Servings: 6
Cooking Time: 8 Minutes
Ingredients:
- 12 prawns
- 2 eggs
- Flour to taste
- Breadcrumbs
- 1 teaspoon oil

Directions:
1. Remove the head of the prawns and shell carefully.
2. Pass the prawns first in the flour, then in the beaten egg and then in the breadcrumbs.
3. At 350 degrees F/ 175 degrees C, preheat your air fryer.
4. Add the prawns and cook for 4 minutes. If the prawns are large, it will be necessary to cook 6 at a time.
5. Turn the prawns and cook for another 4 minutes.
6. They should be served with a yogurt or mayonnaise sauce.

Popcorn Crawfish

Servings: 4
Cooking Time: 18 Minutes
Ingredients:
- ½ cup flour, plus 2 tablespoons
- ½ teaspoon garlic powder
- 1½ teaspoons Old Bay Seasoning
- ½ teaspoon onion powder
- ½ cup beer, plus 2 tablespoons
- 12-ounce package frozen crawfish tail meat, thawed and drained
- oil for misting or cooking spray
- Coating
- 1½ cups panko crumbs

- 1 teaspoon Old Bay Seasoning
- ½ teaspoon ground black pepper

Directions:

1. In a large bowl, mix together the flour, garlic powder, Old Bay Seasoning, and onion powder. Stir in beer to blend.
2. Add crawfish meat to batter and stir to coat.
3. Combine the coating ingredients in food processor and pulse to finely crush the crumbs. Transfer crumbs to shallow dish.
4. Preheat air fryer to 390°F.
5. Pour the crawfish and batter into a colander to drain. Stir with a spoon to drain excess batter.
6. Working with a handful of crawfish at a time, roll in crumbs and place on a cookie sheet. It's okay if some of the smaller pieces of crawfish meat stick together.
7. Spray breaded crawfish with oil or cooking spray and place all at once into air fryer basket.
8. Cook at 390°F for 5minutes. Shake basket or stir and mist again with olive oil or spray. Cook 5 moreminutes, shake basket again, and mist lightly again. Continue cooking 5 more minutes, until browned and crispy.

Shrimp Patties

Servings: 4
Cooking Time: 10 Minutes

Ingredients:

- ½ pound shelled and deveined raw shrimp
- ¼ cup chopped red bell pepper
- ¼ cup chopped green onion
- ¼ cup chopped celery
- 2 cups cooked sushi rice
- ½ teaspoon garlic powder
- ½ teaspoon Old Bay Seasoning
- ½ teaspoon salt
- 2 teaspoons Worcestershire sauce
- ½ cup plain breadcrumbs
- oil for misting or cooking spray

Directions:

1. Finely chop the shrimp. You can do this in a food processor, but it takes only a few pulses. Be careful not to overprocess into mush.
2. Place shrimp in a large bowl and add all other ingredients except the breadcrumbs and oil. Stir until well combined.
3. Preheat air fryer to 390°F.
4. Shape shrimp mixture into 8 patties, no more than ½-inch thick. Roll patties in breadcrumbs and mist with oil or cooking spray.
5. Place 4 shrimp patties in air fryer basket and cook at 390°F for 10 minutes, until shrimp cooks through and outside is crispy.
6. Repeat step 5 to cook remaining shrimp patties.

Curried Sweet-and-spicy Scallops

Servings:3
Cooking Time: 5 Minutes

Ingredients:

- 6 tablespoons Thai sweet chili sauce
- 2 cups Crushed Rice Krispies or other rice-puff cereal
- 2 teaspoons Yellow curry powder, purchased or homemade
- 1 pound Sea scallops
- Vegetable oil spray

Directions:

1. Preheat the air fryer to 400°F.
2. Set up and fill two shallow soup plates or small pie plates on your counter: one for the chili sauce and one for crumbs, mixed with the curry powder.
3. Dip a scallop into the chili sauce, coating it on all sides. Set it in the cereal mixture and turn several times to coat evenly. Gently shake off any excess and set the scallop on a cutting board. Continue dipping and coating the remaining scallops. Coat them all on all sides with the vegetable oil spray.
4. Set the scallops in the basket with as much air space between them as possible. Air-fry undisturbed for 5 minutes, or until lightly browned and crunchy.
5. Remove the basket. Set aside for 2 minutes to let the coating set up. Then gently pour the contents of the basket onto a platter and serve at once.

Lemon Breaded Fish

Servings: 4
Cooking Time: 12 Minutes

Ingredients:

- ½ cup breadcrumbs
- 4 tablespoons vegetable oil
- 1 egg
- 4 fish fillets
- 1 lemon

Directions:

1. Heat the air fryer to reach 355 degrees F/ 180 degrees C.
2. Whisk the oil and breadcrumbs until crumbly.
3. Dip the prepared fish into the egg, then the crumb mixture.
4. Arrange the fish in the cooker and air-fry for 12 minutes.
5. Garnish using the lemon.

Lemon Foil Salmon

Servings: 2
Cooking Time: 12 Minutes

Ingredients:

- 2 x 4-oz. skinless salmon fillets
- 2 tablespoons unsalted butter, melted
- ½ teaspoon garlic powder
- 1 medium lemon
- ½ teaspoon dried dill

Directions:

1. Cut one sheet of aluminum foil into 2 squares measuring roughly 5" x 5". Lay each of the salmon fillets at the center of each piece. Brush both fillets with

a tablespoon of bullet and season with a quarter-teaspoon of garlic powder.

2. Halve the lemon and grate the skin of 1 ½ over the fish. Cut 4 half-slices of lemon, using 2 to top each fillet. Season each fillet with a quarter-teaspoon of dill.

3. Fold the tops and sides of the aluminum foil over the fish to create a kind of packet. Place each 1 in the air fryer.

4. Cook for 12 minutes at 400 degrees F/ 205 degrees C.

5. The salmon is ready when it flakes easily. Serve hot.

Sesame-crusted Tuna Steaks

Servings:3
Cooking Time: 10-13 Minutes
Ingredients:
- ½ cup Sesame seeds, preferably a blend of white and black
- 1½ tablespoons Toasted sesame oil
- 3 6-ounce skinless tuna steaks

Directions:
1. Preheat the air fryer to 400°F.
2. Pour the sesame seeds on a dinner plate. Use ½ tablespoon of the sesame oil as a rub on both sides and the edges of a tuna steak. Set it in the sesame seeds, then turn it several times, pressing gently, to create an even coating of the seeds, including around the steak's edge. Set aside and continue coating the remaining steak(s).
3. When the machine is at temperature, set the steaks in the basket with as much air space between them as possible. Air-fry undisturbed for 10 minutes for medium-rare, or 12 to 13 minutes for cooked through.
4. Use a nonstick-safe spatula to transfer the steaks to serving plates. Serve hot.

Flavor Calamari With Mediterranean Sauce

Servings: 4
Cooking Time: 4 Minutes
Ingredients:
- ½ pound calamari tubes cut into rings, cleaned
- Sea salt, to taste
- Ground black pepper, to season
- ½ cup almond flour
- ½ cup all-purpose flour
- 4 tablespoons parmesan cheese, grated
- ½ cup ale beer
- ¼ teaspoon cayenne pepper
- ½ cup breadcrumbs
- ¼ cup mayonnaise
- ¼ cup Greek-style yogurt
- 1 clove garlic, minced
- 1 tablespoon fresh lemon juice
- 1 teaspoon fresh parsley, chopped
- 1 teaspoon fresh dill, chopped

Directions:
1. Sprinkle salt and black pepper on the calamari.

2. In a bowl, mix the flour, cheese and beer until well combined.

3. In another bowl, mix cayenne pepper and breadcrumbs.

4. Coat the calamari pieces with the flour mixture and then roll them onto the breadcrumb mixture, pressing to coat on all sides.

5. Lightly oil the cooking basket and transfer the calamari pieces in it.

6. Cook the calamari pieces at 400 degrees F/ 205 degrees C for 4 minutes, shaking the basket halfway through.

7. Meanwhile, thoroughly mix the remaining ingredients well.

8. Serve warm calamari with the sauce for dipping.

9. Enjoy!

Holiday Shrimp Scampi

Servings: 4
Cooking Time: 25 Minutes
Ingredients:
- 1 ½ lb peeled shrimp, deveined
- ¼ tsp lemon pepper seasoning
- 6 garlic cloves, minced
- 1 tsp salt
- ½ tsp grated lemon zest
- 3 tbsp fresh lemon juice
- 3 tbsp sunflower oil
- 3 tbsp butter
- 2 tsp fresh thyme leaves
- 1 lemon, cut into wedges

Directions:
1. Preheat the air fryer to 400°F. Combine the shrimp and garlic in a cake pan, then sprinkle with salt and lemon pepper seasoning. Toss to coat, then add the lemon zest, lemon juice, oil, and butter. Place the cake pan in the frying basket and Bake for 10-13 minutes, stirring once until no longer pink. Sprinkle with thyme leaves. Serve hot with lemon wedges on the side.

Salmon Puttanesca En Papillotte With Zucchini

Servings: 2
Cooking Time: 17 Minutes
Ingredients:
- 1 small zucchini, sliced into ¼-inch thick half moons
- 1 teaspoon olive oil
- salt and freshly ground black pepper
- 2 (5-ounce) salmon fillets
- 1 beefsteak tomato, chopped (about 1 cup)
- 1 tablespoon capers, rinsed
- 10 black olives, pitted and sliced
- 2 tablespoons dry vermouth or white wine 2 tablespoons butter
- ¼ cup chopped fresh basil, chopped

Directions:
1. Preheat the air fryer to 400°F.

2. Toss the zucchini with the olive oil, salt and freshly ground black pepper. Transfer the zucchini into the air fryer basket and air-fry for 5 minutes, shaking the basket once or twice during the cooking process.

3. Cut out 2 large rectangles of parchment paper – about 13-inches by 15-inches each. Divide the air-fried zucchini between the two pieces of parchment paper, placing the vegetables in the center of each rectangle.

4. Place a fillet of salmon on each pile of zucchini. Season the fish very well with salt and pepper. Toss the tomato, capers, olives and vermouth (or white wine) together in a bowl. Divide the tomato mixture between the two fish packages, placing it on top of the fish fillets and pouring any juice out of the bowl onto the fish. Top each fillet with a tablespoon of butter.

5. Fold up each parchment square. Bring two edges together and fold them over a few times, leaving some space above the fish. Twist the open sides together and upwards so they can serve as handles for the packet, but don't let them extend beyond the top of the air fryer basket.

6. Place the two packages into the air fryer and air-fry at 400°F for 12 minutes. The packages should be puffed up and slightly browned when fully cooked. Once cooked, let the fish sit in the parchment for 2 minutes.

7. Serve the fish in the parchment paper, or if desired, remove the parchment paper before serving. Garnish with a little fresh basil.

Rosemary Salmon

Servings: 4
Cooking Time: 15 Minutes
Ingredients:
- ½-teaspoon dried rosemary
- ½-teaspoon dried thyme
- ½-teaspoon dried basil
- ½-teaspoon ground coriander
- ½-teaspoon ground cumin
- ½-teaspoon ground paprika
- ½-teaspoon salt
- 1 pound salmon
- 1 tablespoon olive oil

Directions:
1. Mixed up the dried rosemary, thyme, basil, coriander, cumin, paprika, and salt in a suitable bowl.
2. Rub the salmon with the spice mixture gently and sprinkle it with the olive oil.
3. At 375 degrees F/ 190 degrees C, heat your air fryer in advance.
4. Put the prepared salmon on the cooking pan with the baking paper under it.
5. Cook the fish at 375 degrees F/ 190 degrees C for 15 minutes, or until you get the light crunchy crust.
6. Once done, serve and enjoy.

Caper Monkfish

Servings: 4
Cooking Time: 40 Minutes
Ingredients:
- 1 monkfish
- 10 cherry tomatoes
- 50 g cailletier olives
- 5 capers

Directions:
1. Spread aluminum foil inside the air fryer basket and place the monkfish clean and skinless.
2. Add chopped tomatoes, olives, capers, oil, and salt.
3. At 380 degrees F/ 195 degrees C, preheat your Air Fryer.
4. Cook the monkfish for about 40 minutes.

Rainbow Salmon Kebabs

Servings:2
Cooking Time: 8 Minutes
Ingredients:
- 6 ounces boneless, skinless salmon, cut into 1" cubes
- ¼ medium red onion, peeled and cut into 1" pieces
- ½ medium yellow bell pepper, seeded and cut into 1" pieces
- ½ medium zucchini, trimmed and cut into ½" slices
- 1 tablespoon olive oil
- ½ teaspoon salt
- ¼ teaspoon ground black pepper

Directions:
1. Using one 6" skewer, skewer 1 piece salmon, then 1 piece onion, 1 piece bell pepper, and finally 1 piece zucchini. Repeat this pattern with additional skewers to make four kebabs total. Drizzle with olive oil and sprinkle with salt and black pepper.
2. Place kebabs into ungreased air fryer basket. Adjust the temperature to 400°F and set the timer for 8 minutes, turning kebabs halfway through cooking. Salmon will easily flake and have an internal temperature of at least 145°F when done; vegetables will be tender. Serve warm.

Tomato Shrimp Kebab

Servings: 4
Cooking Time: 20 Minutes
Ingredients:
- 1 ½ pounds jumbo shrimp, cleaned, shelled and deveined
- 1 pound cherry tomatoes
- 2 tablespoons butter, melted
- 1 tablespoon Sriracha sauce
- Salt and black pepper, to taste
- ½ teaspoon dried oregano
- ½ teaspoon dried basil
- 1 teaspoon dried parsley flakes
- ½ teaspoon marjoram
- ½ teaspoon mustard seeds

Directions:
1. Toss all the recipe ingredients in a suitable mixing bowl until the shrimp and tomatoes are covered on all sides.
2. Prepare the skewers by soaking them in water for almost 15 minutes.

3. Thread the jumbo shrimp and cherry tomatoes onto skewers.

4. Cook the tomato shrimp kebab in the preheated air fryer at about 400 degrees F/ 205 degrees C for 5 minutes, working with batches. Serve.

Restaurant-style Flounder Cutlets

Servings: 2
Cooking Time: 15 Minutes
Ingredients:
*   1 egg
*   1 cup Pecorino Romano cheese, grated
*   Sea salt and white pepper, to taste
*   1/2 teaspoon cayenne pepper
*   1 teaspoon dried parsley flakes
*   2 flounder fillets

Directions:
1. To make a breading station, whisk the egg until frothy.
2. In another bowl, mix Pecorino Romano cheese, and spices.
3. Dip the fish in the egg mixture and turn to coat evenly; then, dredge in the cracker crumb mixture, turning a couple of times to coat evenly.
4. Cook in the preheated Air Fryer at 390°F for 5 minutes; turn them over and cook another 5 minutes. Enjoy!

Rich Salmon Burgers With Broccoli Slaw

Servings: 4
Cooking Time: 25 Minutes
Ingredients:
*   1 lb salmon fillets
*   1 egg
*   ¼ cup dill, chopped
*   1 cup bread crumbs
*   Salt to taste
*   ½ tsp cayenne pepper
*   1 lime, zested
*   1 tsp fish sauce
*   4 buns
*   3 cups chopped broccoli
*   ½ cup shredded carrots
*   ¼ cup sunflower seeds
*   2 garlic cloves, minced
*   1 cup Greek yogurt

Directions:
1. Preheat air fryer to 360°F. Blitz the salmon fillets in your food processor until they are finely chopped. Remove to a large bowl and add egg, dill, bread crumbs, salt, and cayenne. Stir to combine. Form the mixture into 4 patties. Put them into the frying basket and Bake for 10 minutes, flipping once. Combine broccoli, carrots, sunflower seeds, garlic, salt, lime, fish sauce, and Greek yogurt in a bowl. Serve the salmon burgers onto buns with broccoli slaw. Enjoy!

Fish Piccata With Crispy Potatoes

Servings: 4

Cooking Time: 30 Minutes
Ingredients:
*   4 cod fillets
*   1 tbsp butter
*   2 tsp capers
*   1 garlic clove, minced
*   2 tbsp lemon juice
*   ½ lb asparagus, trimmed
*   2 large potatoes, cubed
*   1 tbsp olive oil
*   Salt and pepper to taste
*   ¼ tsp garlic powder
*   1 tsp dried rosemary
*   1 tsp dried parsley
*   1 tsp chopped dill

Directions:
1. Preheat air fryer to 380°F. Place each fillet on a large piece of foil. Top each fillet with butter, capers, dill, garlic, and lemon juice. Fold the foil over the fish and seal the edges to make a pouch. Mix asparagus, parsley, potatoes, olive oil, salt, rosemary, garlic powder, and pepper in a large bowl. Place asparagus in the frying basket. Roast for 4 minutes, then shake the basket. Top vegetable with foil packets and Roast for another 8 minutes. Turn off air fryer and let it stand for 5 minutes. Serve warm and enjoy.

Beer-battered Fish And Chips

Servings: 4
Cooking Time: 30 Minutes
Ingredients:
*   2 eggs
*   1 cup malty beer, such as Pabst Blue Ribbon
*   1 cup all-purpose flour
*   ½ cup cornstarch
*   1 teaspoon garlic powder
*   Salt
*   Pepper
*   Cooking oil
*   4 (4-ounce) cod fillets

Directions:
1. In a medium bowl, beat the eggs with the beer. In another medium bowl, combine the flour and cornstarch, and season with the garlic powder and salt and pepper to taste.
2. Spray the air fryer basket with cooking oil.
3. Dip each cod fillet in the flour and cornstarch mixture and then in the egg and beer mixture. Dip the cod in the flour and cornstarch a second time.
4. Place the cod in the air fryer. Do not stack. Cook in batches. Spray with cooking oil. Cook for 8 minutes.
5. Open the air fryer and flip the cod. Cook for an additional 7 minutes.
6. Remove the cooked cod from the air fryer, then repeat steps 4 and 5 for the remaining fillets.
7. Serve with Classic French Fries or prepare air-fried frozen fries. Frozen fries will need to be cooked for 18 to 20 minutes at 400ºF.
8. Cool before serving.

Sea Bass With Fruit Salsa

Servings: 4
Cooking Time: 30 Minutes
Ingredients:
- 3 halved nectarines, pitted
- 4 sea bass fillets
- 2 tsp olive oil
- 3 plums, halved and pitted
- 1 cup red grapes
- 1 tbsp lemon juice
- 1 tbsp honey
- ½ tsp dried thyme

Directions:
1. Preheat air fryer to 390°F. Lay the sea bass fillets in the frying basket, then spritz olive oil over the top. Air Fry for 4 minutes. Take the basket out of the fryer and add the nectarines and plums. Pour the grapes over, spritz with lemon juice and honey, then add a pinch of thyme. Put the basket back into the fryer and Bake for 5-9 minutes. The fish should flake when finished, and the fruits should be soft. Serve hot.

Lightened-up Breaded Fish Filets

Servings: 4
Cooking Time: 10 Minutes
Ingredients:
- ½ cup all-purpose flour
- ½ teaspoon cayenne pepper
- 1 teaspoon garlic powder
- ½ teaspoon black pepper
- ¼ teaspoon salt
- 2 eggs, whisked
- 1½ cups panko breadcrumbs
- 1 pound boneless white fish filets
- 1 cup tartar sauce
- 1 lemon, sliced into wedges

Directions:
1. In a medium bowl, mix the flour, cayenne pepper, garlic powder, pepper, and salt.
2. In a shallow dish, place the eggs.
3. In a third dish, place the breadcrumbs.
4. Cover the fish in the flour, dip them in the egg, and coat them with panko. Repeat until all fish are covered in the breading.
5. Liberally spray the metal trivet that fits inside the air fryer basket with olive oil mist. Place the fish onto the trivet, leaving space between the filets to flip. Cook for 5 minutes, flip the fish, and cook another 5 minutes. Repeat until all the fish is cooked.
6. Serve warm with tartar sauce and lemon wedges.

Saucy Shrimp

Servings: 4
Cooking Time: 30 Minutes
Ingredients:
- 1 lb peeled shrimp, deveined
- ½ cup grated coconut
- ¼ cup bread crumbs
- ¼ cup flour
- ¼ tsp smoked paprika
- Salt and pepper to taste
- 1 egg
- 2 tbsp maple syrup
- ½ tsp rice vinegar
- 1 tbsp hot sauce
- ⅛ tsp red pepper flakes
- ¼ cup orange juice
- 1 tsp cornstarch
- ½ cup banana ketchup
- 1 lemon, sliced

Directions:
1. Preheat air fryer to 350°F. Combine coconut, bread crumbs, flour, paprika, black pepper, and salt in a bowl. In a separate bowl, whisk egg and 1 teaspoon water. Dip one shrimp into the egg bowl and shake off excess drips. Dip the shrimp in the bread crumb mixture and coat it completely. Continue the process for all of the shrimp. Arrange the shrimp on the greased frying basket. Air Fry for 5 minutes, then use tongs to flip the shrimp. Cook for another 2-3 minutes.
2. To make the sauce, add maple syrup, banana ketchup, hot sauce, vinegar, and red pepper flakes in a small saucepan over medium heat. Make a slurry in a small bowl with orange juice and cornstarch. Stir in slurry and continue stirring. Bring the sauce to a boil and cook for 5 minutes. When the sauce begins to thicken, remove from heat and allow to sit for 5 minutes. Serve shrimp warm along with sauce and lemon slices on the side.

Lemon Shrimp And Zucchinis

Servings: 4
Cooking Time: 15 Minutes
Ingredients:
- 1 pound shrimp, peeled and deveined
- A pinch of salt and black pepper
- 2 zucchinis, cut into medium cubes
- 1 tablespoon lemon juice
- 1 tablespoon olive oil
- 1 tablespoon garlic, minced

Directions:
1. In a pan that fits the air fryer, combine all the ingredients, toss, put the pan in the machine and cook at 370°F for 15 minutes. Divide between plates and serve right away.

Cajun Salmon

Servings:2
Cooking Time: 7 Minutes
Ingredients:
- 2 boneless, skinless salmon fillets
- 2 tablespoons salted butter, softened
- ⅛ teaspoon cayenne pepper
- ½ teaspoon garlic powder
- 1 teaspoon paprika
- ¼ teaspoon ground black pepper

Directions:

1. Brush both sides of each fillet with butter. In a small bowl, mix remaining ingredients and rub into fish on both sides.

2. Place fillets into ungreased air fryer basket. Adjust the temperature to 390°F and set the timer for 7 minutes. Internal temperature will be 145°F when done. Serve warm.

Crab Ratatouille

Servings:4
Cooking Time: 11 To 14 Minutes
Ingredients:

- 1½ cups peeled, cubed eggplant
- 1 onion, chopped
- 1 red bell pepper, chopped
- 2 large tomatoes, chopped
- 1 tablespoon olive oil
- ½ teaspoon dried thyme
- ½ teaspoon dried basil
- Pinch salt
- Freshly ground black pepper
- 1½ cups cooked crabmeat, picked over

Directions:

1. Combine the eggplant, onion, bell pepper, tomatoes, olive oil, thyme, and basil in a 6-inch metal bowl. Sprinkle with salt and pepper.

2. Roast for 9 minutes, then remove the bowl from the air fryer and stir.

3. Add the crabmeat and roast for 2 to 5 minutes or until the ratatouille is bubbling and the vegetables are tender. Serve immediately.

Mediterranean Sea Scallops

Servings: 2
Cooking Time: 20 Minutes
Ingredients:

- 1 tbsp olive oil
- 1 shallot, minced
- 2 tbsp capers
- 2 cloves garlic, minced
- ½ cup heavy cream
- 3 tbsp butter
- 1 tbsp lemon juice

- Salt and pepper to taste
- ¼ tbsp cumin powder
- ¼ tbsp curry powder
- 1 lb jumbo sea scallops
- 2 tbsp chopped parsley
- 1 tbsp chopped cilantro

Directions:

1. Warm the olive oil in a saucepan over medium heat. Add shallot and stir-fry for 2 minutes until translucent. Stir in capers, cumin, curry, garlic, heavy cream, 1 tbsp of butter, lemon juice, salt, and pepper and cook for 2 minutes until rolling a boil. Low the heat and simmer for 3 minutes until the caper sauce thickens. Turn the heat off.

2. Preheat air fryer at 400°F. In a bowl, add the remaining butter and scallops and toss to coat on all sides. Place scallops in the greased frying basket and Air Fry for 8 minutes, flipping once. Drizzle caper sauce over, scatter with parsley, cilantro and serve.

Tuna Steaks

Servings: 2 Servings
Cooking Time: 30 Minutes
Ingredients:

- 2 skinless yellowfin tuna steaks
- ¼ cup of soy sauce
- ½ teaspoon of rice vinegar
- 2 teaspoons of honey
- 1 teaspoon of sesame or olive oil
- 1 teaspoon of grated ginger
- Lime wedges and avocado-cucumber salsa, for serving

Directions:

1. Mix soy sauce, ginger, honey, vinegar, and oil in a large mixing bowl. Put the tuna steaks in the bowl. Keep covered for 20–30 minutes in the fridge.

2. Preheat your air fryer to 380°F. Cover the inside of air fryer basket with the perforated parchment paper.

3. Put the marinated tuna steaks in the air fryer basket in a single layer. Cook at 380°F for 4 minutes. Let it rest for 1–2 minutes before serving.

4. Serve with your favorite salsa and lime wedges. Enjoy your Tuna Steaks!

Chapter 8: Poultry Recipes

Garlic Chicken Popcorn

Servings: 1
Cooking Time: 15 Minutes
Ingredients:
- 1-pound skinless, boneless chicken breast
- 1 teaspoon chili flakes
- 1 teaspoon garlic powder
- ½ cup flour
- 1 tablespoon olive oil cooking spray

Directions:
1. Pre-heat your air fryer at 365 degrees F/ 185 degrees C. Spray with olive oil.
2. Cut the chicken breasts into cubes and place in a suitable bowl.
3. Toss with the chili flakes, garlic powder, and additional seasonings to taste.
4. Add the coconut flour and toss once more.
5. Cook the chicken in the air fryer for ten minutes almost.
6. Flip and continue cooking for 5 minutes before serving.

Chicken Fajitas

Servings: 4
Cooking Time:10 To 15 Minutes
Ingredients:
- 4 (5-ounce) low-sodium boneless skinless chicken breasts, cut into 4-by-½-inch strips
- 1 tablespoon freshly squeezed lemon juice
- 2 teaspoons olive oil
- 2 teaspoons chili powder
- 2 red bell peppers, sliced (see Tip)
- 4 low-sodium whole-wheat tortillas
- ⅓ cup nonfat sour cream
- 1 cup grape tomatoes, sliced (see Tip)

Directions:
1. In a large bowl, mix the chicken, lemon juice, olive oil, and chili powder. Toss to coat. Transfer the chicken to the air fryer basket. Add the red bell peppers. Grill for 10 to 15 minutes, or until the chicken reaches an internal temperature of 165°F on a meat thermometer.
2. Assemble the fajitas with the tortillas, chicken, bell peppers, sour cream, and tomatoes. Serve immediately.

Lemon Garlic Chicken

Servings:4
Cooking Time: 16 To 19 Minutes
Ingredients:
- 4 (5-ounce / 142-g) low-sodium boneless, skinless chicken breasts, cut into 4-by-½-inch strips
- 2 teaspoons olive oil
- 2 tablespoons cornstarch
- 3 garlic cloves, minced
- ½ cup low-sodium chicken broth
- ¼ cup freshly squeezed lemon juice
- 1 tablespoon honey
- ½ teaspoon dried thyme

- Brown rice, cooked (optional)

Directions:
1. Preheat the air fryer to 400°F (204°C).
2. In a large bowl, mix the chicken and olive oil. Sprinkle with the cornstarch. Toss to coat.
3. Add the garlic and transfer to a metal pan. Bake in the air fryer for 10 minutes, stirring once during cooking.
4. Add the chicken broth, lemon juice, honey, and thyme to the chicken mixture. Bake for 6 to 9 minutes more, or until the sauce is slightly thickened and the chicken reaches an internal temperature of 165°F (74°C) on a meat thermometer. Serve over hot cooked brown rice, if desired.

Air Fryer Naked Chicken Tenders

Servings:4
Cooking Time: 7 Minutes
Ingredients:
- Seasoning:
- 1 teaspoon kosher salt
- ½ teaspoon garlic powder
- ½ teaspoon onion powder
- ½ teaspoon chili powder
- ¼ teaspoon sweet paprika
- ¼ teaspoon freshly ground black pepper
- Chicken:
- 8 chicken breast tenders (1 pound / 454 g total)
- 2 tablespoons mayonnaise

Directions:
1. Preheat the air fryer to 375°F (191°C).
2. For the seasoning: In a small bowl, combine the salt, garlic powder, onion powder, chili powder, paprika, and pepper.
3. For the chicken: Place the chicken in a medium bowl and add the mayonnaise. Mix well to coat all over, then sprinkle with the seasoning mix.
4. Working in batches, arrange a single layer of the chicken in the air fryer basket. Air fry for 6 to 7 minutes, flipping halfway, until cooked through in the center. Serve immediately.

Garlic Turkey With Tomato Mix

Servings: 4
Cooking Time: 25 Minutes
Ingredients:
- 1 pound turkey meat, cubed and browned
- A pinch of salt and black pepper
- 1 green bell pepper, chopped
- 3 garlic cloves, chopped
- 1 and ½ tsps. cumin, ground
- 12 ounces veggies stock
- 1 cup tomatoes, chopped

Directions:
1. Mix the turkey, salt, black pepper, green bell pepper, garlic cloves, ground cumin, veggies stock, and the chopped tomatoes together in a baking pan that fits in your air fryer.
2. Toss well to season.

3. Cook in your air fryer at 380 degrees F/ 195 degrees C for 25 minutes.
4. When the cooking time runs out, remove from the air fryer.
5. Serve hot on plates and enjoy!

Dill Chicken Strips

Servings:4
Cooking Time: 10 Minutes
Ingredients:
- 2 whole boneless, skinless chicken breasts, halved lengthwise
- 1 cup Italian dressing
- 3 cups finely crushed potato chips
- 1 tablespoon dried dill weed
- 1 tablespoon garlic powder
- 1 large egg, beaten
- Cooking spray

Directions:
1. In a large resealable bag, combine the chicken and Italian dressing. Seal the bag and refrigerate to marinate at least 1 hour.
2. In a shallow dish, stir together the potato chips, dill, and garlic powder. Place the beaten egg in a second shallow dish.
3. Remove the chicken from the marinade. Roll the chicken pieces in the egg and the potato chip mixture, coating thoroughly.
4. Preheat the air fryer to 325ºF (163ºC). Line the air fryer basket with parchment paper.
5. Place the coated chicken on the parchment and spritz with cooking spray.
6. Bake for 5 minutes. Flip the chicken, spritz it with cooking spray, and bake for 5 minutes more until the outsides are crispy and the insides are no longer pink. Serve immediately.

Spiced Duck Legs

Servings: 2
Cooking Time: 30 Minutes
Ingredients:
- ½ tbsp. fresh thyme, chopped
- ½ tbsp. fresh parsley, chopped
- 2 duck legs
- 1 garlic clove, minced
- 1 tsp. five spice powder
- Salt and black pepper, as required

Directions:
1. Gently grease an air fryer basket.
2. Before cooking, heat your air fryer to 340 degrees F/ 170 degrees C.
3. In a bowl, combine together herbs, salt, black pepper, garlic, and five spice powder.
4. Rub the garlic mixture over the duck legs. Then transfer to the air fryer basket.
5. Cook in the preheated air fryer at 390 degrees F/ 200 degrees C for 25 minutes.

6. When the cooking time is up, cook for 5 more minutes if needed.
7. Remove from the air fryer and serve hot. Enjoy!

Baked Chicken Nachos

Servings:4
Cooking Time: 7 Minutes
Ingredients:
- 50 tortilla chips
- 2 cups shredded cooked chicken breast, divided
- 2 cups shredded Mexican-blend cheese, divided
- ½ cup sliced pickled jalapeño peppers, divided
- ½ cup diced red onion, divided

Directions:
1. Preheat the air fryer to 300°F.
2. Use foil to make a bowl shape that fits the shape of the air fryer basket. Place half tortilla chips in the bottom of foil bowl, then top with 1 cup chicken, 1 cup cheese, ¼ cup jalapeños, and ¼ cup onion. Repeat with remaining chips and toppings.
3. Place foil bowl in the air fryer basket and cook 7 minutes until cheese is melted and toppings heated through. Serve warm.

Quick Air Fried Chicken Breast

Servings: 4
Cooking Time: 22 Minutes
Ingredients:
- 4 chicken breasts, skinless and boneless
- ½ teaspoon dried oregano
- ½ teaspoon dried basil
- ½ teaspoon dried thyme
- ½ teaspoon garlic powder
- 2 tablespoons olive oil
- ⅛ teaspoon black pepper
- ½ teaspoon salt

Directions:
1. In a suitable bowl, mix together olive oil, oregano, basil, thyme, garlic powder, black pepper, and salt.
2. Rub herb oil mixture all over chicken breasts.
3. Grease its air fryer basket with cooking spray.
4. Place the herbed chicken in the air fryer basket and cook at 360 degrees F/ 180 degrees C for almost 10 minutes.
5. Flip the chicken and continue cooking for 8-12 minutes more or until the internal temperature of chicken reaches at 165 degrees F/ 75 degrees C.
6. Serve and enjoy.

Whole Turkey With Gravy

Servings: 12 Servings
Cooking Time: 3 Hours 25 Minutes
Ingredients:
- 1 whole turkey (about 14 pounds)
- 1/3 cup of sliced butter
- 1 ½ cups of chicken broth
- ¾ cup of flour
- 4 sliced garlic cloves

- 1 tablespoon of salt
- Pinch of black pepper, to taste

Directions:
1. Take the giblets out and dry the turkey with a paper towel.
2. Place the garlic and butter slices in between the breast and the skin. Grease the turkey with oil and season with pepper and salt.
3. Put the lower rack inside the air fryer and spray it with some oil. Place the turkey breast-side down in the air fryer and pour in ½ cup of broth over the top. Put the extender ring and cover with a lid.
4. Cook at 350ºF for 2.5–3 hours. Baste with the broth every 30–40 minutes. You use the remaining part of the broth for the first 2 batches; for other ones you use the broth and juice from the bottom of the air fryer.
5. After cooking for about 2 hours, flip the turkey skin-side down, baste, and cook for about 30–60 minutes until it reaches the internal temperature of 165ºF in the thickest parts. Let it cool for 20 minutes.
6. Meantime, cook the gravy. Take the lower rack out from the air fryer, remove the chunks from the broth. Add flour and 1 cup from the air fryer broth in a mixing bowl. Whisk it until you reach smooth consistency. Transfer the prepared flour mixture to the air fryer basket. Whisk well until smooth. Cover the air fryer with a lid and cook at 400ºF for 10 minutes until thickened, stirring occasionally.
7. Serve warm and enjoy your Whole Turkey with Gravy!

Balsamic Turkey In Hoisin Sauce

Servings: 4
Cooking Time: 50 Minutes
Ingredients:
- 2 pounds turkey drumsticks
- 2 tablespoons balsamic vinegar
- 2 tablespoons dry white wine
- 1 tablespoon sesame oil
- 1 sprig rosemary, chopped
- Salt, to taste
- Ground black pepper, to your liking
- 2 ½ tablespoons butter, melted
- For the Hoisin Sauce:
- 2 tablespoons hoisin sauce
- 1 tablespoon mustard

Directions:
1. Before cooking, heat your air fryer to 350 degrees F/ 175 degrees C.
2. In a mixing dish, add the turkey drumsticks, vigar, sesame oil, rosemary, and wine. Marinate the mixture for 3 hours.
3. To season, add salt and pepper in the marinate.
4. Drizzle over with the melted butter.
5. Transfer the turkey drumsticks inside an air fryer basket.
6. Cook in the preheated air fryer at 350 degrees F/ 175 degrees C for 30 to 35 minutes, in batches if possible.

7. During cooking, flip the drumsticks from to time to ensure even cook.
8. To make the hoisin sauce, mix all the sauce ingredients.
9. When the cooking time is up, drizzle the sauce over the turkey and cook again for 5 minutes.
10. When cooked, let it rest for about 10 minutes.
11. Carve the turkey into your desired size and serve. Enjoy!
12. While the turkey drumsticks are roasting, prepare the Hoisin sauce by mixing the ingredients. After that, drizzle the turkey with the sauce mixture; roast for a further 5 minutes.
13. Then allow the turkey to rest for about 10 minutes before carving and serving. Bon appétit!

Chicken Salad With White Dressing

Servings: 2
Cooking Time: 20 Minutes
Ingredients:
- 2 chicken breasts, cut into strips
- ¼ cup diced peeled red onion
- ½ peeled English cucumber, diced
- 1 tbsp crushed red pepper flakes
- 1 cup Greek yogurt
- 3 tbsp light mayonnaise
- 1 tbsp mustard
- 1 tsp chopped dill
- 1 tsp chopped mint
- 1 tsp lemon juice
- 2 cloves garlic, minced
- Salt and pepper to taste
- 3 cups mixed greens
- 10 Kalamata olives, halved
- 1 tomato, diced
- ¼ cup feta cheese crumbles

Directions:
1. Preheat air fryer at 350ºF. In a small bowl, whisk the Greek yogurt, mayonnaise, mustard, cucumber, dill, mint, salt, lemon juice, and garlic, and let chill the resulting dressing covered in the fridge until ready to use. Sprinkle the chicken strips with salt and pepper. Place them in the frying basket and Air Fry for 10 minutes, tossing once. Place the mixed greens and pepper flakes in a salad bowl. Top each with red onion, olives, tomato, feta cheese, and grilled chicken. Drizzle with the dressing and serve.

Smoky Chicken Fajita Bowl

Servings:4
Cooking Time: 35 Minutes + Chilling Time
Ingredients:
- 1 jalapeño, sliced and seeded
- ½ cup queso fresco crumbles
- 1 tbsp olive oil
- 2 tsp flour
- ¼ tsp chili powder
- ¼ tsp fajita seasoning
- ¼ tsp smoked paprika

- ¼ tsp ground cumin
- ½ tsp granular honey
- ⅛ tsp onion powder
- ⅛ tsp garlic powder
- 1 lb chicken breast strips
- 4 tomatoes, diced
- ½ diced red onion
- 4 tbsp sour cream
- 1 avocado, diced

Directions:
1. Combine the olive oil, flour, all the spices, and chicken strips in a bowl. Let chill in the fridge for 30 minutes.
2. Preheat air fryer to 400°F. Place the chicken strips in the frying basket and Air Fry for 8 minutes, shaking once. Divide between 4 medium bowls. Add tomatoes, jalapeño, onion, queso fresco, sour cream, and avocado to the bowls. Serve right away.

Jerk Chicken Wraps

Servings:4
Cooking Time: 15 Minutes
Ingredients:
- 1 pound boneless, skinless chicken tenderloins
- 1 cup jerk marinade
- Olive oil
- 4 large low-carb tortillas
- 1 cup julienned carrots
- 1 cup peeled cucumber ribbons
- 1 cup shredded lettuce
- 1 cup mango or pineapple chunks

Directions:
1. In a medium bowl, coat the chicken with the jerk marinade, cover, and refrigerate for 1 hour.
2. Spray a fryer basket lightly with olive oil.
3. Place the chicken in the fryer basket in a single layer and spray lightly with olive oil. You may need to cook the chicken in batches. Reserve any leftover marinade.
4. Air fry for 8 minutes. Turn the chicken over and brush with some of the remaining marinade. Cook until the chicken reaches an internal temperature of at least 165°F, an additional 5 to 7 minutes.
5. To assemble the wraps, fill each tortilla with ¼ cup carrots, ¼ cup cucumber, ¼ cup lettuce, and ¼ cup mango. Place one quarter of the chicken tenderloins on top and roll up the tortilla. These are great served warm or cold.

Crispy Parmesan Chicken Breasts

Servings: 3
Cooking Time: 15 Minutes
Ingredients:
- 2 6-ounces boneless chicken breasts, cut into tenders
- ¾ cup buttermilk
- 1½ teaspoons Worcestershire sauce, divided
- ½ teaspoon smoked paprika, divided
- Salt and black pepper, as required
- ½ cup all-purpose flour

- 1½ cups panko breadcrumbs
- ¼ cup Parmesan cheese, finely grated
- 2 tablespoons butter, melted
- 2 large eggs

Directions:
1. In a suitable bowl, mix together buttermilk, ¾ teaspoon of Worcestershire sauce, ¼ teaspoon of paprika, salt, and black pepper.
2. Add in the chicken tenders and refrigerate overnight.
3. In a suitable bowl, mix the flour, remaining paprika, salt, and black pepper.
4. Place the remaining Worcestershire sauce and eggs in a third bowl and beat until well combined.
5. Mix well the panko, Parmesan, and butter in a fourth bowl.
6. Remove the chicken tenders from bowl and discard the buttermilk.
7. Coat the chicken tenders with flour mixture, then dip into egg mixture and finally coat with the panko mixture.
8. At 400 degrees F/ 205 degrees C, preheat your Air Fryer. Oil its air fryer basket.
9. Arrange chicken tenders into the prepared air fryer basket in 2 batches in a single layer.
10. Air fry for about 13-15 minutes, flipping once halfway through.
11. Remove from Air Fryer and transfer the chicken tenders onto a serving platter.
12. Serve hot.

Dijon Chicken Breasts

Servings: 6
Cooking Time: 24 Minutes
Ingredients:
- 6 (6-oz, each) Boneless, skinless chicken breasts
- 2 tablespoons Fresh rosemary, minced
- 3 tablespoons Honey
- 1 tablespoon Dijon mustard
- Black pepper and salt to taste

Directions:
1. Combine the mustard, honey, black pepper, rosemary and salt in a suitable bowl. Rub the chicken with this mixture.
2. Grease its air fryer basket with oil.
3. Air fry the chicken at 350 degrees F/ 175 degrees C for 20 to 24 minutes or until the chicken' inner doneness reaches 165 degrees F/ 75 degrees C.
4. Serve.

Turkey Sausage With Veggies

Servings: 2
Cooking Time: 15 Minutes
Ingredients:
- 4 turkey sausages
- ½ pound Brussels sprouts, trimmed and halved
- 1 teaspoon olive oil
- Sea salt, to taste
- Ground black pepper, to taste
- ½ teaspoon cayenne pepper

- ½ teaspoon shallot powder
- ¼ teaspoon dried dill weed

Directions:
1. Arrange the turkey sausage in the air fryer basket.
2. Mix the Brussels sprouts, spices, and olive oil together in a mixing dish and toss well. Spread the Brussels sprouts around the sausages.
3. Cook in your air fryer at 380 degrees F/ 195 degrees C for 15 minutes. Halfway through cooking, shake the basket.
4. Enjoy!

Tuscan Stuffed Chicken

Servings: 4
Cooking Time: 30 Minutes
Ingredients:
- 1/3 cup ricotta cheese
- 1 cup Tuscan kale, chopped
- 4 chicken breasts
- 1 tbsp chicken seasoning
- Salt and pepper to taste
- 1 tsp paprika

Directions:
1. Preheat air fryer to 370°F. Soften the ricotta cheese in a microwave-safe bowl for 15 seconds. Combine in a bowl along with Tuscan kale. Set aside. Cut 4-5 slits in the top of each chicken breast about ¾ of the way down. Season with chicken seasoning, salt, and pepper.
2. Place the chicken with the slits facing up in the greased frying basket. Lightly spray the chicken with oil. Bake for 6-8 minutes. Slide-out and stuff the cream cheese mixture into the chicken slits. Sprinkle ½ tsp of paprika and cook for another 3 minutes. Serve and enjoy!

Indian-inspired Chicken Skewers

Servings:4
Cooking Time: 40 Minutes + Chilling Time
Ingredients:
- 1 lb boneless, skinless chicken thighs, cubed
- 1 red onion, diced
- 1 tbsp grated ginger
- 2 tbsp lime juice
- 1 cup canned coconut milk
- 2 tbsp tomato paste
- 2 tbsp olive oil
- 1 tbsp ground cumin
- 1 tbsp ground coriander
- 1 tsp cayenne pepper
- 1 tsp ground turmeric
- ½ tsp red chili powder
- ¼ tsp curry powder
- 2 tsp salt
- 2 tbsp chopped cilantro

Directions:
1. Toss red onion, ginger, lime juice, coconut milk, tomato paste, olive oil, cumin, coriander, cayenne pepper, turmeric, chili powder, curry powder, salt, and chicken until fully coated. Let chill in the fridge for 2 hours.

2. Preheat air fryer to 350°F. Thread chicken onto 8 skewers and place them on a kebab rack. Place rack in the frying basket and Air Fry for 12 minutes. Discard marinade. Garnish with cilantro to serve.

Crispy Chicken Strips

Servings:4
Cooking Time: 20 Minutes
Ingredients:
- 1 tablespoon olive oil
- 1 pound (454 g) boneless, skinless chicken tenderloins
- 1 teaspoon salt
- ½ teaspoon freshly ground black pepper
- ½ teaspoon paprika
- ½ teaspoon garlic powder
- ½ cup whole-wheat seasoned bread crumbs
- 1 teaspoon dried parsley
- Cooking spray

Directions:
1. Preheat the air fryer to 370°F (188°C). Spray the air fryer basket lightly with cooking spray.
2. In a medium bowl, toss the chicken with the salt, pepper, paprika, and garlic powder until evenly coated.
3. Add the olive oil and toss to coat the chicken evenly.
4. In a separate, shallow bowl, mix together the bread crumbs and parsley.
5. Coat each piece of chicken evenly in the bread crumb mixture.
6. Place the chicken in the air fryer basket in a single layer and spray it lightly with cooking spray. You may need to cook them in batches.
7. Air fry for 10 minutes. Flip the chicken over, lightly spray it with cooking spray, and air fry for an additional 8 to 10 minutes, until golden brown. Serve.

Crispy Tender Parmesan Chicken

Servings:2
Cooking Time: 20 Minutes
Ingredients:
- 1 tablespoon butter, melted
- 2 chicken breasts
- 2 tablespoons parmesan cheese
- 6 tablespoons almond flour

Directions:
1. Preheat the air fryer for 5 minutes.
2. Combine the almond flour and parmesan cheese in a plate.
3. Drizzle the chicken breasts with butter.
4. Dredge in the almond flour mixture.
5. Place in the fryer basket.
6. Cook for 20 minutes at 350°F.

Fennel & Chicken Ratatouille

Servings:4
Cooking Time: 30 Minutes
Ingredients:
- 1 lb boneless, skinless chicken thighs, cubed
- 2 tbsp grated Parmesan cheese

- 1 eggplant, cubed
- 1 zucchini, cubed
- 1 bell pepper, diced
- 1 fennel bulb, sliced
- 1 tsp salt
- 1 tsp Italian seasoning
- 2 tbsp olive oil
- 1 can diced tomatoes
- 1 tsp pasta sauce
- 2 tbsp basil leaves

Directions:
1. Preheat air fryer to 400ºF. Mix the chicken, eggplant, zucchini, bell pepper, fennel, salt, Italian seasoning, and oil in a bowl. Place the chicken mixture in the frying basket and Air Fry for 7 minutes. Transfer it to a cake pan. Mix in tomatoes along with juices and pasta sauce. Air Fry for 8 minutes. Scatter with Parmesan and basil.Serve.

Chicken & Rice Sautée

Servings: 4
Cooking Time: 25 Minutes
Ingredients:
- 1 can pineapple chunks, drained, ¼ cup juice reserved
- 1 cup cooked long-grain rice
- 1 lb chicken breasts, cubed
- 1 red onion, chopped
- 1 tbsp peanut oil
- 1 peeled peach, cubed
- 1 tbsp cornstarch
- ½ tsp ground ginger
- ¼ tsp chicken seasoning

Directions:
1. Preheat air fryer to 400°F. Combine the chicken, red onion, pineapple, and peanut oil in a metal bowl, then put the bowl in the fryer. Air Fry for 9 minutes, remove and stir. Toss the peach in and put the bowl back into the fryer for 3 minutes. Slide out and stir again. Mix the reserved pineapple juice, corn starch, ginger, and chicken seasoning in a bowl, then pour over the chicken mixture and stir well. Put the bowl back into the fryer and cook for 3 more minutes or until the chicken is cooked through and the sauce is thick. Serve over cooked rice.

Chilean-style Chicken Empanadas

Servings: 4
Cooking Time: 25 Minutes
Ingredients:
- 4 oz chorizo sausage, casings removed and crumbled
- 1 tbsp olive oil
- 4 oz chicken breasts, diced
- ¼ cup black olives, sliced
- 1 tsp chili powder
- 1 tsp paprika
- ¼ cup raisins
- 4 empanada shells

Directions:

1. Preheat air fryer to 350°F. Warm the oil in a skillet over medium heat. Sauté the chicken and chorizo, breaking up the chorizo, 3-4 minutes. Add the raisins, chili powder, paprika, and olives and stir. Kill the heat and let the mixture cool slightly. Divide the chorizo mixture between the empanada shells and fold them over to cover the filling. Seal edges with water and press down with a fork to secure. Place the empanadas in the frying basket. Bake for 15 minutes, flipping once until golden. Serve warm.

Fajita Chicken Strips

Servings:4
Cooking Time: 15 Minutes
Ingredients:
- 1 pound (454 g) boneless, skinless chicken tenderloins, cut into strips
- 3 bell peppers, any color, cut into chunks
- 1 onion, cut into chunks
- 1 tablespoon olive oil
- 1 tablespoon fajita seasoning mix
- Cooking spray

Directions:
1. Preheat the air fryer to 370ºF (188ºC).
2. In a large bowl, mix together the chicken, bell peppers, onion, olive oil, and fajita seasoning mix until completely coated.
3. Spray the air fryer basket lightly with cooking spray.
4. Place the chicken and vegetables in the air fryer basket and lightly spray with cooking spray.
5. Air fry for 7 minutes. Shake the basket and air fry for an additional 5 to 8 minutes, until the chicken is cooked through and the veggies are starting to char.
6. Serve warm.

Zesty Ranch Chicken Drumsticks

Servings: 4
Cooking Time: 20 Minutes
Ingredients:
- 8 chicken drumsticks
- 1 teaspoon salt
- ½ teaspoon ground black pepper
- ¼ cup dry ranch seasoning
- ½ cup panko bread crumbs
- ½ cup grated Parmesan cheese

Directions:
1. Preheat the air fryer to 375°F.
2. Sprinkle drumsticks with salt, pepper, and ranch seasoning.
3. In a paper lunch bag, combine bread crumbs and Parmesan. Add drumsticks to the bag and shake to coat. Spritz with cooking spray.
4. Place drumsticks in the air fryer basket and cook 20 minutes, turning halfway through cooking time, until the internal temperature reaches at least 165°F. Serve warm.

Low-carb Naked Chicken Wings

Servings: 4
Cooking Time: 15 Minutes
Ingredients:

- 8 whole chicken wings
- 1 teaspoon garlic powder
- Chicken seasoning or rub
- Pepper
- Cooking oil

Directions:
1. Season the wings with the garlic powder and chicken seasoning and pepper to taste.
2. Place the chicken wings in the air fryer. It is okay to stack them on top of each other. Spray the chicken with cooking oil. Cook for 10 minutes.
3. Remove the basket and shake it to ensure all of the chicken pieces will cook fully.
4. Return the basket and cook the chicken for an additional 5 minutes.
5. Cool before serving.

Tender Chicken With Parmesan Cheese

Servings: 2
Cooking Time: 20 Minutes
Ingredients:
- 1 tablespoon butter, melted
- 2 chicken breasts
- 2 tablespoons parmesan cheese
- 6 tablespoons almond flour

Directions:
1. At 350 degrees F/ 175 degrees C, preheat your Air Fryer.
2. Combine the 6 tablespoons of almond flour and parmesan cheese in a plate.
3. Drizzle the chicken breasts with butter.
4. Dredge in the almond flour mixture.
5. Place in the air fryer basket.
6. Cook for 20 minutes at 350 degrees F/ 175 degrees C.
7. When cooked, serve and enjoy.

Fried Chicken Halves

Servings: 4
Cooking Time: 75 Minutes
Ingredients:
- 16 oz whole chicken
- 1 tablespoon dried thyme
- 1 teaspoon ground cumin
- 1 teaspoon salt
- 1 tablespoon avocado oil

Directions:
1. Cut the chicken into halves and sprinkle it with dried thyme, cumin, and salt. Then brush the chicken halves with avocado oil. Preheat the air fryer to 365°F. Put the chicken halves in the air fryer and cook them for 60 minutes. Then flip the chicken halves on another side and cook them for 15 minutes more.

Taquitos

Servings: 12
Cooking Time: 6 Minutes Per Batch
Ingredients:

- 1 teaspoon butter
- 2 tablespoons chopped green onions
- 1 cup cooked chicken, shredded
- 2 tablespoons chopped green chiles
- 2 ounces Pepper Jack cheese, shredded
- 4 tablespoons salsa
- ½ teaspoon lime juice
- ¼ teaspoon cumin
- ½ teaspoon chile powder
- ⅛ teaspoon garlic powder
- 12 corn tortillas
- oil for misting or cooking spray

Directions:
1. Melt butter in a saucepan over medium heat. Add green onions and sauté a minute or two, until tender.
2. Remove from heat and stir in the chicken, green chiles, cheese, salsa, lime juice, and seasonings.
3. Preheat air fryer to 390°F.
4. To soften refrigerated tortillas, wrap in damp paper towels and microwave for 30 to 60 seconds, until slightly warmed.
5. Remove one tortilla at a time, keeping others covered with the damp paper towels. Place a heaping tablespoon of filling into tortilla, roll up and secure with toothpick. Spray all sides with oil or cooking spray.
6. Place taquitos in air fryer basket, either in a single layer or stacked. To stack, leave plenty of space between taquitos and alternate the direction of the layers, 4 on the bottom lengthwise, then 4 more on top crosswise.
7. Cook for 6minutes or until brown and crispy.
8. Repeat steps 6 and 7 to cook remaining taquitos.
9. Serve hot with guacamole, sour cream, salsa or all three!

Hawaiian Chicken

Servings: 4
Cooking Time: 25 Minutes
Ingredients:
- 1 can diced pineapple
- 1 kiwi, sliced
- 2 tbsp coconut aminos
- 1 tbsp honey
- 3 garlic cloves, minced
- Salt and pepper to taste
- ½ tsp paprika
- 1 lb chicken breasts

Directions:
1. Preheat air fryer to 360°F. Stir together pineapple, kiwi, coconut aminos, honey, garlic, salt, paprika, and pepper in a small bowl. Arrange the chicken in a single layer in a baking dish. Spread half of the pineapple mixture over the top of the chicken. Transfer the dish into the frying basket. Roast for 8 minutes, then flip the chicken. Spread the rest of the pineapple mixture over the top of the chicken and Roast for another 8-10 until the chicken is done. Allow sitting for 5 minutes. Serve and enjoy!

Chicken Wrapped In Bacon

Servings: 6
Cooking Time: 25 Minutes
Ingredients:
- 6 rashers unsmoked back bacon
- 1 small chicken breast
- 1 tbsp. garlic soft cheese

Directions:
1. Cut the chicken breast into six bite-sized pieces.
2. Spread the soft cheese across one side of each slice of bacon.
3. Put the chicken on top of the cheese and wrap the bacon around it, holding it in place with a toothpick.
4. Transfer the wrapped chicken pieces to the Air Fryer and cook for 15 minutes at 350°F.

Cheesy Chicken Nuggets

Servings:4
Cooking Time: 15 Minutes
Ingredients:
- 1 pound ground chicken thighs
- ½ cup shredded mozzarella cheese
- 1 large egg, whisked
- ½ teaspoon salt
- ¼ teaspoon dried oregano
- ¼ teaspoon garlic powder

Directions:
1. In a large bowl, combine all ingredients. Form mixture into twenty nugget shapes, about 2 tablespoons each.
2. Place nuggets into ungreased air fryer basket, working in batches if needed. Adjust the temperature to 375°F and set the timer for 15 minutes, turning nuggets halfway through cooking. Let cool 5 minutes before serving.

Crispy Chicken Nuggets

Servings: 4
Cooking Time: 40 Minutes
Ingredients:
- 2 slices bread crumbs
- 9 ounces chicken breast, chopped
- 1 teaspoon garlic, minced
- 1 teaspoon tomato ketchup
- 2 medium eggs
- 1 tablespoon olive oil
- 1 teaspoon. paprika
- 1 teaspoon parsley
- Salt and pepper to taste

Directions:
1. To make the batter, combine together the paprika, pepper, salt, oil, and breadcrumbs.
2. Whisk one egg in a separate bowl.
3. Whisk the egg, with ketchup and parsley over the chopped chicken and press to coat well.
4. Make several nuggets from the chicken mixture and dip each in the egg.
5. Then coat the chicken with breadcrumbs.
6. Cook the breaded chicken in your air fryer at 390 degrees F/ 200 degrees C for 10 minutes.

7. If desired, serve the chicken nuggets with your favorite sauce.

Tempero Baiano Brazilian Chicken

Servings:4
Cooking Time: 20 Minutes
Ingredients:
- 1 teaspoon cumin seeds
- 1 teaspoon dried oregano
- 1 teaspoon dried parsley
- 1 teaspoon ground turmeric
- ½ teaspoon coriander seeds
- 1 teaspoon kosher salt
- ½ teaspoon black peppercorns
- ½ teaspoon cayenne pepper
- ¼ cup fresh lime juice
- 2 tablespoons olive oil
- 1½ pounds (680 g) chicken drumsticks

Directions:
1. In a clean coffee grinder or spice mill, combine the cumin, oregano, parsley, turmeric, coriander seeds, salt, peppercorns, and cayenne. Process until finely ground.
2. In a small bowl, combine the ground spices with the lime juice and oil. Place the chicken in a resealable plastic bag. Add the marinade, seal, and massage until the chicken is well coated. Marinate at room temperature for 30 minutes or in the refrigerator for up to 24 hours.
3. Preheat the air fryer to 400°F (204°C).
4. Place the drumsticks skin-side up in the air fryer basket and air fry for 20 to 25 minutes, turning the drumsticks halfway through the cooking time. Use a meat thermometer to ensure that the chicken has reached an internal temperature of 165°F (74°C). Serve immediately.

Glazed Chicken Drumsticks

Servings:2
Cooking Time: 20 Minutes
Ingredients:
- 4 chicken drumsticks
- 3 tablespoons soy sauce
- 2 tablespoons brown sugar
- 1 teaspoon minced garlic
- 1 teaspoon minced fresh ginger
- 1 teaspoon toasted sesame oil
- ½ teaspoon red pepper flakes
- ½ teaspoon kosher salt
- ½ teaspoon black pepper

Directions:
1. Preheat the air fryer to 400°F (204°C).
2. Line a round baking pan with aluminum foil. (If you don't do this, you'll either end up scrubbing forever or throwing out the pan.) Arrange the drumsticks in the prepared pan.
3. In a medium bowl, stir together the soy sauce, brown sugar, garlic, ginger, sesame oil, red pepper flakes, salt, and black pepper. Pour the sauce over the drumsticks and toss to coat.
4. Place the pan in the air fryer basket. Air fry for 20 minutes, turning the drumsticks halfway through the

cooking time. Use a meat thermometer to ensure the chicken has reached an internal temperature of 165°F (74°C). Serve immediately.

Chicken Tenders With Italian Seasoning

Servings: 2
Cooking Time: 10 Minutes
Ingredients:
- 2 eggs, lightly beaten
- 1 ½ pounds chicken tenders
- ½ teaspoon onion powder
- ½ teaspoon garlic powder
- 1 teaspoon paprika
- 1 teaspoon Italian seasoning
- 2 tablespoons' ground flax seed
- 1 cup almond flour
- ½ teaspoon black pepper
- 1 teaspoon salt

Directions:
1. At 400 degrees F/ 205 degrees C, preheat your Air fryer.
2. Season chicken with black pepper and salt.
3. In a suitable bowl, whisk eggs to combine.
4. In a shallow dish, mix together almond flour, all seasonings, and flaxseed.
5. Dip chicken into the egg then coats with almond flour mixture and place on a plate.
6. Grease its air fryer basket with cooking spray.
7. Place ½ chicken tenders in air fryer basket and cook for almost 10 minutes, turning halfway through.
8. Cook remaining chicken tenders using same steps.
9. Serve and enjoy.

Crispy Chicken Nuggets With Turnip

Servings: 3
Cooking Time: 32 Minutes
Ingredients:
- 1 egg
- ½ teaspoon cayenne pepper
- ⅓ cup panko crumbs
- ¼ teaspoon Romano cheese, grated
- 2 teaspoons canola oil
- 1 pound chicken breast, cut into slices
- 1 medium-sized turnip, trimmed and sliced
- ½ teaspoon garlic powder
- Sea salt, to taste
- Ground black pepper, to taste

Directions:
1. Whisk the egg together with the cayenne pepper until frothy in a bowl.
2. Mix the cheese together with the panko crumbs in another shallow until well combined.
3. Dredge the chicken slices firstly in the egg mixture, then in the panko mixture until coat well.
4. Then using 1 teaspoon of canola oil brush the slices.
5. To season, add salt and pepper.
6. Before cooking, heat your air fryer to 380 degrees F/ 195 degrees C.

7. Cook the chicken slices in the air fryer for 12 minutes. Shake the basket halfway through cooking.
8. When done, the internal temperature of their thickest part should read 165 degrees F/ 75 degrees C.
9. Remove from the air fryer and reserve. Keep warm.
10. With the remaining canola oil, drizzle over the turnip slices.
11. To season, add salt, pepper, and garlic powder.
12. Cook the slices in your air fryer at 370 degrees F/ 185 degrees C for about 20 minutes.
13. Serve the parsnip slices with chicken nuggets. Enjoy!

Chicken Breasts Wrapped In Bacon

Servings: 4
Cooking Time: 35 Minutes
Ingredients:
- ¼ cup mayonnaise
- ¼ cup sour cream
- 3 tbsp ketchup
- 1 tbsp yellow mustard
- 1 tbsp light brown sugar
- 1 lb chicken tenders
- 1 tsp dried parsley
- 8 bacon slices

Directions:
1. Preheat the air fryer to 370°F. Combine the mayonnaise, sour cream, ketchup, mustard, and brown sugar in a bowl and mix well, then set aside. Sprinkle the chicken with the parsley and wrap each one in a slice of bacon. Put the wrapped chicken in the frying basket in a single layer and Air Fry for 18-20 minutes, flipping once until the bacon is crisp. Serve with sauce.

Italian Herb Stuffed Chicken

Servings: 4
Cooking Time: 30 Minutes
Ingredients:
- 2 tbsp olive oil
- 3 tbsp balsamic vinegar
- 3 garlic cloves, minced
- 1 tomato, diced
- 2 tbsp Italian seasoning
- 1 tbsp chopped fresh basil
- 1 tsp thyme, chopped
- 4 chicken breasts

Directions:
1. Preheat air fryer to 370°F. Combine the olive oil, balsamic vinegar, garlic, thyme, tomato, half of the Italian seasoning, and basil in a medium bowl. Set aside.
2. Cut 4-5 slits into the chicken breasts ¾ of the way through. Season with the rest of the Italian seasoning and place the chicken with the slits facing up, in the greased frying basket. Bake for 7 minutes. Spoon the bruschetta mixture into the slits of the chicken. Cook for another 3 minutes. Allow chicken to sit and cool for a few minutes. Serve and enjoy!

Chicken And Onion Sausages

Servings: 4
Cooking Time: 10 Minutes
Ingredients:
- 1 garlic clove, diced
- 1 spring onion, chopped
- 1 cup ground chicken
- ½ teaspoon salt
- ½ teaspoon ground black pepper
- 4 sausage links
- 1 teaspoon olive oil

Directions:
1. Mix together the ground chicken, ground black pepper, onion, and the diced garlic clove in a mixing dish to make the filling.
2. Fill the sausage links with the chicken mixture.
3. Then cut the sausages into halves and make sure the endings of the sausage halves are secured.
4. Before cooking, heat your air fryer to 365 degrees F/ 185 degrees C.
5. Brush olive oil over the sausages. Arrange the chicken and onion sausage in the air fryer basket and cook in the preheated air fryer for 10 minutes.
6. Then flip the sausage to ensure even cook. Cook again for 5 minutes or more. Or increase the temperature to 390 degrees F/ 200 degrees C and cook for 8 minutes for a faster result.

Nutty Chicken Tenders

Servings:4
Cooking Time: 12 Minutes
Ingredients:
- 1 pound (454 g) chicken tenders
- 1 teaspoon kosher salt
- 1 teaspoon black pepper
- ½ teaspoon smoked paprika
- ¼ cup coarse mustard
- 2 tablespoons honey
- 1 cup finely crushed pecans

Directions:
1. Preheat the air fryer to 350ºF (177ºC).
2. Place the chicken in a large bowl. Sprinkle with the salt, pepper, and paprika. Toss until the chicken is coated with the spices. Add the mustard and honey and toss until the chicken is coated.
3. Place the pecans on a plate. Working with one piece of chicken at a time, roll the chicken in the pecans until both sides are coated. Lightly brush off any loose pecans. Place the chicken in the air fryer basket.
4. Bake for 12 minutes, or until the chicken is cooked through and the pecans are golden brown.
5. Serve warm.

Sticky Drumsticks

Servings: 4
Cooking Time: 45 Minutes
Ingredients:
- 1 lb chicken drumsticks
- 1 tbsp chicken seasoning
- 1 tsp dried chili flakes
- Salt and pepper to taste
- ¼ cup honey
- 1 cup barbecue sauce

Directions:
1. Preheat air fryer to 390°F. Season drumsticks with chicken seasoning, chili flakes, salt, and pepper. Place one batch of drumsticks in the greased frying basket and Air Fry for 18-20 minutes, flipping once until golden.
2. While the chicken is cooking, combine honey and barbecue sauce in a small bowl. Remove the drumsticks to a serving dish. Drizzle honey-barbecue sauce over and serve.

Hawaiian Tropical Chicken

Servings:4
Cooking Time: 15 Minutes
Ingredients:
- 4 boneless, skinless chicken thighs (about 1½ pounds / 680 g)
- 1 (8-ounce / 227-g) can pineapple chunks in juice, drained, ¼ cup juice reserved
- ¼ cup soy sauce
- ¼ cup sugar
- 2 tablespoons ketchup
- 1 tablespoon minced fresh ginger
- 1 tablespoon minced garlic
- ¼ cup chopped scallions

Directions:
1. Use a fork to pierce the chicken all over to allow the marinade to penetrate better. Place the chicken in a large bowl or large resealable plastic bag.
2. Set the drained pineapple chunks aside. In a small microwave-safe bowl, combine the pineapple juice, soy sauce, sugar, ketchup, ginger, and garlic. Pour half the sauce over the chicken; toss to coat. Reserve the remaining sauce. Marinate the chicken at room temperature for 30 minutes, or cover and refrigerate for up to 24 hours.
3. Preheat the air fryer to 350ºF (177ºC).
4. Place the chicken in the air fryer basket, discarding marinade. Bake for 15 minutes, turning halfway through the cooking time.
5. Meanwhile, microwave the reserved sauce on high for 45 to 60 seconds, stirring every 15 seconds, until the sauce has the consistency of a thick glaze.
6. At the end of the cooking time, use a meat thermometer to ensure the chicken has reached an internal temperature of 165ºF (74ºC).
7. Transfer the chicken to a serving platter. Pour the sauce over the chicken. Garnish with the pineapple chunks and scallions before serving.

Buttered Chicken Thighs

Servings: 4
Cooking Time: 30 Minutes
Ingredients:
- 4 bone-in chicken thighs, skinless
- 2 tbsp butter, melted
- 1 tsp garlic powder
- 1 tsp lemon zest
- Salt and pepper to taste
- 1 lemon, sliced

Directions:
1. Preheat air fryer to 380°F.Stir the chicken thighs in the butter, lemon zest, garlic powder, and salt. Divide the chicken thighs between 4 pieces of foil and sprinkle with black pepper, and then top with slices of lemon. Bake in the air fryer for 20-22 minutes until golden. Serve.

Chicken Fillets With Lemon Pepper & Cheddar Cheese

Servings: 2
Cooking Time: 14 Minutes
Ingredients:
- 1 lemon pepper
- ¼ cup Cheddar cheese, shredded
- 8 oz. chicken fillets
- ½ teaspoon dried cilantro
- 1 teaspoon coconut oil, melted
- ¼ teaspoon smoked paprika

Directions:
1. Cut the lemon pepper into halves and remove the seeds.
2. Then cut the chicken fillet into 2 fillets.
3. Make the horizontal cuts in every chicken fillet.
4. Then sprinkle the chicken fillets with smoked paprika and dried cilantro. After this, fill them with lemon pepper halves and Cheddar cheese.
5. At 385 degrees F/ 195 degrees C, preheat your air fryer.
6. Put the chicken fillets in the preheated Air Fryer and sprinkle with melted coconut oil. Cook the chicken for 14 minutes.
7. Carefully transfer the chicken fillets in the serving plates.
8. Serve.

Guajillo Chile Chicken Meatballs

Servings:4
Cooking Time: 30 Minutes
Ingredients:
- 1 lb ground chicken
- 1 large egg
- ½ cup bread crumbs
- 1 tbsp sour cream
- 2 tsp brown mustard
- 2 tbsp grated onion
- 2 tbsp tomato paste
- 1 tsp ground cumin
- 1 tsp guajillo chile powder
- 2 tbsp olive oil

Directions:
1. Preheat air fryer to 350ºF. Mix the ground chicken, egg, bread crumbs, sour cream, mustard, onion, tomato paste, cumin, and chili powder in a bowl. Form into 16 meatballs. Place the meatballs in the greased frying basket and Air Fry for 8-10 minutes, shaking once until browned and cooked through. Serve immediately.

Garlic Chicken With Bacon

Servings: 2
Cooking Time: 15 Minutes
Ingredients:
- 4 rashers smoked bacon
- 2 chicken filets
- ½ teaspoon coarse sea salt
- ¼ teaspoon black pepper, preferably freshly ground
- 1 teaspoon garlic, minced
- 1 (2-inch) piece ginger, peeled and minced
- 1 teaspoon. black mustard seeds
- 1 teaspoon mild curry powder
- ½ cup coconut milk
- ½ cup parmesan cheese, grated

Directions:
1. Before cooking, heat your air fryer to 400 degrees F/ 205 degrees C.
2. In the air fryer basket, place the smoked bacon.
3. Cook in your air fryer for 5 to 7 minutes. Set aside for later use.
4. Add the salt, chicken fillets, garlic, mustard seed, milk, curry powder, black pepper, and ginger in a mixing dish.
5. Refrigerate for about 30 minutes to make the marinate.
6. Add the grated parmesan cheese in a second separate bowl.
7. Then dip the parmesan bowl and coat well. Place in the air fryer basket. Decrease the air fryer to 380 degrees F/ 195 degrees C and set the timer for 6 minutes. Start to cook.
8. When the cooking time is up, flip and cook again for 6 minutes.
9. Repeat the prepare cooking steps for the remaining ingredients.
10. Serve with the cooked bacon.

Chicken Tikka

Servings: 4
Cooking Time: 15 Minutes
Ingredients:
- ¼ cup plain Greek yogurt
- 1 clove garlic, minced
- 1 tablespoon ketchup
- 1 tablespoon extra-virgin olive oil
- 1 tablespoon lemon juice
- ½ teaspoon salt
- ½ teaspoon ground cumin

- ½ teaspoon paprika
- ¼ teaspoon ground cinnamon
- ½ teaspoon ground black pepper
- ½ teaspoon cayenne pepper
- 1 pound boneless, skinless chicken thighs

Directions:

1.   In a large bowl, stir together the yogurt, garlic, ketchup, olive oil, lemon juice, salt, cumin, paprika, cinnamon, black pepper, and cayenne pepper until combined.

2.   Add the chicken thighs to the bow and fold the yogurt-spice mixture over the chicken thighs until they're covered with the marinade. Cover with plastic wrap and place in the refrigerator for 30 minutes.

3.   When ready to cook the chicken, remove from the refrigerator and preheat the air fryer to 370°F.

4.   Liberally spray the air fryer basket with olive oil mist. Place the chicken thighs into the air fryer basket, leaving space between the thighs to turn.

5.   Cook for 10 minutes, turn the chicken thighs, and cook another 5 minutes (or until the internal temperature reaches 165°F).

6.   Remove the chicken from the air fryer and serve warm with desired sides.

Turkey Wings With Thai-style Sauce

Servings: 4
Cooking Time: 40 Minutes

Ingredients:

- ¾ pound turkey wings, cut into pieces
- 1 teaspoon ginger powder
- 1 teaspoon garlic powder
- ¾ teaspoon paprika
- 2 tablespoons soy sauce
- 1 handful minced lemongrass
- Salt flakes and black pepper to taste
- 2 tablespoons rice wine vinegar
- ¼ cup peanut butter
- 1 tablespoon sesame oil
- ½ cup Thai sweet chili sauce

Directions:

1.   Boil the turkey wings in a suitable saucepan full of water for 20 minutes.

2.   Put the turkey wings in a suitable bowl and cover them with the remaining ingredients, minus the Thai sweet chili sauce.

3.   Transfer to the Air Fryer and fry for 20 minutes at 350 degrees F/ 175 degrees C, turning once halfway through the cooking time.

4.   Ensure they are cooked through before serving with the Thai sweet chili sauce, as well as some lemon wedges if desired.

Pickle Brined Fried Chicken

Servings: 4
Cooking Time: 47 Minutes

Ingredients:

- 4 bone-in, skin-on chicken legs, cut into drumsticks and thighs (about 3½ pounds)
- pickle juice from a 24-ounce jar of kosher dill pickles
- ½ cup flour
- salt and freshly ground black pepper
- 2 eggs
- 1 cup fine breadcrumbs
- 1 teaspoon salt
- 1 teaspoon freshly ground black pepper
- ½ teaspoon ground paprika
- ⅛ teaspoon ground cayenne pepper
- vegetable or canola oil in a spray bottle

Directions:

1.   Place the chicken in a shallow dish and pour the pickle juice over the top. Cover and transfer the chicken to the refrigerator to brine in the pickle juice for 3 to 8 hours.

2.   When you are ready to cook, remove the chicken from the refrigerator to let it come to room temperature while you set up a dredging station. Place the flour in a shallow dish and season well with salt and freshly ground black pepper. Whisk the eggs in a second shallow dish. In a third shallow dish, combine the breadcrumbs, salt, pepper, paprika and cayenne pepper.

3.   Preheat the air fryer to 370°F.

4.   Remove the chicken from the pickle brine and gently dry it with a clean kitchen towel. Dredge each piece of chicken in the flour, then dip it into the egg mixture, and finally press it into the breadcrumb mixture to coat all sides of the chicken. Place the breaded chicken on a plate or baking sheet and spray each piece all over with vegetable oil.

5.   Air-fry the chicken in two batches. Place two chicken thighs and two drumsticks into the air fryer basket. Air-fry for 10 minutes. Then, gently turn the chicken pieces over and air-fry for another 10 minutes. Remove the chicken pieces and let them rest on plate – do not cover. Repeat with the second batch of chicken, air-frying for 20 minutes, turning the chicken over halfway through.

6.   Lower the temperature of the air fryer to 340°F. Place the first batch of chicken on top of the second batch already in the basket and air-fry for an additional 7 minutes. Serve warm and enjoy.

Sweet-and-sour Drumsticks

Servings:4
Cooking Time: 23 To 25 Minutes

Ingredients:

- 6 chicken drumsticks
- 3 tablespoons lemon juice, divided
- 3 tablespoons low-sodium soy sauce, divided
- 1 tablespoon peanut oil
- 3 tablespoons honey
- 3 tablespoons brown sugar
- 2 tablespoons ketchup
- ¼ cup pineapple juice

Directions:
1. Preheat the air fryer to 350ºF (177ºC).
2. Sprinkle the drumsticks with 1 tablespoon of lemon juice and 1 tablespoon of soy sauce. Place in the air fryer basket and drizzle with the peanut oil. Toss to coat. Bake for 18 minutes or until the chicken is almost done.
3. Meanwhile, in a metal bowl, combine the remaining 2 tablespoons of lemon juice, the remaining 2 tablespoons of soy sauce, honey, brown sugar, ketchup, and pineapple juice.
4. Add the cooked chicken to the bowl and stir to coat the chicken well with the sauce.
5. Place the metal bowl in the basket. Bake for 5 to 7 minutes or until the chicken is glazed and registers 165ºF (74ºC) on a meat thermometer. Serve warm.

Stir-fried Chicken With Pineapple

Servings:4
Cooking Time: 11 To 15 Minutes
Ingredients:
- 2 boneless, skinless chicken breasts
- 2 tablespoons cornstarch
- 1 egg white, lightly beaten
- 1 tablespoon olive or peanut oil
- 1 onion, sliced
- 1 red bell pepper, chopped
- 1 (8-ounce) can pineapple tidbits, drained, juice reserved
- 2 tablespoons reduced-sodium soy sauce

Directions:
1. Cut the chicken breasts into cubes and put into a medium bowl. Add the cornstarch and egg white and mix together thoroughly. Set aside.
2. In a 6-inch metal bowl, combine the oil and the onion. Cook in the air fryer for 2 to 3 minutes or until the onion is crisp and tender.
3. Drain the chicken and add to the bowl with the onions; stir well. Cook for 7 to 9 minutes or until the chicken is thoroughly cooked to 165°F.
4. Stir the chicken mixture, then add the pepper, pineapple tidbits, 3 tablespoons of the reserved pineapple liquid, and the soy sauce, and stir again. Cook for 2 to 3 minutes or until the food is cooked and the sauce is slightly thickened.

Chicken Wings With Paprika & Parmesan

Servings: 4
Cooking Time: 15 Minutes

Ingredients:
- 2 pounds Chicken wings, cut into drumettes, pat dried
- ½ cup plus 6 tablespoons Parmesan, grated
- 1 teaspoon Herbs de Provence
- 1 teaspoon Paprika
- Salt to taste

Directions:
1. Combine the parmesan, herbs, paprika, and salt in a suitable bowl and rub the chicken with this mixture.
2. At 350 degrees F/ 175 degrees C, preheat your Air fryer.
3. Grease the basket with cooking spray.
4. Cook for almost 15 minutes. Flip once at the halfway through the cooking time.
5. Garnish with parmesan and serve.

Curried Orange Honey Chicken

Servings:4
Cooking Time: 16 To 19 Minutes
Ingredients:
- ¾ pound (340 g) boneless, skinless chicken thighs, cut into 1-inch pieces
- 1 yellow bell pepper, cut into 1½-inch pieces
- 1 small red onion, sliced
- Olive oil for misting
- ¼ cup chicken stock
- 2 tablespoons honey
- ¼ cup orange juice
- 1 tablespoon cornstarch
- 2 to 3 teaspoons curry powder

Directions:
1. Preheat the air fryer to 370ºF (188ºC).
2. Put the chicken thighs, pepper, and red onion in the air fryer basket and mist with olive oil.
3. Roast for 12 to 14 minutes or until the chicken is cooked to 165ºF (74ºC), shaking the basket halfway through cooking time.
4. Remove the chicken and vegetables from the air fryer basket and set aside.
5. In a metal bowl, combine the stock, honey, orange juice, cornstarch, and curry powder, and mix well. Add the chicken and vegetables, stir, and put the bowl in the basket.
6. Return the basket to the air fryer and roast for 2 minutes. Remove and stir, then roast for 2 to 3 minutes or until the sauce is thickened and bubbly.
7. Serve warm.

Chapter 9: Vegetable Side Dishes Recipes

Tasty Cauliflower Croquettes

Servings: 4
Cooking Time: 20 Minutes
Ingredients:
- 1 pound cauliflower florets
- 2 eggs
- 1 tablespoon olive oil
- 2 tablespoons scallions, chopped
- 1 garlic clove, minced
- 1 cup Colby cheese, shredded
- ½ cup parmesan cheese, grated
- Salt and black pepper, to taste
- ¼ teaspoon dried dill weed
- 1 teaspoon paprika

Directions:
1. Bring the salted water in a pot and blanch the cauliflower florets until al dente, for about 3 to 4 minutes. Drain well and pulse in a food processor.
2. Add the remaining ingredients; mix to combine well. Shape the cauliflower mixture into bite-sized tots.
3. At 375 degrees F/ 190 degrees C, heat your air fryer in advance.
4. Grease its air fryer basket with cooking spray.
5. Cook the cauliflower croquettes in the preheated air fryer for almost 16 minutes, shaking halfway through the cooking time. Serve with your favorite sauce for dipping. Serve!

Creamy Cauliflower Mash

Servings: 4
Cooking Time: 20 Minutes
Ingredients:
- 2 pounds cauliflower florets
- 1 teaspoon olive oil
- 2 ounces parmesan, grated
- 4 ounces butter, soft
- Juice of ½ lemon
- Zest of ½ lemon, grated
- Salt and black pepper to the taste

Directions:
1. Before cooking, heat your air fryer with the air fryer basket to 380 degrees F/ 195 degrees C.
2. Add the cauliflower in the preheated air fryer basket and add oil to rub well.
3. Cook in your air fryer for 20 minutes.
4. When cooked, remove the cauliflower to a bowl. Mash well and place the remaining ingredients in the bowl. Stir well.
5. Serve on plates as a side dish.

Cheddar Mushroom Cakes

Servings: 4
Cooking Time: 8 Minutes
Ingredients:
- 9 ounces mushrooms, finely chopped
- ¼ cup coconut flour
- 1 teaspoon salt
- 1 egg, beaten
- 3 ounces Cheddar cheese, shredded
- 1 teaspoon dried parsley
- ½ teaspoon ground black pepper
- 1 teaspoon sesame oil
- 1 ounce spring onion, chopped

Directions:
1. Mix the coconut flour, salt, dried parsley, minced onion, ground black pepper, egg, and the chopped mushrooms until smooth.
2. Then add Cheddar cheese. Use a fork to stir.
3. Before cooking, heat your air fryer to 385 degrees F/ 195 degrees C.
4. Line baking paper over the air fryer pan.
5. Use a spoon to make medium-size patties from the mixture. Then arrange evenly on the pan.
6. Sprinkle the patties with sesame oil and cook in your air fryer for 4 minutes from each side.

Simple Zucchini Ribbons

Servings:4
Cooking Time: 15 Minutes
Ingredients:
- 2 zucchini
- 2 tsp butter, melted
- ¼ tsp garlic powder
- ¼ tsp chili flakes
- 8 cherry tomatoes, halved
- Salt and pepper to taste

Directions:
1. Preheat air fryer to 275ºF. Cut the zucchini into ribbons with a vegetable peeler. Mix them with butter, garlic, chili flakes, salt, and pepper in a bowl. Transfer to the frying basket and Air Fry for 2 minutes. Toss and add the cherry tomatoes. Cook for another 2 minutes. Serve.

Awesome Chicken Taquitos

Servings: 4
Cooking Time: 12 Minutes
Ingredients:
- 1 cup shredded mozzarella cheese
- ¼ cup salsa
- ¼ cup Greek yogurt
- Salt and black pepper
- 8 flour tortillas

Directions:
1. In a suitable bowl, mix chicken, cheese, salsa, sour cream, salt, and black pepper.
2. Spray 1 side of the tortilla with cooking spray.
3. Lay 2 tablespoon of the chicken mixture at the center of the non-oiled side the tortillas.
4. Roll tightly around the mixture. Arrange taquitos on your air fryer basket.
5. Cook for almost 12 minutes at 380 degrees F/ 195 degrees C.
6. Serve.

Herb-roasted Vegetables

Servings: 4
Cooking Time: 14 To 18 Minutes
Ingredients:

- 1 red bell pepper, sliced
- 1 (8-ounce) package sliced mushrooms
- 1 cup green beans, cut into 2-inch pieces
- ⅓ cup diced red onion
- 3 garlic cloves, sliced
- 1 teaspoon olive oil (see Tip)
- ½ teaspoon dried basil
- ½ teaspoon dried tarragon

Directions:

1. In a medium bowl, mix the red bell pepper, mushrooms, green beans, red onion, and garlic. Drizzle with the olive oil. Toss to coat.
2. Add the herbs and toss again.
3. Place the vegetables in the air fryer basket. Roast for 14 to 18 minutes, or until tender. Serve immediately.

Crispy Pickles With Parmesan

Servings: 4
Cooking Time: 6 Minutes
Ingredients:

- 16 dill pickles, sliced
- 1 egg, lightly beaten
- ½ cup almond flour
- 3 tablespoon parmesan cheese, grated
- ½ cup pork rind, crushed

Directions:

1. Take 3 bowls. Mix together pork rinds and cheese in the first bowl.
2. In a second bowl, add the egg.
3. In the third bowl, spread the almond flour for coating.
4. Coat each pickle slice with almond flour then dip in egg and finally coat with pork and cheese mixture.
5. Grease its air fryer basket with cooking spray.
6. Place coated pickles in the air fryer basket.
7. Cook pickles for 6 minutes at 370 degrees F/ 185 degrees C.
8. Serve and enjoy.

Southwestern Sweet Potato Wedges

Servings: 4
Cooking Time: 30 Minutes
Ingredients:

- 2 sweet potatoes, peeled and cut into ½-inch wedges
- 2 tsp olive oil
- 2 tbsp cornstarch
- 1 tsp garlic powder
- ¼ tsp ground allspice
- ¼ tsp paprika
- ⅛ tsp cayenne pepper

Directions:

1. Preheat air fryer to 400°F. Place the sweet potatoes in a bowl. Add some olive oil and toss to coat, then transfer to the frying basket. Roast for 8 minutes.

Sprinkle the potatoes with cornstarch, garlic powder, allspice, paprika, and cayenne, then toss. Put the potatoes back into the fryer and Roast for 12-17 more minutes. Shake the basket a couple of times while cooking. The potatoes should be golden and crispy. Serve warm.

Loaded Sweet Potatoes

Servings: 4
Cooking Time: 40 Minutes
Ingredients:

- 4 sweet potatoes
- 2 tablespoons butter
- 2 tablespoons honey
- 1 teaspoon cinnamon
- ½ teaspoon vanilla extract

Directions:

1. Using a fork, poke three holes in the top of each sweet potato.
2. Place the sweet potatoes in the air fryer. Cook for 40 minutes.
3. Meanwhile, in a small, microwave-safe bowl, melt the butter and honey together in the microwave for 15 to 20 seconds.
4. Remove the bowl from the microwave. Add the cinnamon and vanilla extract to the butter and honey mixture, and stir.
5. Remove the cooked sweet potatoes from the air fryer and allow them to cool for 5 minutes.
6. Cut open each sweet potato. Drizzle the butter mixture over each, and serve.

Garlicky Vegetable Rainbow Fritters

Servings: 2
Cooking Time: 12 Minutes
Ingredients:

- 1 zucchini, grated and squeezed
- 1 cup corn kernels
- ½ cup canned green peas
- 4 tablespoons all-purpose flour
- 2 tablespoons fresh shallots, minced
- 1 teaspoon fresh garlic, minced
- 1 tablespoon peanut oil
- Salt and black pepper, to taste
- 1 teaspoon cayenne pepper

Directions:

1. In a suitable mixing bowl, thoroughly combine all the recipe ingredients until everything is well incorporated.
2. Shape the mixture into patties.
3. Grease its air fryer basket with cooking spray.
4. Cook the patties in the preheated air fryer at about 365 degrees F/ 185 degrees C for 6 minutes almost.
5. Flip and cook for a 6 minutes more.
6. Serve immediately and enjoy!

Mozzarella Spinach Mash

Servings: 4
Cooking Time: 13 Minutes
Ingredients:
- 3 cups spinach, chopped
- ½ cup Mozzarella, shredded
- 4 bacon slices, chopped
- 1 teaspoon butter
- 1 cup heavy cream
- ½ teaspoon salt
- ½ jalapeno pepper, chopped

Directions:
1. In the air fryer basket, place the chopped bacon slices.
2. Cook in your air fryer at 400 degrees F/ 205 degrees C for 8 minutes.
3. During cooking, stir the bacon with a spatula from time to time.
4. In the air fryer casserole mold, add the cooked bacon.
5. Add spinach, heavy cream, salt, and jalapeno pepper, Mozzarella, and butter. Gently stir the mixture.
6. Cook the mash at 400 degrees F/ 205 degrees C for 5 minutes.
7. Using a spoon, carefully stir the spinach mash.

Black Bean And Tomato Chili

Servings:6
Cooking Time: 23 Minutes
Ingredients:
- 1 tablespoon olive oil
- 1 medium onion, diced
- 3 garlic cloves, minced
- 1 cup vegetable broth
- 3 cans black beans, drained and rinsed
- 2 cans diced tomatoes
- 2 chipotle peppers, chopped
- 2 teaspoons cumin
- 2 teaspoons chili powder
- 1 teaspoon dried oregano
- ½ teaspoon salt

Directions:
1. Over a medium heat, fry the garlic and onions in the olive oil for 3 minutes.
2. Add the remaining ingredients, stirring constantly and scraping the bottom to prevent sticking.
3. Preheat the air fryer to 400ºF (204ºC).
4. Take a dish and place the mixture inside. Put a sheet of aluminum foil on top.
5. Transfer to the air fryer and bake for 20 minutes.
6. When ready, plate up and serve immediately.

Golden Pickles

Servings:4
Cooking Time: 15 Minutes
Ingredients:
- 14 dill pickles, sliced
- ¼ cup flour
- ⅛ teaspoon baking powder
- Pinch of salt
- 2 tablespoons cornstarch plus 3 tablespoons water
- 6 tablespoons panko bread crumbs
- ½ teaspoon paprika
- Cooking spray

Directions:
1. Preheat the air fryer to 400ºF (204ºC).
2. Drain any excess moisture out of the dill pickles on a paper towel.
3. In a bowl, combine the flour, baking powder and salt.
4. Throw in the cornstarch and water mixture and combine well with a whisk.
5. Put the panko bread crumbs in a shallow dish along with the paprika. Mix thoroughly.
6. Dip the pickles in the flour batter, before coating in the bread crumbs. Spritz all the pickles with the cooking spray.
7. Transfer to the air fryer basket and air fry for 15 minutes, or until golden brown.
8. Serve immediately.

Herbed Potatoes With Tomato Sauce

Servings: 4
Cooking Time: 16 Minutes
Ingredients:
- 2 pounds potatoes; cubed
- 4 garlic cloves; minced
- 1 yellow onion; chopped.
- 1 cup tomato sauce
- ½ teaspoon oregano; dried
- ½ teaspoon parsley; dried
- 2 tablespoons basil; chopped
- 2 tablespoons olive oil

Directions:
1. Heat up a pan that fits your air fryer with the oil over medium heat, add onion; stir and cook for 1-2 minutes.
2. Add garlic, potatoes, parsley, tomato sauce and oregano; stir, introduce in your air fryer and cook at almost 370 degrees F/ 185 degrees C and cook for 16 minutes.
3. Add basil, toss everything, divide among plates and serve.

Baked Shishito Peppers

Servings: 2
Cooking Time: 15 Minutes
Ingredients:
- 6 oz shishito peppers
- 1 tsp olive oil
- 1 tsp salt
- ¼ cup soy sauce

Directions:
1. Preheat air fryer at 375ºF. Combine all ingredients in a bowl. Place peppers in the frying basket and Bake for 8 minutes until the peppers are blistered, shaking once. Serve with soy sauce for dipping.

Potato-nut Casserole Dish

Servings: 4
Cooking Time: 30 Minutes
Ingredients:
- 3 pounds sweet potatoes; scrubbed
- ¼ cup milk
- 2 tablespoons white flour
- ¼ teaspoon allspice; ground
- ½ teaspoon nutmeg; ground
- Salt to the taste
- For the topping:
- ½ cup almond flour
- ½ cup walnuts; soaked, drained and ground
- ¼ cup sugar
- 1 teaspoon cinnamon powder
- 5 tablespoons butter
- ¼ cup pecans; soaked, drained and ground
- ¼ cup coconut; shredded
- 1 tablespoon chia seeds

Directions:
1. Place potatoes in your air fryer basket, prick them with a fork and cook at almost 360 degrees F/ 180 degrees C, for 30 minutes.
2. Meanwhile; in a bowl, mix almond flour with pecans, walnuts, ¼ cup coconut, ¼ cup sugar, chia seeds, 1 teaspoon cinnamon and the butter and stir everything.
3. Transfer potatoes to a cutting board, cool them, peel and place them in a baking dish that fits your air fryer.
4. Add milk, flour, salt, nutmeg and allspice and stir
5. Add crumble mix you've made earlier on top; place dish in your air fryer's basket and Cook at almost 400 degrees F/ 205 degrees C, for almost 8 minutes.
6. Divide among plates and serve as a side dish.

Twice-baked Potatoes

Servings:8
Cooking Time: 50 Minutes
Ingredients:
- 4 large russet potatoes
- 4 slices bacon
- 2 tablespoons butter
- ½ cup milk
- 1 teaspoon garlic powder
- Salt
- Pepper
- 2 scallions, green parts (white parts optional), chopped
- 2 tablespoons sour cream
- 1¼ cups shredded Cheddar cheese, divided

Directions:
1. Using a fork, poke three holes into the top of each potato.
2. Place the potatoes in the air fryer. Cook for 40 minutes.
3. Meanwhile, in a skillet over medium-high heat, cook the bacon for about 5 to 7 minutes, flipping to evenly crisp. Drain on paper towels, crumble, and set aside.

4. Remove the cooked potatoes from the air fryer and allow them to cool for 10 minutes.
5. While the potatoes cool, heat a saucepan over medium-high heat. Add the butter and milk. Stir. Allow the mixture to cook for 2 to 3 minutes, until the butter has melted.
6. Halve each of the potatoes lengthwise. Scoop half of the flesh out of the middle of each potato half, leaving the flesh on the surrounding edges. This will hold the potato together when you stuff it.
7. Place the potato flesh in a large bowl and mash with a potato masher. Add the warm butter and milk mixture and stir to combine. Season with the garlic powder and salt and pepper to taste.
8. Add the cooked bacon, scallions, sour cream, and 1 cup of Cheddar cheese. Stir to combine.
9. Stuff each potato half with 1 to 2 tablespoons of the mashed potato mixture. Sprinkle the remaining ¼ cup of Cheddar cheese on top of the potato halves.
10. Place 4 potato halves in the air fryer. Do not stack. Cook for 2 to 3 minutes, or until the cheese has melted.
11. Remove the cooked potatoes from the air fryer, then repeat step 10 for the remaining 4 potato halves.
12. Cool before serving.

Sweet Potatoes With Zucchini

Servings:4
Cooking Time: 20 Minutes
Ingredients:
- 2 large-sized sweet potatoes, peeled and quartered
- 1 medium zucchini, sliced
- 1 Serrano pepper, deseeded and thinly sliced
- 1 bell pepper, deseeded and thinly sliced
- 1 to 2 carrots, cut into matchsticks
- ¼ cup olive oil
- 1½ tablespoons maple syrup
- ½ teaspoon porcini powder
- ¼ teaspoon mustard powder
- ½ teaspoon fennel seeds
- 1 tablespoon garlic powder
- ½ teaspoon fine sea salt
- ¼ teaspoon ground black pepper
- Tomato ketchup, for serving

Directions:
1. Put the sweet potatoes, zucchini, peppers, and the carrot into the air fryer basket. Coat with a drizzling of olive oil.
2. Preheat the air fryer to 350ºF (177ºC).
3. Air fry the vegetables for 15 minutes.
4. In the meantime, prepare the sauce by vigorously combining the other ingredients, except for the tomato ketchup, with a whisk.
5. Lightly grease a baking dish.
6. Transfer the cooked vegetables to the baking dish, pour over the sauce and coat the vegetables well.
7. Increase the temperature to 390ºF (199ºC) and air fry the vegetables for an additional 5 minutes.
8. Serve warm with a side of ketchup.

Parmesan Risotto

Servings: 6
Cooking Time: 20 Minutes
Ingredients:
- 2 tablespoons butter, melted
- 1 pound cauliflower, riced
- 2 garlic cloves, minced
- ½ cup chicken stock
- 1 cup heavy cream
- 1 cup parmesan, grated
- 3 tablespoons. sun-dried tomatoes
- ½ teaspoon nutmeg, ground

Directions:
1. Add the cauliflower and rest of the recipe ingredients to air fryer basket.
2. Air fryer at almost 360 degrees F/ 180 degrees C for 20 minutes almost.
3. Serve.

Chipotle Chickpea Tacos

Servings: 4
Cooking Time: 10 Minutes
Ingredients:
- 2 cans chickpeas, drained and rinsed
- ¼ cup adobo sauce
- ¾ teaspoon salt
- ¼ teaspoon ground black pepper
- 8 medium flour tortillas, warmed
- 1 ½ cups chopped avocado
- ½ cup chopped fresh cilantro

Directions:
1. Preheat the air fryer to 375°F.
2. In a large bowl, toss chickpeas, adobo, salt, and pepper to fully coat.
3. Using a slotted spoon, place chickpeas in the air fryer basket and cook 10 minutes, shaking the basket twice during cooking, until tender.
4. To assemble, scoop ¼ cup chickpeas into a tortilla, then top with avocado and cilantro. Repeat with remaining tortillas and filling. Serve warm.

Cashew Stuffed Mushrooms

Servings:6
Cooking Time: 15 Minutes
Ingredients:
- 1 cup basil
- ½ cup cashew, soaked overnight
- ½ cup nutritional yeast
- 1 tablespoon lemon juice
- 2 cloves garlic
- 1 tablespoon olive oil
- Salt, to taste
- 1 pound (454 g) baby Bella mushroom, stems removed

Directions:
1. Preheat the air fryer to 400°F (204°C).
2. Prepare the pesto. In a food processor, blend the basil, cashew nuts, nutritional yeast, lemon juice, garlic and olive oil to combine well. Sprinkle with salt as desired.
3. Turn the mushrooms cap-side down and spread the pesto on the underside of each cap.
4. Transfer to the air fryer and air fry for 15 minutes.
5. Serve warm.

Veggie Fritters

Servings: 4
Cooking Time: 35 Minutes
Ingredients:
- ¼ cup crumbled feta cheese
- 1 grated zucchini
- ¼ cup Parmesan cheese
- 2 tbsp minced onion
- 1 tbs powder garlic
- 1 tbsp flour
- 1 tbsp cornmeal
- 1 tbsp butter, melted
- 1 egg
- 2 tsp chopped dill
- 2 tsp chopped parsley
- Salt and pepper to taste
- 1 cup bread crumbs

Directions:
1. Preheat air fryer at 350°F. Squeeze grated zucchini between paper towels to remove excess moisture. In a bowl, combine all ingredients except breadcrumbs. Form mixture into 12 balls, about 2 tbsp each. In a shallow bowl, add breadcrumbs. Roll each ball in breadcrumbs, covering all sides. Place fritters on an ungreased pizza pan. Place in the frying basket and Air Fry for 11 minutes, flipping once. Serve.

Spinach And Cheese-stuffed Mushrooms

Servings:4
Cooking Time: 10 Minutes
Ingredients:
- Olive oil
- 4 ounces reduced-fat cream cheese, softened
- ¾ cup shredded Italian blend cheese
- ¼ cup whole-wheat bread crumbs
- 1 egg
- ¼ teaspoon salt
- ¼ teaspoon freshly ground black pepper
- 1 cup fresh baby spinach, chopped
- 20 large mushrooms, stems removed

Directions:
1. Spray a fryer basket lightly with olive oil.
2. In a medium bowl, use an electric mixer to combine the cream cheese, Italian blend cheese, bread crumbs, egg, salt, and pepper.
3. Add the spinach and stir with a spoon to combine.
4. Spoon the mixture into each mushroom, pressing the mixture into the mushroom and leaving a little bit popping out of the top.

5. Place the stuffed mushrooms in a single layer in the fryer basket. Spray lightly with olive oil. You may need to cook these in more than one batch.

6. Air fry until the mushrooms have started to brown lightly and the cheese is lightly brown on top, 7 to 10 minutes.

Steakhouse Baked Potatoes

Servings: 3
Cooking Time: 55 Minutes
Ingredients:
- 3 10-ounce russet potatoes
- 2 tablespoons Olive oil
- 1 teaspoon Table salt

Directions:
1. Preheat the air fryer to 375°F.
2. Poke holes all over each potato with a fork. Rub the skin of each potato with 2 teaspoons of the olive oil, then sprinkle ¼ teaspoon salt all over each potato.
3. When the machine is at temperature, set the potatoes in the basket in one layer with as much air space between them as possible. Air-fry for 50 minutes, turning once, or until soft to the touch but with crunchy skins. If the machine is at 360°F, you may need to add up to 5 minutes to the cooking time.
4. Use kitchen tongs to gently transfer the baked potatoes to a wire rack. Cool for 5 or 10 minutes before serving.

Spiced Balsamic Asparagus

Servings:4
Cooking Time: 10 Minutes
Ingredients:
- 4 tablespoons olive oil, plus more for spraying
- 4 tablespoons balsamic vinegar
- 1½ pounds asparagus, trimmed
- Salt
- Freshly ground black pepper

Directions:
1. Spray a fryer basket lightly with olive oil.
2. In a medium shallow bowl, whisk together the 4 tablespoons of olive oil and balsamic vinegar to make a marinade.
3. Lay the asparagus in the bowl so they are completely covered by the oil and vinegar mixture and let marinate for 5 minutes.
4. Place the asparagus in a single layer in the air fryer and sprinkle with salt and pepper. You may need to cook them in batches.
5. Air fry for 5 minutes. Shake the basket and cook until the asparagus is tender and lightly browned, 3 to 5 more minutes.

Curried Brussels Sprouts

Servings: 4
Cooking Time:15 To 17 Minutes
Ingredients:
- 1 pound Brussels sprouts, ends trimmed, discolored leaves removed, halved lengthwise

- 2 teaspoons olive oil
- 3 teaspoons curry powder, divided
- 1 tablespoon freshly squeezed lemon juice

Directions:
1. In a large bowl, toss the Brussels sprouts with the olive oil and 1 teaspoon of curry powder. Transfer to the air fryer basket. Roast for 12 minutes, shaking the basket once during cooking.
2. Sprinkle with the remaining 2 teaspoons of the curry powder and the lemon juice. Shake again. Roast for 3 to 5 minutes more, or until the Brussels sprouts are browned and crisp (see Tip). Serve immediately.

Cauliflower Bake With Basil Pesto

Servings: 6
Cooking Time: 20 Minutes
Ingredients:
- 1 cup heavy whipping cream
- 2 tablespoons basil pesto
- Salt and black pepper to the taste
- Juice of ½ lemon
- 1 pound cauliflower, florets separated
- 4 ounces cherry tomatoes, halved
- 3 tablespoons ghee, melted
- 7 ounces cheddar cheese, grated

Directions:
1. Drizzle a suitable baking pan with ghee.
2. Gently toss together the lemon juice, pesto, cream, and the cauliflower in the pan.
3. Add the tomatoes and cover the top with cheese.
4. Cook in your air fryer at 380 degrees F/ 195 degrees C for 20 minutes.
5. Serve on plates as a side dish.

Buttered Kale Mix

Servings: 2
Cooking Time: 12 Minutes
Ingredients:
- 3 tablespoons butter, melted
- 2 cups kale leaves
- Black pepper and salt to taste
- ½ cup yellow onion, chopped
- 2 teaspoons turmeric powder

Directions:
1. Place all the recipe ingredients in a pan that fits your air fryer and mix well.
2. Put the pan in the air fryer and cook at almost 250 degrees F/ 120 degrees C for 12 minutes.
3. Divide between plates and serve.

Flavorful Radish Salad

Servings: 4
Cooking Time: 30 Minutes
Ingredients:
- 1 ½ pounds radishes, trimmed and halved
- 2 tablespoons olive oil
- Pepper and salt, as needed
- For the Salad:

- 1 teaspoon olive oil
- 1 tablespoon balsamic vinegar
- ½ pound mozzarella, sliced
- 1 teaspoon honey
- Pepper and salt, as needed

Directions:

1. Mix thoroughly the salt, black pepper, oil, and the radishes in medium sized bowl.
2. On a flat kitchen surface, plug your air fryer and turn it on.
3. Before cooking, heat your air fryer to 350 degrees F/ 175 degrees C for 4 to 5 minutes.
4. Place the mixture onto the air fryer basket.
5. Cook in your air fryer for 3 minutes.
6. In another medium sized bowl, mix thoroughly the cheese and fried radish.
7. Mix the remaining ingredients in a small bowl. Drizzle over the salad to serve.

Asparagus & Cherry Tomato Roast

Servings: 6
Cooking Time: 20 Minutes

Ingredients:

- 2 tbsp dill, chopped
- 2 cups cherry tomatoes
- 1 ½ lb asparagus, trimmed
- 2 tbsp olive oil
- 3 garlic cloves, minced
- ½ tsp salt

Directions:

1. Preheat air fryer to 380ºF. Add all ingredients to a bowl, except for dill, and toss until the vegetables are well coated with the oil. Pour the vegetable mixture into the frying basket and Roast for 11-13 minutes, shaking once. Serve topped with fresh dill.

Mediterranean Air Fried Veggies

Servings:4
Cooking Time: 6 Minutes

Ingredients:

- 1 large zucchini, sliced
- 1 cup cherry tomatoes, halved
- 1 parsnip, sliced
- 1 green pepper, sliced
- 1 carrot, sliced
- 1 teaspoon mixed herbs
- 1 teaspoon mustard
- 1 teaspoon garlic purée
- 6 tablespoons olive oil
- Salt and ground black pepper, to taste

Directions:

1. Preheat the air fryer to 400ºF (204ºC).
2. Combine all the ingredients in a bowl, making sure to coat the vegetables well.
3. Transfer to the air fryer and air fry for 6 minutes, ensuring the vegetables are tender and browned.

4. Serve immediately.

Roast Sweet Potatoes With Parmesan

Servings: 4
Cooking Time: 30 Minutes

Ingredients:

- 2 peeled sweet potatoes, sliced
- ¼ cup grated Parmesan
- 1 tsp olive oil
- 1 tbsp balsamic vinegar
- 1 tsp dried rosemary

Directions:

1. Preheat air fryer to 400°F. Place the sweet potatoes and some olive oil in a bowl and shake to coat. Spritz with balsamic vinegar and rosemary, then shake again. Put the potatoes in the frying basket and Roast for 18-25 minutes, shaking at least once until the potatoes are soft. Sprinkle with Parmesan cheese and serve warm.

Spicy Bean Stuffed Potatoes

Servings: 4
Cooking Time: 60 Minutes

Ingredients:

- 1 lb russet potatoes, scrubbed and perforated with a fork
- 1 can diced green chilies, including juice
- 1/3 cup grated Mexican cheese blend
- 1 green bell pepper, diced
- 1 yellow bell pepper, diced
- ¼ cup torn iceberg lettuce
- 2 tsp olive oil
- 2 tbsp sour cream
- ½ tsp chili powder
- 2-3 jalapeños, sliced
- 1 red bell pepper, chopped
- Salt and pepper to taste
- 1/3 cup canned black beans
- 4 grape tomatoes, sliced
- ¼ cup chopped parsley

Directions:

1. Preheat air fryer at 400ºF. Brush olive oil over potatoes. Place them in the frying basket and Bake for 45 minutes, turning at 30 minutes mark. Let cool on a cutting board for 10 minutes until cool enough to handle. Slice each potato lengthwise and scoop out all but a ¼" layer of potato to form 4 boats.
2. Mash potato flesh, sour cream, green chilies, cheese, chili powder, jalapeños, green, yellow, and red peppers, salt, and pepper in a bowl until smooth. Fold in black beans. Divide between potato skin boats. Place potato boats in the frying basket and Bake for 2 minutes. Remove them to a serving plate. Top each boat with lettuce, tomatoes, and parsley. Sprinkle tops with salt and serve.

Roasted Salsa

Servings:2
Cooking Time: 30 Minutes
Ingredients:
- 2 large San Marzano tomatoes, cored and cut into large chunks
- ½ medium white onion, peeled and large-diced
- ½ medium jalapeño, seeded and large-diced
- 2 cloves garlic, peeled and diced
- ½ teaspoon salt
- 1 tablespoon coconut oil
- ¼ cup fresh lime juice

Directions:
1. Place tomatoes, onion, and jalapeño into an ungreased 6" round nonstick baking dish. Add garlic, then sprinkle with salt and drizzle with coconut oil.
2. Place dish into air fryer basket. Adjust the temperature to 300°F and set the timer for 30 minutes. Vegetables will be dark brown around the edges and tender when done.
3. Pour mixture into a food processor or blender. Add lime juice. Process on low speed 30 seconds until only a few chunks remain.
4. Transfer salsa to a sealable container and refrigerate at least 1 hour. Serve chilled.

Spicy Fries

Servings:4
Cooking Time: 20 Minutes
Ingredients:
- 2 tsp olive oil
- 2 tsp cayenne pepper
- 1 tsp paprika
- Salt and black pepper

Directions:
1. Place the fries into a bowl and sprinkle with oil, cayenne, paprika, salt, and black pepper. Toss and place them in the fryer. Cook for 7 minutes at 360°F, until golden and crispy. Give it a toss after 7-8 minutes and continue cooking for another 8 minutes. Serve.

Green Beans And Tomatoes Recipe

Servings: 4
Cooking Time:25 Minutes
Ingredients:
- 1-pint cherry tomatoes
- 2 tbsp. olive oil
- 1 lb. green beans
- Salt and black pepper to the taste

Directions:
1. In a bowl; mix cherry tomatoes with green beans, olive oil, salt and pepper, toss, transfer to your air fryer and cook at 400 °F, for 15 minutes. Divide among plates and serve right away

Lemon Tempeh

Servings: 4
Cooking Time: 12 Minutes
Ingredients:
- 1 teaspoon lemon juice
- 1 tablespoon sunflower oil
- ¼ teaspoon ground coriander
- 6 oz tempeh, chopped

Directions:
1. Sprinkle the tempeh with lemon juice, sunflower oil, and ground coriander. Massage the tempeh gently with the help of the fingertips. After this, preheat the air fryer to 325ºF. Put the tempeh in the air fryer and cook it for 12 minutes. Flip the tempeh every 2 minutes during cooking.

Roasted Baby Carrots

Servings: 6
Cooking Time: 20 Minutes
Ingredients:
- 1 lb baby carrots
- 2 tbsp olive oil
- ¼ cup raw honey
- ¼ tsp ground cinnamon
- ¼ tsp ground nutmeg
- ¼ cup pecans, chopped

Directions:
1. Preheat air fryer to 360°F. Place the baby carrots with olive oil, honey, nutmeg and cinnamon in a bowl and toss to coat. Pour into the air fryer and Roast for 6 minutes. Shake the basket, sprinkle the pecans on top, and roast for 6 minutes more. Serve and enjoy!

Herbed Zucchini Poppers

Servings: 4
Cooking Time: 30 Minutes
Ingredients:
- 1 tbsp grated Parmesan cheese
- 2 zucchini, sliced
- 1 cup breadcrumbs
- 2 eggs, beaten
- Salt and pepper to taste
- 1 tsp dry tarragon
- 1 tsp dry dill

Directions:
1. Preheat air fryer to 390°F. Place the breadcrumbs, Parmesan, tarragon, dill, salt, and pepper in a bowl and stir to combine. Dip the zucchini into the beaten eggs, then coat with Parmesan-crumb mixture. Lay the zucchini slices on the greased frying basket in an even layer. Air Fry for 14-16 minutes, shaking the basket several times during cooking. When ready, the zucchini will be crispy and golden brown. Serve hot and enjoy!

Garlic And Sesame Carrots

Servings:6
Cooking Time: 16 Minutes
Ingredients:
- 1 pound baby carrots
- 1 tablespoon sesame oil
- ½ teaspoon dried dill
- Pinch salt
- Freshly ground black pepper

- 6 cloves garlic, peeled
- 3 tablespoons sesame seeds

Directions:

1. Place the baby carrots in a medium bowl. Drizzle with sesame oil, add the dill, salt, and pepper, and toss to coat well.
2. Place the carrots in the basket of the air fryer. Roast for 8 minutes, shaking the basket once during cooking time.
3. Add the garlic to the air fryer. Roast for 8 minutes, shaking the basket once during cooking time, or until the garlic and carrots are lightly browned.
4. Transfer to a serving bowl and sprinkle with the sesame seeds before serving.

Zucchini Boats With Ham And Cheese

Servings: 4
Cooking Time: 12 Minutes

Ingredients:

- 2 6-inch-long zucchini
- 2 ounces Thinly sliced deli ham, any rind removed, meat roughly chopped
- 4 Dry-packed sun-dried tomatoes, chopped
- ⅓ cup Purchased pesto
- ¼ cup Packaged mini croutons
- ¼ cup (about 1 ounce) Shredded semi-firm mozzarella cheese

Directions:

1. Preheat the air fryer to 375°F .
2. Split the zucchini in half lengthwise and use a flatware spoon or a serrated grapefruit spoon to scoop out the insides of the halves, leaving at least a ¼-inch border all around the zucchini half. (You can save the scooped out insides to add to soups and stews—or even freeze it for a much later use.)
3. Mix the ham, sun-dried tomatoes, pesto, croutons, and half the cheese in a bowl until well combined. Pack this mixture into the zucchini "shells." Top them with the remaining cheese.
4. Set them stuffing side up in the basket without touching (even a fraction of an inch between them is enough room). Air-fry undisturbed for 12 minutes, or until softened and browned, with the cheese melted on top.
5. Use a nonstick-safe spatula to transfer the zucchini boats stuffing side up on a wire rack. Cool for 5 or 10 minutes before serving.

Hawaiian Brown Rice

Servings: 4
Cooking Time: 12 Minutes

Ingredients:

- ¼ pound ground sausage
- 1 teaspoon butter
- ¼ cup minced onion
- ¼ cup minced bell pepper
- 2 cups cooked brown rice
- 1 8-ounce can crushed pineapple, drained

Directions:

1. Shape sausage into 3 or 4 thin patties. Cook at 390°F for 6 to 8minutes or until well done. Remove from air fryer, drain, and crumble. Set aside.
2. Place butter, onion, and bell pepper in baking pan. Cook at 390°F for 1 minute and stir. Cook 4 minutes longer or just until vegetables are tender.
3. Add sausage, rice, and pineapple to vegetables and stir together.
4. Cook at 390°F for 2 minutes, until heated through.

Spicy Dill Pickle Fries

Servings:4
Cooking Time: 15 Minutes

Ingredients:

- Olive oil
- 1 cup whole-wheat flour
- 1 teaspoon paprika
- 1 egg
- 1⅓ cups whole-wheat panko bread crumbs
- 1 (24-ounce) jar spicy dill pickle spears

Directions:

1. Spray a fryer basket lightly with olive oil.
2. In a small, shallow bowl, combine the whole-wheat flour and paprika.
3. In another small, shallow bowl, whisk the egg.
4. Put the panko bread crumbs in another small.
5. Pat the pickle spears dry with paper towels.
6. Dip each pickle spear in the flour mixture, coat in the egg, and dredge in the panko bread crumbs.
7. Place each pickle spear in the fryer basket in a single layer, leaving a little space between each one. Spray the pickles lightly with olive oil. You may need to cook them in batches.
8. Air fry for 7 minutes. Turn the pickles over and cook until lightly browned and crispy, another 5 to 8 minutes.

Garlic Parmesan-roasted Cauliflower

Servings:6
Cooking Time: 15 Minutes

Ingredients:

- 1 medium head cauliflower, leaves and core removed, cut into florets
- 2 tablespoons salted butter, melted
- ½ tablespoon salt
- 2 cloves garlic, peeled and finely minced
- ½ cup grated Parmesan cheese, divided

Directions:

1. Toss cauliflower in a large bowl with butter. Sprinkle with salt, garlic, and ¼ cup Parmesan.
2. Place florets into ungreased air fryer basket. Adjust the temperature to 350°F and set the timer for 15 minutes, shaking basket halfway through cooking. Cauliflower will be browned at the edges and tender when done.
3. Transfer florets to a large serving dish and sprinkle with remaining Parmesan. Serve warm.

Dijon Roast Cabbage

Servings:4
Cooking Time: 10 Minutes
Ingredients:
- 1 small head cabbage, cored and sliced into 1"-thick slices
- 2 tablespoons olive oil, divided
- ½ teaspoon salt
- 1 tablespoon Dijon mustard
- 1 teaspoon apple cider vinegar
- 1 teaspoon granular erythritol

Directions:
1. Drizzle each cabbage slice with 1 tablespoon olive oil, then sprinkle with salt. Place slices into ungreased air fryer basket, working in batches if needed. Adjust the temperature to 350°F and set the timer for 10 minutes. Cabbage will be tender and edges will begin to brown when done.
2. In a small bowl, whisk remaining olive oil with mustard, vinegar, and erythritol. Drizzle over cabbage in a large serving dish. Serve warm.

Avocado Fries

Servings:6
Cooking Time: 8 Minutes
Ingredients:
- Olive oil
- 4 slightly under-ripe avocados, cut in half, pits removed
- 1½ cups whole-wheat panko bread crumbs
- ¾ teaspoon freshly ground black pepper
- 1½ teaspoons paprika
- ¾ teaspoon salt
- 3 eggs

Directions:
1. Spray a fryer basket lightly with olive oil.
2. Carefully remove the skin from the avocado leaving the flesh intact. Cut each avocado half lengthwise into 5 to 6 slices. Set aside.
3. In a small bowl, mix together the panko bread crumbs, black pepper, paprika, and salt.
4. In a separate small bowl, whisk the eggs.
5. Coat each avocado slice in the egg and then in the panko mixture, pressing the panko mixture gently into the avocado so it sticks.
6. Place the avocado slices in the fryer basket in a single layer. Lightly spray with olive oil. You may need to cook them in batches.
7. Air fry for 3 to 4 minutes. Turn the slices over and spray lightly with olive oil.
8. Air fry until light brown and crispy, 3 to 4 more minutes.

Fingerling Potatoes

Servings: 4
Cooking Time: 15 Minutes
Ingredients:
- 1 pound fingerling potatoes

- 1 tablespoon light olive oil
- ½ teaspoon dried parsley
- ½ teaspoon lemon juice
- coarsely ground sea salt

Directions:
1. Cut potatoes in half lengthwise.
2. In a large bowl, combine potatoes, oil, parsley, and lemon juice. Stir well to coat potatoes.
3. Place potatoes in air fryer basket and cook at 360°F for 15 minutes or until lightly browned and tender inside.
4. Sprinkle with sea salt before serving.

Roasted Thyme Asparagus

Servings: 4
Cooking Time: 20 Minutes
Ingredients:
- 1 lb asparagus, trimmed
- 2 tsp olive oil
- 3 garlic cloves, minced
- 2 tbsp balsamic vinegar
- ½ tsp dried thyme
- ½ red chili, finely sliced

Directions:
1. Preheat air fryer to 380°F. Put the asparagus and olive oil in a bowl and stir to coat, then put them in the frying basket. Toss some garlic over the asparagus and Roast for 4-8 minutes until crisp-tender. Spritz with balsamic vinegar and toss in some thyme leaves. Top with red chili slices and serve.

Lush Vegetable Salad

Servings:4
Cooking Time: 10 Minutes
Ingredients:
- 6 plum tomatoes, halved
- 2 large red onions, sliced
- 4 long red pepper, sliced
- 2 yellow pepper, sliced
- 6 cloves garlic, crushed
- 1 tablespoon extra-virgin olive oil
- 1 teaspoon paprika
- ½ lemon, juiced
- Salt and ground black pepper, to taste
- 1 tablespoon baby capers

Directions:
1. Preheat the air fryer to 420ºF (216ºC).
2. Put the tomatoes, onions, peppers, and garlic in a large bowl and cover with the extra-virgin olive oil, paprika, and lemon juice. Sprinkle with salt and pepper as desired.
3. Line the inside of the air fryer basket with aluminum foil. Put the vegetables inside and air fry for 10 minutes, ensuring the edges turn brown.
4. Serve in a salad bowl with the baby capers.

Super Veg Rolls

Servings:6
Cooking Time: 10 Minutes
Ingredients:
- 2 potatoes, mashed
- ¼ cup peas
- ¼ cup mashed carrots
- 1 small cabbage, sliced
- ¼ cups beans
- 2 tablespoons sweetcorn
- 1 small onion, chopped
- ½ cup bread crumbs
- 1 packet spring roll sheets
- ½ cup cornstarch slurry

Directions:
1. Preheat the air fryer to 390ºF (199ºC).
2. Boil all the vegetables in water over a low heat. Rinse and allow to dry.
3. Unroll the spring roll sheets and spoon equal amounts of vegetable onto the center of each one. Fold into spring rolls and coat each one with the slurry and bread crumbs.
4. Air fry the rolls in the preheated air fryer for 10 minutes.
5. Serve warm.

Parsley Cabbage

Servings: 4
Cooking Time: 20 Minutes
Ingredients:
- 2 ounces butter, melted
- 1 green cabbage head, shredded 1 and ½ cups heavy cream
- ¼ cup parsley, chopped
- 1 tablespoon sweet paprika
- 1 teaspoon lemon zest, grated

Directions:
1. Heat butter on a suitable cooking pan.
2. Then add cabbage and cook for 5 minutes.
3. Place the remaining ingredients in the pan. Toss well and transfer the pan into your air fryer.
4. Cook in your air fryer at 380 degrees F/ 195 degrees C for 5 minutes.
5. Serve on plates as a side dish.

Turmeric Cauliflower Patties

Servings: 2
Cooking Time: 10 Minutes
Ingredients:
- ¼ cup cauliflower, shredded
- 1 egg yolk
- ½ teaspoon ground turmeric
- ¼ teaspoon onion powder
- ¼ teaspoon salt
- 2 ounces Cheddar cheese, shredded
- ¼ teaspoon baking powder
- 1 teaspoon heavy cream

- 1 tablespoon coconut flakes
- Cooking spray

Directions:
1. Squeeze the shredded cauliflower and put it in the bowl.
2. Add egg yolk, ground turmeric, baking powder, onion powder, heavy cream, salt, and coconut flakes.
3. Then melt Cheddar cheese and add it in the cauliflower mixture.
4. Stir the ingredients until you get the smooth mass.
5. After this, make the medium size cauliflower patties.
6. At 365 degrees F/ 185 degrees C, preheat your air fryer.
7. Grease its air fryer basket with cooking spray and put the patties inside.
8. Cook them for almost 5 minutes from each side.
9. Serve warm.

Rice And Eggplant Bowl

Servings:4
Cooking Time: 10 Minutes
Ingredients:
- ¼ cup sliced cucumber
- 1 teaspoon salt
- 1 tablespoon sugar
- 7 tablespoons Japanese rice vinegar
- 3 medium eggplants, sliced
- 3 tablespoons sweet white miso paste
- 1 tablespoon mirin rice wine
- 4 cups cooked sushi rice
- 4 spring onions
- 1 tablespoon toasted sesame seeds

Directions:
1. Coat the cucumber slices with the rice wine vinegar, salt, and sugar.
2. Put a dish on top of the bowl to weight it down completely.
3. In a bowl, mix the eggplants, mirin rice wine, and miso paste. Allow to marinate for half an hour.
4. Preheat the air fryer to 400ºF (204ºC).
5. Put the eggplant slices in the air fryer and air fry for 10 minutes.
6. Fill the bottom of a serving bowl with rice and top with the eggplants and pickled cucumbers.
7. Add the spring onions and sesame seeds for garnish. Serve immediately.

Wilted Brussels Sprout Slaw

Servings: 4
Cooking Time: 18 Minutes
Ingredients:
- 2 Thick-cut bacon strip(s), halved widthwise (gluten-free, if a concern)
- 4½ cups Bagged shredded Brussels sprouts
- ¼ teaspoon Table salt
- 2 tablespoons White balsamic vinegar
- 2 teaspoons Worcestershire sauce (gluten-free, if a concern)

- 1 teaspoon Dijon mustard (gluten-free, if a concern)
- ¼ teaspoon Ground black pepper

Directions:

1. Preheat the air fryer to 375°F .
2. When the machine is at temperature, lay the bacon strip halves in the basket in one layer and air-fry for 10 minutes, or until crisp.
3. Use kitchen tongs to transfer the bacon pieces to a wire rack. Put the shredded Brussels sprouts in a large bowl. Drain any fat from the basket or the tray under the basket onto the Brussels sprouts. Add the salt and toss well to coat.
4. Put the Brussels sprout shreds in the basket, spreading them out into as close to an even layer as you can. Air-fry for 8 minutes, tossing the basket's contents at least three times, until wilted and lightly browned.
5. Pour the contents of the basket into a serving bowl. Chop the bacon and add it to the Brussels sprouts. Add the vinegar, Worcestershire sauce, mustard, and pepper. Toss well to blend the dressing and coat the Brussels sprout shreds. Serve warm.

Cholula Onion Rings

Servings: 4
Cooking Time: 30 Minutes

Ingredients:

- 1 large Vidalia onion
- ½ cup chickpea flour
- 1/3 cup milk
- 2 tbsp lemon juice
- 2 tbsp Cholula hot sauce
- 1 tsp allspice
- 2/3 cup bread crumbs

Directions:

1. Preheat air fryer to 380°F. Cut ½-inch off the top of the onion's root, then cut into ½-inch thick rings. Set aside. Combine the chickpea flour, milk, lemon juice, hot sauce, and allspice in a bowl. In another bowl, add in breadcrumbs. Submerge each ring into the flour batter until well coated, then dip into the breadcrumbs, and Air Fry for 14 minutes until crispy, turning once. Serve.

Chapter 10: Desserts And Sweets Recipes

Grilled Spiced Fruit

Servings: 4
Cooking Time:3 To 5 Minutes
Ingredients:

- 2 peaches, peeled, pitted, and thickly sliced
- 3 plums, halved and pitted
- 3 nectarines, halved and pitted
- 1 tablespoon honey
- ½ teaspoon ground cinnamon
- ¼ teaspoon ground allspice
- Pinch cayenne pepper

Directions:

1. Thread the fruit, alternating the types, onto 8 bamboo (see Tip, here) or metal skewers that fit into the air fryer.
2. In a small bowl, stir together the honey, cinnamon, allspice, and cayenne. Brush the glaze onto the fruit.
3. Grill the skewers for 3 to 5 minutes, or until lightly browned and caramelized. Cool for 5 minutes and serve.

Rich Blueberry Biscuit Shortcakes

Servings: 4
Cooking Time: 35 Minutes
Ingredients:

- 1 lb blueberries, halved
- ¼ cup granulated sugar
- 1 tsp orange zest
- 1 cup heavy cream
- 1 tbsp orange juice
- 2 tbsp powdered sugar
- ¼ tsp cinnamon
- ¼ tsp nutmeg
- 2 cups flour
- 1 egg yolk
- 1 tbsp baking powder
- ½ tsp baking soda
- ½ tsp cornstarch
- ½ tsp salt
- ½ tsp vanilla extract
- ½ tsp honey
- 4 tbsp cold butter, cubed
- 1 ¼ cups buttermilk

Directions:

1. Combine blueberries, granulated sugar, and orange zest in a bowl. Let chill the topping covered in the fridge until ready to use. Beat heavy cream, orange juice, egg yolk, vanilla extract and powdered sugar in a metal bowl until peaks form. Let chill the whipped cream covered in the fridge until ready to use.
2. Preheat air fryer at 350ºF. Combine flour, cinnamon, nutmeg, baking powder, baking soda, cornstarch, honey, butter cubes, and buttermilk in a bowl until a sticky dough forms. Flour your hands and form dough into 8 balls. Place them on a lightly greased pizza pan. Place pizza pan in the frying basket and Air Fry for 8 minutes. Transfer biscuits to serving plates and cut them in half. Spread blueberry mixture to each biscuit bottom and

place tops of biscuits. Garnish with whipped cream and serve.

Cherry Turnovers

Servings:8
Cooking Time: 20 Minutes
Ingredients:

- 1 (17-ounce) box frozen puff pastry dough, thawed (see Prep tip)
- 1 (10-ounce) can cherry pie filling
- 1 egg white, beaten
- Cooking oil

Directions:

1. Unfold both sheets of puff pastry dough and cut each into 4 squares for 8 squares total.
2. Spoon ½ to 1 tablespoon of cherry pie filling onto the center of each square. Do not overfill or the filling will leak out the turnover.
3. Use a cooking brush or your fingers to brush the edges of the squares with the egg white.
4. Fold the dough over diagonally to close each turnover. Using the back of a fork, press lines into the open edges of each turnover to seal.
5. Spray the air fryer basket with cooking oil.
6. Place the turnovers in the air fryer, being careful not to let them touch. Do not stack. Cook in batches. Spray the turnovers with cooking oil. Cook for 8 minutes.
7. Cool for 3 or 4 minutes before removing from the air fryer. The turnovers may stick to the basket if not cooled.
8. Repeat steps 6 and 7 for the remaining turnovers.

Vanilla Spread

Servings: 4
Cooking Time: 5 Minutes
Ingredients:

- 2 oz. walnuts, chopped
- 5 teaspoons coconut oil
- ½ teaspoon vanilla extract
- 1 tablespoon Erythritol
- 1 teaspoon of cocoa powder

Directions:

1. Preheat the air fryer to 350F.
2. Put the walnuts in the mason jar, then add the coconut oil, vanilla extract, Erythritol and cocoa powder.
3. Stir the walnut mixture with a spoon until smooth.
4. Arrange the mason jar with Nutella to your air fryer and cook at 350 degrees F/ 175 degrees C for 5 minutes.
5. Before serving, stir Nutella.

Fried Oreos

Servings: 12
Cooking Time: 6 Minutes Per Batch
Ingredients:

- oil for misting or nonstick spray
- 1 cup complete pancake and waffle mix
- 1 teaspoon vanilla extract
- ½ cup water, plus 2 tablespoons
- 12 Oreos or other chocolate sandwich cookies
- 1 tablespoon confectioners' sugar

Directions:
1. Spray baking pan with oil or nonstick spray and place in basket.
2. Preheat air fryer to 390°F.
3. In a medium bowl, mix together the pancake mix, vanilla, and water.
4. Dip 4 cookies in batter and place in baking pan.
5. Cook for 6minutes, until browned.
6. Repeat steps 4 and 5 for the remaining cookies.
7. Sift sugar over warm cookies.

Fiesta Pastries

Servings:8
Cooking Time:20 Minutes
Ingredients:
- ½ of apple, peeled, cored and chopped
- 1 teaspoon fresh orange zest, grated finely
- 7.05-ounce prepared frozen puff pastry, cut into 16 squares
- ½ tablespoon white sugar
- ½ teaspoon ground cinnamon

Directions:
1. Preheat the Air fryer to 390°F and grease an Air fryer basket.
2. Mix all ingredients in a bowl except puff pastry.
3. Arrange about 1 teaspoon of this mixture in the center of each square.
4. Fold each square into a triangle and slightly press the edges with a fork.
5. Arrange the pastries in the Air fryer basket and cook for about 10 minutes.
6. Dish out and serve immediately.

Easy Chocolate Donuts

Servings:8
Cooking Time: 8 Minutes
Ingredients:
- 1 (8-ounce / 227-g) can jumbo biscuits
- Cooking oil
- Chocolate sauce, for drizzling

Directions:
1. Preheat the air fryer to 375°F (191°C)
2. Separate the biscuit dough into 8 biscuits and place them on a flat work surface. Use a small circle cookie cutter or a biscuit cutter to cut a hole in the center of each biscuit. You can also cut the holes using a knife.
3. Spray the air fryer basket with cooking oil.
4. Put 4 donuts in the air fryer. Do not stack. Spray with cooking oil. Air fry for 4 minutes.
5. Open the air fryer and flip the donuts. Air fry for an additional 4 minutes.
6. Remove the cooked donuts from the air fryer, then repeat steps 3 and 4 for the remaining 4 donuts.
7. Drizzle chocolate sauce over the donuts and enjoy while warm.

British Bread Pudding

Servings: 4
Cooking Time: 30 Minutes

Ingredients:
- 4 bread slices
- 1 cup milk
- ¼ cup sugar
- 2 eggs, beaten
- 1 tbsp vanilla extract
- ½ tsp ground cinnamon

Directions:
1. Preheat air fryer to 320°F. Slice bread into bite-size pieces. Set aside in a small cake pan. Mix the milk, sugar, eggs, vanilla extract, and cinnamon in a bowl until well combined. Pour over the bread and toss to coat.Bake for 20 minutes until crispy and all liquid is absorbed. Slice into 4 pieces. Serve and enjoy!

Tasty Cheesecake Bites

Servings: 12
Cooking Time: 2 Minutes
Ingredients:
- 8 ounces cream cheese, softened
- ½ cup plus 2 tablespoons sugar, divided
- 4 tablespoons heavy cream, divided
- ½ teaspoon vanilla extract
- ½ cup almond flour

Directions:
1. In a stand mixer, mix add cream cheese, ½ cup sugar, vanilla extract and 2 tablespoons of heavy cream.
2. Using a paddle attachment, pour the mixture onto a baking sheet lined with baking paper.
3. Freeze for about 30 minutes.
4. In a suitable bowl, place the remaining cream.
5. Add the almond flour and remaining sugar in another bowl and mix well.
6. Dip each cheesecake bite into the cream and then top with the flour mixture.
7. Set the air frying time to 2 minutes on your air fryer.
8. Set the temperature setting to 300 degrees F/ 150 degrees C.
9. Place pan in air fry basket and place in the air fryer.

Dark Chocolate Oatmeal Cookies

Servings:30
Cooking Time:8 To 13 Minutes
Ingredients:
- 3 tablespoons unsalted butter
- 2 ounces dark chocolate, chopped (see Tip)
- ½ cup packed brown sugar
- 2 egg whites
- 1 teaspoon pure vanilla extract
- 1 cup quick-cooking oatmeal
- ½ cup whole-wheat pastry flour
- ½ teaspoon baking soda
- ¼ cup dried cranberries

Directions:
1. In a medium metal bowl, mix the butter and dark chocolate. Bake in the air fryer for 1 to 3 minutes, or until the butter and chocolate melt. Stir until smooth.

2. Beat in the brown sugar, egg whites, and vanilla until smooth.

3. Stir in the oatmeal, pastry flour, and baking soda.

4. Stir in the cranberries. Form the dough into about 30 (1-inch) balls. Bake the dough balls, in batches of 8, in the air fryer basket for 7 to 10 minutes, or until set.

5. Carefully remove the cookies from the air fryer and cool on a wire rack. Repeat with the remaining dough balls.

Sage Cream

Servings: 4
Cooking Time: 30 Minutes
Ingredients:
- 7 cups red currants
- 1 cup swerve
- 1 cup water
- 6 sage leaves

Directions:
1. In a pan that fits your air fryer, mix all the ingredients, toss, put the pan in the fryer and cook at 330°F for 30 minutes. Discard sage leaves, divide into cups and serve cold.

Strawberry Cups

Servings: 8
Cooking Time: 10 Minutes
Ingredients:
- 16 strawberries, halved
- 2 tablespoons coconut oil
- 2 cups chocolate chips, melted

Directions:
1. In a pan that fits your air fryer, mix the strawberries with the oil and the melted chocolate chips, toss gently, put the pan in the air fryer and cook at 340°F for 10 minutes. Divide into cups and serve cold.

Black Forest Hand Pies

Servings:6
Cooking Time: 15 Minutes
Ingredients:
- 3 tablespoons milk or dark chocolate chips
- 2 tablespoons thick, hot fudge sauce
- 2 tablespoons chopped dried cherries
- 1 (10-by-15-inch) sheet puff pastry, thawed
- 1 egg white, beaten
- 2 tablespoons sugar
- ½ teaspoon cinnamon

Directions:
1. In a small bowl, combine the chocolate chips, fudge sauce, and dried cherries.

2. Roll out the puff pastry on a floured surface. Cut into 6 squares with a sharp knife.

3. Divide the chocolate chip mixture onto the center of each puff pastry square. Fold the squares in half to make triangles. Firmly press the edges with the tines of a fork to seal.

4. Brush the triangles on all sides sparingly with the beaten egg white. Sprinkle the tops with sugar and cinnamon.

5. Place in the air fryer basket and bake for 15 minutes or until the triangles are golden brown. The filling will be hot, so cool for at least 20 minutes before serving.

Nutella® Torte

Servings: 6
Cooking Time: 55 Minutes
Ingredients:
- ¼ cup unsalted butter, softened
- ½ cup sugar
- 2 eggs
- 1 teaspoon vanilla
- 1¼ cups Nutella® (or other chocolate hazelnut spread), divided
- ¼ cup flour
- 1 teaspoon baking powder
- ¼ teaspoon salt
- dark chocolate fudge topping
- coarsely chopped toasted hazelnuts

Directions:
1. Cream the butter and sugar together with an electric hand mixer until light and fluffy. Add the eggs, vanilla, and ¾ cup of the Nutella® and mix until combined. Combine the flour, baking powder and salt together, and add these dry ingredients to the butter mixture, beating for 1 minute.

2. Preheat the air fryer to 350°F.

3. Grease a 7-inch cake pan with butter and then line the bottom of the pan with a circle of parchment paper. Grease the parchment paper circle as well. Pour the batter into the prepared cake pan and wrap the pan completely with aluminum foil. Lower the pan into the air fryer basket with an aluminum sling (fold a piece of aluminum foil into a strip about 2-inches wide by 24-inches long). Fold the ends of the aluminum foil over the top of the dish before returning the basket to the air fryer. Air-fry for 30 minutes. Remove the foil and air-fry for another 25 minutes.

4. Remove the cake from air fryer and let it cool for 10 minutes. Invert the cake onto a plate, remove the parchment paper and invert the cake back onto a serving platter. While the cake is still warm, spread the remaining ½ cup of Nutella® over the top of the cake. Melt the dark chocolate fudge in the microwave for about 10 seconds so it melts enough to be pourable. Drizzle the sauce on top of the cake in a zigzag motion. Turn the cake 90 degrees and drizzle more sauce in zigzags perpendicular to the first zigzags. Garnish the edges of the torte with the toasted hazelnuts and serve.

Honey-roasted Pears

Servings:4
Cooking Time: 20 Minutes
Ingredients:
- 2 large Bosc pears, halved and deseeded

- 3 tablespoons honey
- 1 tablespoon unsalted butter
- ½ teaspoon ground cinnamon
- ¼ cup walnuts, chopped
- ¼ cup part skim low-fat ricotta cheese, divided

Directions:
1. Preheat the air fryer to 350ºF (177ºC).
2. In a baking pan, place the pears, cut side up.
3. In a small microwave-safe bowl, melt the honey, butter, and cinnamon. Brush this mixture over the cut sides of the pears.
4. Pour 3 tablespoons of water around the pears in the pan. Roast the pears for 20 minutes, or until tender when pierced with a fork and slightly crisp on the edges, basting once with the liquid in the pan.
5. Carefully remove the pears from the pan and place on a serving plate. Drizzle each with some liquid from the pan, sprinkle the walnuts on top, and serve with a spoonful of ricotta cheese.

Midnight Nutella Banana Sandwich

Servings: 2
Cooking Time: 8 Minutes
Ingredients:
- butter, softened
- 4 slices white bread
- ¼ cup chocolate hazelnut spread
- 1 banana

Directions:
1. Preheat the air fryer to 370°F.
2. Spread the softened butter on one side of all the slices of bread and place the slices buttered side down on the counter. Spread the chocolate hazelnut spread on the other side of the bread slices. Cut the banana in half and then slice each half into three slices lengthwise. Place the banana slices on two slices of bread and top with the remaining slices of bread to make two sandwiches. Cut the sandwiches in half – this will help them all fit in the air fryer at once. Transfer the sandwiches to the air fryer.
3. Air-fry at 370°F for 5 minutes. Flip the sandwiches over and air-fry for another 2 to 3 minutes, or until the top bread slices are nicely browned. Pour yourself a glass of milk or a midnight nightcap while the sandwiches cool slightly and enjoy!

Delicious Spiced Apples

Servings: 6
Cooking Time: 10 Minutes
Ingredients:
- 4 small apples, sliced
- 1 tsp apple pie spice
- 1/2 cup erythritol
- 2 tbsp coconut oil, melted

Directions:
1. Add apple slices in a mixing bowl and sprinkle sweetener, apple pie spice, and coconut oil over apple and toss to coat.

2. Transfer apple slices in air fryer dish. Place dish in air fryer basket and cook at 350°F for 10 minutes.
3. Serve and enjoy.

Vanilla Cheesecake

Servings:6
Cooking Time: 10 Minutes
Ingredients:
- 2 eggs
- 16 ounces cream cheese, softened
- 2 tablespoons sour cream
- ½ teaspoon fresh lemon juice
- 1 teaspoon vanilla
- ¾ cup erythritol

Directions:
1. Before cooking, heat your air fryer to 350 degrees F/ 175 degrees C.
2. In a large bowl, mix the whisked eggs, vanilla, lemon juice, and sweetener together and use a hand mixer to beat until smooth.
3. Then beat in cream cheese and sour cream until fluffy.
4. Divide the batter into 2 4-inch springform pan that fits in your air fryer.
5. Cook in your air fryer at 350 degrees F/ 175 degrees C for 8 to 10 minutes.
6. When cooked, remove from the air fryer and set it aside to cool completely.
7. Transfer in the fridge to reserve.
8. Serve and enjoy!

Brownies After Dark

Servings: 4
Cooking Time: 13 Minutes
Ingredients:
- 1 egg
- ½ cup granulated sugar
- ¼ teaspoon salt
- ½ teaspoon vanilla
- ¼ cup butter, melted
- ¼ cup flour, plus 2 tablespoons
- ¼ cup cocoa
- cooking spray
- Optional
- vanilla ice cream
- caramel sauce
- whipped cream

Directions:
1. Beat together egg, sugar, salt, and vanilla until light.
2. Add melted butter and mix well.
3. Stir in flour and cocoa.
4. Spray 6 x 6-inch baking pan lightly with cooking spray.
5. Spread batter in pan and cook at 330°F for 13 minutes. Cool and cut into 4 large squares or 16 small brownie bites.

Molten Chocolate Almond Cakes

Servings: 3
Cooking Time: 13 Minutes
Ingredients:
- butter and flour for the ramekins
- 4 ounces bittersweet chocolate, chopped
- ½ cup (1 stick) unsalted butter
- 2 eggs
- 2 egg yolks
- ¼ cup sugar
- ½ teaspoon pure vanilla extract, or almond extract
- 1 tablespoon all-purpose flour
- 3 tablespoons ground almonds
- 8 to 12 semisweet chocolate discs (or 4 chunks of chocolate)
- cocoa powder or powdered sugar, for dusting
- toasted almonds, coarsely chopped

Directions:
1. Butter and flour three (6-ounce) ramekins. (Butter the ramekins and then coat the butter with flour by shaking it around in the ramekin and dumping out any excess.)
2. Melt the chocolate and butter together, either in the microwave or in a double boiler. In a separate bowl, beat the eggs, egg yolks and sugar together until light and smooth. Add the vanilla extract. Whisk the chocolate mixture into the egg mixture. Stir in the flour and ground almonds.
3. Preheat the air fryer to 330°F.
4. Transfer the batter carefully to the buttered ramekins, filling halfway. Place two or three chocolate discs in the center of the batter and then fill the ramekins to ½-inch below the top with the remaining batter. Place the ramekins into the air fryer basket and air-fry at 330°F for 13 minutes. The sides of the cake should be set, but the centers should be slightly soft. Remove the ramekins from the air fryer and let the cakes sit for 5 minutes. (If you'd like the cake a little less molten, air-fry for 14 minutes and let the cakes sit for 4 minutes.)
5. Run a butter knife around the edge of the ramekins and invert the cakes onto a plate. Lift the ramekin off the plate slowly and carefully so that the cake doesn't break. Dust with cocoa powder or powdered sugar and serve with a scoop of ice cream and some coarsely chopped toasted almonds.

Black And Blue Clafoutis

Servings: 2
Cooking Time: 15minutes
Ingredients:
- 6-inch pie pan
- 3 large eggs
- ½ cup sugar
- 1 teaspoon vanilla extract
- 2 tablespoons butter, melted 1 cup milk
- ½ cup all-purpose flour*
- 1 cup blackberries
- 1 cup blueberries

- 2 tablespoons confectioners' sugar

Directions:
1. Preheat the air fryer to 320°F.
2. Combine the eggs and sugar in a bowl and whisk vigorously until smooth, lighter in color and well combined. Add the vanilla extract, butter and milk and whisk together well. Add the flour and whisk just until no lumps or streaks of white remain.
3. Scatter half the blueberries and blackberries in a greased (6-inch) pie pan or cake pan. Pour half of the batter (about 1¼ cups) on top of the berries and transfer the tart pan to the air fryer basket. You can use an aluminum foil sling to help with this by taking a long piece of aluminum foil, folding it in half lengthwise twice until it is roughly 26-inches by 3-inches. Place this under the pie dish and hold the ends of the foil to move the pie dish in and out of the air fryer basket. Tuck the ends of the foil beside the pie dish while it cooks in the air fryer.
4. Air-fry at 320°F for 15 minutes or until the clafoutis has puffed up and is still a little jiggly in the center. Remove the clafoutis from the air fryer, invert it onto a plate and let it cool while you bake the second batch. Serve the clafoutis warm, dusted with confectioners' sugar on top.

Lemony Blackberry Crisp

Servings:1
Cooking Time: 20 Minutes
Ingredients:
- 2 tablespoons lemon juice
- ⅓ cup powdered erythritol
- ¼ teaspoon xantham gum
- 2 cup blackberries
- 1 cup crunchy granola

Directions:
1. Preheat the air fryer to 350ºF (177ºC).
2. In a bowl, combine the lemon juice, erythritol, xantham gum, and blackberries. Transfer to a round baking dish and cover with aluminum foil.
3. Put the dish in the air fryer and bake for 12 minutes.
4. Take care when removing the dish from the air fryer. Give the blackberries a stir and top with the granola.
5. Return the dish to the air fryer and bake for an additional 3 minutes, this time at 320ºF (160ºC). Serve once the granola has turned brown and enjoy.

Lemon Berries Stew

Servings: 4
Cooking Time: 20 Minutes
Ingredients:
- 1 pound strawberries, halved
- 4 tablespoons stevia
- 1 tablespoon lemon juice
- 1 and ½ cups water

Directions:
1. In a pan that fits your air fryer, mix all the ingredients, toss, put it in the fryer and cook at 340°F for 20 minutes. Divide the stew into cups and serve cold.

Chickpea Brownies

Servings:6
Cooking Time: 20 Minutes
Ingredients:
- Vegetable oil
- 1 (15-ounce / 425-g) can chickpeas, drained and rinsed
- 4 large eggs
- ⅓ cup coconut oil, melted
- ⅓ cup honey
- 3 tablespoons unsweetened cocoa powder
- 1 tablespoon espresso powder (optional)
- 1 teaspoon baking powder
- 1 teaspoon baking soda
- ½ cup chocolate chips

Directions:
1. Preheat the air fryer to 325ºF (163ºC).
2. Generously grease a baking pan with vegetable oil.
3. In a blender or food processor, combine the chickpeas, eggs, coconut oil, honey, cocoa powder, espresso powder (if using), baking powder, and baking soda. Blend or process until smooth. Transfer to the prepared pan and stir in the chocolate chips by hand.
4. Set the pan in the air fryer basket and bake for 20 minutes, or until a toothpick inserted into the center comes out clean.
5. Let cool in the pan on a wire rack for 30 minutes before cutting into squares.
6. Serve immediately.

Stuffed Apples

Servings: 4
Cooking Time:12 To 17 Minutes
Ingredients:
- 4 medium apples, rinsed and patted dry (see Tip)
- 2 tablespoons freshly squeezed lemon juice
- ¼ cup golden raisins
- 3 tablespoons chopped walnuts
- 3 tablespoons dried cranberries
- 2 tablespoons packed brown sugar
- ⅓ cup apple cider

Directions:
1. Cut a strip of peel from the top of each apple and remove the core, being careful not to cut through the bottom of the apple. Sprinkle the cut parts of the apples with lemon juice and place in a 6-by-2-inch pan.
2. In a small bowl, stir together the raisins, walnuts, cranberries, and brown sugar. Stuff one-fourth of this mixture into each apple.
3. Pour the apple cider around the apples in the pan.
4. Bake in the air fryer for 12 to 17 minutes, or until the apples are tender when pierced with a fork. Serve immediately.

Plum Apple Crumble With Cranberries

Servings: 6-7
Cooking Time: 25 Minutes
Ingredients:
- 2 ½ ounces caster sugar
- ⅓ cup oats
- ⅔ cup flour
- ½ stick butter, chilled
- 1 tablespoon cold water
- 1 tablespoon honey
- ½ teaspoon ground mace
- ¼ pound plums, pitted and chopped
- ¼ pound apples, cored and chopped
- 1 tablespoon lemon juice
- ½ teaspoon vanilla paste
- 1 cup cranberries

Directions:
1. On a flat kitchen surface, plug your air fryer and turn it on.
2. Gently coat your cake pan with cooking oil or spray.
3. Before cooking, heat your air fryer to 390 degrees F/ 200 degrees C for about 4 to 5 minutes.
4. Mix the lemon juice, sugar, honey, mace, apples, and plums in a medium sized bowl.
5. Place the fruits onto the cake pan.
6. In a second medium sized bowl, mix thoroughly the rest of the ingredients and add the fruit mixture on the top. Transfer to the cake pan.
7. Bake the apple crumble in the preheated air fryer for 20 minutes.
8. When cooked, remove from the air fryer and serve warm.

Olive Oil Cake

Servings:8
Cooking Time: 30 Minutes
Ingredients:
- 2 cups blanched finely ground almond flour
- 5 large eggs, whisked
- ¾ cup extra-virgin olive oil
- ⅓ cup granular erythritol
- 1 teaspoon vanilla extract
- 1 teaspoon baking powder

Directions:
1. In a large bowl, mix all ingredients. Pour batter into an ungreased 6" round nonstick baking dish.
2. Place dish into air fryer basket. Adjust the temperature to 300°F and set the timer for 30 minutes. The cake will be golden on top and firm in the center when done.
3. Let cake cool in dish 30 minutes before slicing and serving.

Chocolate Peanut Butter Molten Cupcakes

Servings:8
Cooking Time: 10 To 13 Minutes
Ingredients:
- Nonstick baking spray with flour
- 1⅓ cups chocolate cake mix (from 15-ounce box)
- 1 egg

- 1 egg yolk
- ¼ cup safflower oil
- ¼ cup hot water
- ⅓ cup sour cream
- 3 tablespoons peanut butter
- 1 tablespoon powdered sugar

Directions:

1. Double up 16 foil muffin cups to make 8 cups. Spray each lightly with nonstick spray; set aside.
2. In a medium bowl, combine the cake mix, egg, egg yolk, safflower oil, water, and sour cream, and beat until combined.
3. In a small bowl, combine the peanut butter and powdered sugar and mix well. Form this mixture into 8 balls.
4. Spoon about ¼ cup of the chocolate batter into each muffin cup and top with a peanut butter ball. Spoon remaining batter on top of the peanut butter balls to cover them.
5. Arrange the cups in the air fryer basket, leaving some space between each. Bake for 10 to 13 minutes or until the tops look dry and set.
6. Let the cupcakes cool for about 10 minutes, then serve warm.

Pumpkin Brownies

Servings: 4
Cooking Time: 30 Minutes
Ingredients:

- ¼ cup canned pumpkin
- ½ cup maple syrup
- 2 eggs, beaten
- 1 tbsp vanilla extract
- ¼ cup tapioca flour
- ¼ cup flour
- ½ tsp baking powder

Directions:

1. Preheat air fryer to 320°F. Mix the pumpkin, maple syrup, eggs, and vanilla extract in a bowl. Toss in tapioca flour, flour, and baking powder until smooth. Pour the batter into a small round cake pan and Bake for 20 minutes until a toothpick comes out clean. Let cool completely before slicing into 4 brownies. Serve and enjoy!

Coconut-custard Pie

Servings: 4
Cooking Time: 20 Minutes
Ingredients:

- 1 cup milk
- ¼ cup plus 2 tablespoons sugar
- ¼ cup biscuit baking mix
- 1 teaspoon vanilla
- 2 eggs
- 2 tablespoons melted butter
- cooking spray
- ½ cup shredded, sweetened coconut

Directions:

1. Place all ingredients except coconut in a medium bowl.
2. Using a hand mixer, beat on high speed for 3minutes.
3. Let sit for 5minutes.
4. Preheat air fryer to 330°F.
5. Spray a 6-inch round or 6 x 6-inch square baking pan with cooking spray and place pan in air fryer basket.
6. Pour filling into pan and sprinkle coconut over top.
7. Cook pie at 330°F for 20 minutes or until center sets.

Recipes Index

Printed in Great Britain
by Amazon